JR rev. $37.50 (cloth)

                                              Joel Swerk

Topics for Rev.

  Altruism

  Civic Religion

  identity

  mentalité

  symbol ? (16) IS speaks of blood as "symbolic" — funny, idealists cannot
      accept materiality of any sort. Blood IS blood, life, not a symbol !

  group vs. individual dynamics   (critical issue)

                    _____

                        de Maistre

                        Crisy

"Durkheimian" — def'd p. 51 "from Hubert-Mauss to Bataille"
                        p. 163

"Catholic sacrificial mentality" 80

latency 102

Stravinskis politics — 141f.

CONTESTING
SACRIFICE

Is Steinmetz foll. some established professional practice in his use of the term *intransigent* Catholicism?

CONTESTING SACRIFICE

Religion, Nationalism, and Social Thought in France

Ivan Strenski

THE UNIVERSITY OF CHICAGO PRESS
CHICAGO & LONDON

IVAN STRENSKI is the Holstein Family Community Professor of Religious Studies at the
University of California, Riverside. He is the author most recently of *Durkheim and the Jews
of France* (1997), also published by the University of Chicago Press.

The University of Chicago Press, Chicago 60637
The University of Chicago Press, Ltd., London
© 2002 by The University of Chicago
All rights reserved. Published 2002
Printed in the United States of America
11 10 09 08 07 06 05 04 03 02   1 2 3 4 5

ISBN: 0-226-77736-7 (cloth)

Library of Congress Cataloging-in-Publication Data

Strenski, Ivan.
    Contesting sacrifice : religion, nationalism, and social thought in France / Ivan Strenski.
        p.   cm.
    Includes index.
    ISBN 0-226-77736-7 (alk. paper)
    1. Christianity and politics—France—History. 2. Sacrifice— France—History. 3. Christi-
anity and politics—Catholic Church—History. 4. Sacrifice—Christianity—History of doctrines. I. Title.

  BX1530 .S84 2002
  291.3'4'0944—dc21

                                                                          2001007062

⊗The paper used in this publication meets the minimum requirements of the American
National Standard for Information Sciences—Permanence of Paper for Printed Library
Materials, ANSI z39.48-1992.

For Chantal Auger, Daniel-Marc Auger,
Blake Hamilton, Miranda Hamilton,
Megan Strenski, and Christian Ten Eyck

When hope is crushed, the heart is crushed,
but a wish come true fills you with joy.

Proverbs 13:12

Contents

Acknowledgments

I wish to thank the many colleagues and friends who read, commented upon, and in other ways aided this project: Greg Alles, Philippe Besnard, Grace Davie, Winston Davis, Michel Despland, Wendy Doniger, Mary Douglas, Wendell Dietrich, Louis Dumont, Antoine Faivre, Marcel Fournier, Tamar Frankiel, Ernest Frerichs, Calvin Goldscheider, Cristiano Grottanelli, Halina Grzymała-Moszczynska, Richard Hecht, Robert Alun Jones, Diane Jonte-Pace, Henrika Kuklick, Bruce Lincoln, Jacob Neusner, Pat O'Brien, Bill Pickering, Douglas Parrott, Sam Preus, Norman Ravitch, Michèle Richman, Erik Sand, Robert Segal, Ninian Smart, Ellen Marie Strenski, Jennie Strenski, Jan Szmyd, Carlos Vélez-Ibañez, and Irwin Wall.

For generous use of library facilities, I should also like to thank in Paris the Bibliothèque de l'Alliance Israelite Universelle, especially its Bibliothècaire, Madame Yvonne Levyne; the Bibliothèque de l'Histoire du Protestantisme Français; the Bibliothèque Nationale; and Archives Nationales. In California, I salute the Young Reference Library of the University of California, Los Angeles, and the tireless, cheerful, and efficient staff of the Rivera Library of the University of California, Riverside, especially its Interlibrary Loan Services.

Thanks finally are due also to the Holstein Family Community Endowment in Religious Studies for much-appreciated financial support.

1

SACRIFICE, RELIGION, AND POLITICS

Sacrifice without End

Sacrifice has been one of the most contentious and divisive notions of religion and politics in the West. From the time of Luther, differences between Catholics and Protestants could in a way be reduced to conflicts over the Mass and its sacrificial conception of the Eucharist.[1] But perhaps nowhere has Eucharistic sacrifice aroused such bitter political and religious historical controversy as in France.[2] There, as early as 1534, assaults on the Catholic Mass were launched in what has come to be known as the "Affair of the Placards." In a coordinated campaign against the sacrificial Eucharist, posters denouncing the Eucharist and Mass were put up simultaneously in public places (one even on the door of the king's bedchamber!) on a single night in several principal cities of the realm. Royal repression followed swiftly, but so also did Protestant reactions. Shortly thereafter, Calvinist Antoine Marcourt denounced royal repression with a new placard of his own outlining a detailed theological argument against the Mass and its sacrificial Eucharist. This pattern of attack and response continued over many years, culminating in the infamous St. Bartholomew's Day massacre of France's Protestant leadership in 1572 and in the

1

French Wars of Religion.[3] Protestant attacks on the Mass were understood by one and all as skillful blows to the very heart of Catholic life and identity. After all, in the twenty-second session of the Council of Trent on 17 September 1562, the vast majority of the assembly made sure to define the core of Catholic identity by asserting the sacrificial character of the Eucharist over Protestant objections.[4]

Likewise, in the domain of civic and personal ethics, the question of the status and extent of personal sacrifice in behalf of the collectivity has posed terrible alternatives for Western moralists ever since the dawn of the modern era. The relative weight of the demands of the community over against the rights of individuals, the opposition between altruism and self-interest, in no small part have set the terms of our politics and public policy debates. Given that France is one of the principal points of origin for Western notions of citizenship, civic duty, nationalism, and the like, France also becomes a major source of examples for the working out of relations between self-interest and sacrifice. Whether in the course of the ordinary duties of citizenship or in the extraordinary demands made in wartime, France has been the venue for some of the classic contests between devotion to individual rights and dignity over against the imperatives of life within communities. The French Revolution's rhetoric of sacrifice for the "nation" has perhaps set the standard for calls to patriotic sacrifice ever since.

French moral philosophers of the nineteenth century were also preoccupied with questions of whether the standard of sacrifice in a republic should be a total "giving up" of one's person to the service of the community or whether it was enough for it to be the less extreme "giving of" one's person and possessions for the sake of the community? Are we today required to be "saints" or "citizens"? How much of the individualism inherent to the very nature of personal life in the modern nation-state are we required to sacrifice for the very existence of that nation-state?

These academic debates were conducted in contexts anything but academic. Contending positions were played out against the background of the real threat of civil war, renewed revolution, or *revanche* as well as decades-long preparations for a war of revenge against Germany for the defeat of 1871. Thus, when we reach the height of the nationalist agitation at the end of the nineteenth century, the French literature of "sacrifice" is as rich and elaborated as perhaps any that could be named. Not only that, but so too was French strategic thinking about the conduct of war itself. There, French soldiers were expected to display their devotion to the *patrie* in unleashing the notorious "Gallic fury" in reckless—sacrificial—attacks "to the death" along an often impregnable front. The celebrated Dreyfus Affair could arguably be said to have been conceived at the time as a debate over whether one man ought to be sacrificed for the sake of the honor of the army and nation. France has indeed had its fill of serious talk of sacrifice.

Unfortunately for those seeking simple solutions, no handy "Excalibur" is ready to slice neatly through the dilemmas thrown up by sacrifice, whether between Protestants and Catholics in the religious domain or between self-interest and altruism in the domain of civic ethics. Yet, while liberation from theological and moral anguish does not seem imminent, perhaps we can at least deepen our understanding of the discourse of sacrifice by which we seem trapped. Perhaps we can better understand the discourse about sacrifice and the dynamic of its role in modern society by understanding its history in a particular context like that of France. In doing so, we may even get some purchase on our moral dilemmas. I believe we can better see what talk about sacrifice has really concerned if we consider it in the historical contexts in which it has been particularly conspicuous and influential. The history of France helps us then to put sacrifice into perspective. It lets us see "around the edges" of a notion to which there have always been alternatives, but alternatives that were not always fully appreciated. In part, getting perspective on sacrifice is part of what I have set out to achieve in the present work.

In gaining this perspective, the discourse of sacrifice in France presents an excellent, perhaps even privileged, venue of inquiry. Dating from the early seventeenth century, and summing up in a way the lessons of the religio-political rhetoric of the Wars of Religion, France can cite a school of Roman Catholic theology defined by its determination to articulate a theory of sacramental sacrifice, a theory so influential that it has been said to have defined Catholicism in France's golden age. It was likewise in France that one of the major political events of past hundred years with lasting effects too numerous to mention here—the Dreyfus Case—was fought out in the public arena in terms of the rhetoric of sacrifice. During World War One, another major watershed in the formation of the mentality of the twentieth century, France was also the home of a theory of mass warfare that pushed sacrifice to the fore—so much so that this military failure may single-handedly have been responsible for the bad odor into which the notion of sacrifice has fallen ever since. And, perhaps not accidentally, France is also home to the leading thinkers taken with the idea of sacrifice. Here, I count Émile Durkheim, Joseph de Maistre, Jules Michelet, George Bataille, René Girard, and perhaps most influential of all, that pair of inseparable Durkheimian team members, Henri Hubert and Marcel Mauss.[5] They authored what some would still argue remains the single-most influential book ever written on sacrifice, if not the required point of departure for almost every subsequent theoretical effort

3

in the field. Indeed, I have argued elsewhere that it merits being credited as the "first theory" of sacrifice.[6]

Thus, when we survey French religious and political history, we find a rich field of discourse about sacrifice. French saints, theologians, and mystics thought *about* sacrifice in the religious sphere, and they thought *with* it. Religious folk assumed without question a certain notion of what sacrifice was. This ideal of sacrifice was not the calculated, prudent, "giving *of*" part of one's life or treasure typical of bourgeois morality. It was, rather, a total annihilating surrender of the self, a complete "giving up" of oneself. Sacrifice served thereby to achieve expiation for sin. Similarly, when French military men, politicians, social thinkers, philosophers, belle-lettrists, or ordinary citizens thought *about* sacrifice in the social sphere, they too thought *with* the same notion as the French saints, theologians, and mystics—even when they became critical and thought *against* it.

In this book, I shall be arguing several related theses about the nature of sacrificial discourse in France.

First, beginning in France in the seventeenth century, Catholic thinkers laid down this classic definition of sacrifice as a cosmic drama involving self-annihilation and expiation. I further argue that the place we need to seek the first most prominent and well worked out sources of French talk about sacrifice is in the Roman Catholic theology of the Golden Age. As we will see, this discourse of sacrifice is developed within the Eucharistic theology articulated at that time against the challenges presented by the Reformation.

Second, the notion of sacrifice stipulated in Catholic discourse has carried far beyond its own context of origin and has been either silently assumed or independently rediscovered ever since then by Catholics and non-Catholics alike. It is, in this sense, "embedded" or "entrenched" in French thought and recurs there as conditions dictate. Although one need not employ the same epistemological language as French nationalist writers of the fin-de-siècle, Micheline Tison-Braun, author of a massive study of the conflict between individual and collectivity in the works of modern French literature, well captures the spirit of an entrenched mentality apparently at work in French thinking about sacrifice in and around the time of the First World War. She observed of Adrien Bertrand, one of the masters of the literature of the First World War, what seems like talk of embedded or entrenched spiritual notions of sacrifice.

Indeed, Bertrand reversed the traditional relationship between effects and causes; it is not the intensity of patriotism that calls forth sacrifice. Nor is it, furthermore, social pressure that induces or imposes it. It is piety—communion and service—that seemed to Bertrand to be a *structure of the spirit* that in encountering brute social facts—whether in the form of instincts to gregariousness or resistance to them—made a mere biological symbiosis into a spiritual unity and transformed a common human swarm into a real fatherland.[7]

Sometimes the persistence of such a sacrificial "spirit," to use Tison-Braun's language, seems like a matter of direct continuity, as indeed at times it may be. Thus, writing in a time of virulent anticlericalism, Georges Goyau, that prolific commentator of the contemporary scene of the end of the last century, refers confidently to a "subconscious" Catholicism that "still survives in the soul of France."[8] That "subconscious" Catholicism, says Georges Goyau in 1918, is the very thing which "incites" the French "to sacrifice."[9] Thus, for adherents of the ideal of continuity, despite centuries-long traditions of native Protestantism, Free thought, anticlericalism, militant atheism, as well as the admiration for ancient Roman models of sacrifice during the French Revolution, classic Roman Catholic structures of thought and affect persist beneath the surface of much of the political culture of France.[10] To be sure, there is much in this claim, given the persistence of Catholic institutions to provide a constant real base of social formations in which such a Eucharistic ideology of sacrifice might inhere. A contemporary author, Suzanne Desan echoes Goyau and speaks of the Roman Catholicism of France as going "beyond adherence to specific beliefs and forms of devotion; for many it meant . . . a way of life and a vast frame of cultural references."[11] Chief among these "cultural references" derived from Catholic models of thought is, I am arguing in this book, a particularly durable discourse about sacrifice with a plausible Catholic pedigree and lineage, even if the discourse about sacrifice in France may derive from other sources or be generated "spontaneously," so to speak.

But, having laid out a case for social and historical "influences" and continuities in sacrificial discourse in France, I am not insisting on it. Continuity and influence may not provide the sole, or even most defensible, account for the recurrence of a particular kind of sacrificial discourse in France—even if one were to speculate about supposed "unconscious" continuities as perhaps the words of Goyau and Desan suggest. Sometimes, even among the most virulent Catholic thinkers, such as Joseph de Maistre, for example, we search in vain for clear indications of influence from the classic Eucharistic theologies of sacrifice of the Catholic Golden Age. While it is not unreasonable to believe that de Maistre was schooled in the theology of the Catholic Golden Age, solid evidence is lacking. Or, if we turn, as we will, to the French Revolution, we likewise find discourse about sacrifice reminiscent of the Catholic Golden Age, but, again, without, solid—at least textual—evidence for continuity. This is particularly so in light of the great and easily substantiated debt of the French Revolution to the exemplars provided by ancient Rome. Then, if we turn to modern times and search the theory of sacrifice made rightly famous by sociologists like Émile Durkheim and his creative followers, Henri Hubert and Marcel Mauss, while we find affinities with the Eucharistic theologies of sacrifice of the Catholic Golden Age, we would be wrong, as I shall argue, to claim that the anticlerical Durkheimians were in the business of carrying on Catholic theological ideas.[12]

In any event, the argument of this book does not depend on claims of direct "influence" or putative continuity, unconscious or otherwise. Indeed, as I shall argue in conclusion, the persistence of discourses about sacrifice testifies perhaps more eloquently to the structural requisites that human social life places on us all. This is to say that the persistence of talk about sacrifice seems to mean that many believe that it is in the very nature of viable social life that sacrifice—in some description—will be required. Coming to this conclusion does not require historical precedent, although it never hurts to have available a vivid cultural lexicon for expressing sacrificial ideas, such as the Catholic Eucharistic theology in France provided. Third, in the period which most concerns me—the late nineteenth and early twentieth centuries—I am arguing that we simply cannot understand talk about sacrifice in the many domains in which it was a critical idea unless we understand this cultural lexicon provided by the religious and political history of France. To wit, I claim that even today, when we read the Girards, Batailles, Yourcenars, Huysmans, Balzacs, Claudels, Maurrases, Barrèses, Derridas, and such, we cannot generally understand their talk of sacrifice, unless we know more about their French background—both in terms of the social conditions favoring talk about sacrifice as well as the stock of cultural knowledge available to them to express their concerns.[13] In the conclusion of my study, I shall in fact argue that the most influential of all theoretical works on sacrifice, Henri Hubert and Marcel Mauss's *Sacrifice: Its Nature and Functions* deliberately attempted to contest and overthrow what was in effect the classic Catholic definition of sacrifice so deeply entrenched in French religious and political culture.[14] This was at the same time an attempt to overthrow a form of social life implicit in Catholic ideas of sacrifice and to put in its place a new concept of sacrifice more conducive to the kind of society Hubert and Mauss desired. More recently, the same dynamic of using Catholic ideas as an implicit foil against which to articulate ideas about sacrifice can be seen as much of the burden of the life's work of René Girard, who might be said to be dedicated to the thoroughgoing discrediting of what amounts to the Catholic notion of sacrifice and with it the entire form of social life resting on victimization implicit in it. Interestingly enough Girard links himself with Hubert and Mauss as an ally struggling against the hegemony of Catholic sacrificial symbolism.[15]

Symbols and Meanings: Controlled/Contested/Entrenched

Mention of attempts to unseat the Catholic notion of sacrifice brings me to another large purpose in doing this study. Tracing the fortunes of this dominant notion of sacrifice occupies much of the narrative of this book. But more than that, I believe a certain logic of contestation can be discerned within this history. To wit, whenever the dominant notion was asserted, and because it was well understood how critical the delineation of the ideal of sacrifice was, it was also contested. I shall tell this story of the discourses of sacrifice not only from the point of view of the "winners"— the dominant Catholic discourse—but also from the disadvantaged point of view of those defeated in this centuries-long combat over the symbol of sacrifice. My history of the discourse about sacrifice in France is then a history of a process of struggle to control the meaning of sacrifice.

Focusing on the process of contest and struggle, however, demands that a few distinctions be made among key terms. These are the concepts of control, entrenchment or embeddedness, and ownership. Consider entrenchment or embeddedness first.

Using an example more familiar to our own time, one could say, for example, that the national flag of the American Confederacy carries certain entrenched or embedded meanings clear to all. When it is displayed today in the American South to represent the body politic or even a university's football team, it is not surprising that African Americans, for example, take offense. The racist meanings of the "Stars and Bars" are so deeply *embedded* or *entrenched* in it that disclaimers to the contrary are naturally taken as insincere, naive, or worse. Symbols with embedded or entrenched meanings take on a certain incorrigible fixity and thus are resistant to the individual or often even collective will to dissociate those meanings from the symbol itself. Thus, if people brandish the "Stars and Bars" in certain contexts and then counter charges of racism by disclaiming any such intention, they are rightly judged to be insincere, naive, or worse. This is because the meanings of a symbol like the Confederate flag have attained a certain normative or taken-for-granted status. Individual intentions do not count. Proposed new meanings are thus judged "artificial." To be accepted they would require justification and argument; entrenched meanings are "natural" and integral parts of the cultural landscape. Entrenched meanings become all-purpose points of reference then, either to support or indeed to reject what has been so entrenched.

Beyond being entrenched or embedded within a culture in this way, one can go further to speak of a group's "owning" or "controlling" a certain notion or symbol like the "Stars and Bars" or sacrifice. In the case of sacrifice in France, the entrenched idea of sacrifice can, I shall argue, be traced to an origin. It is the historical product of a particular and strongly self-identified social group. This group fought certain key battles in French history, imprinting, with relative permanence, a certain vision of things. In the United States, this situation would be analogous to the meaning or symbolic status of the Confederate flag being in the hands of the political right wing in the American South. In this sense, it can be said to be "owned" or "controlled" by that group, so much so that, say, African Americans would be powerless to employ the "Stars and Bars" to promote, for example, an agenda of racial harmony and dignity.

In this book, I want to make the case that in France a certain meaning of sacrifice became entrenched and controlled by an identifiable element of French political and religious culture, what I shall call somewhat anachronistically, "intransigent Roman Catholicism." One should note, however, that I carefully distinguish the notion of "intransigent" Catholicism from what is often called "conservative" or "traditional" Catholicism, even if the intransigents would like to obscure the distinction. As we will see, intransigence often played the role of usurper and innovator in French Catholic history, rather than one of preserving or "conserving" Catholic "traditions," many of which bear little resemblance to the claims of the intransigents. Yet, primarily because intransigent Catholicism was able to play a dominant role at crucial junctures in French history and in critical strata of French society, it was able to "entrench" and, for a while and to some degree, "control" the national French discourse about sacrifice. Eventually, the control of the meaning of sacrifice slipped from the hands of the intransigent Roman Catholics, only to be assumed by the forces of nationalism. I shall first trace out a series of major points in which this conception of sacrifice emerged and then explore episodes in which it was reinforced and challenged.

Religious Culture and the Pursuit of Politics

This book also assumes that in order to understand the nature and content of political discourse, especially in France, it will be necessary, from case to case, to understand political discourse in relation to religious culture.[16] In France, for the bulk of its modern history, and in particular in connection with the subject of sacrifice, religion and politics were intricately connected. Official and actual separation of church and state, it should be recalled, did not come about until 1905, even though the ideal of separation of politics and religion had been official policy since Napoleon, not to mention being embraced by the Third Republic's free thinkers and nineteenth-century Catholic liberals such as Montalambert, Lamennais, and Lacordaire.[17] There are good reasons why political culture in France has been particularly susceptible to religious notions like sacrifice, and reasons that carry implications for studies of religion and politics comparatively and in other contexts.

First, the actual pursuit of politics in a given context occurs within what one may call a political culture, a realm of real or imagined legitimate behaviors. Different peoples just "do" politics in different ways. They "do" politics according to the different manners, customs, and assumptions prevailing among themselves. One, but only one, of these features of a culture is religion. In the American context, for example, our traditions and institutions of political and economic individualism can be said to have been conditioned by the religious culture of Calvinist Protestantism. In politics, the reformed tradition established an ideal of the sacredness of the individual, which established a certain taken-for-granted culture of respect for individual rights, in turn conditioning well-known aspects of major American political institutions. The same, I believe, is true regarding the role of Catholic ideas of sacrifice for French political culture. If Max Weber taught us about the Protestant ethic and the spirit of capitalism, I hope this present book may teach us about what one could call a Catholic "ethic" of sacrifice and the spirit of a certain kind of politics.

Second, the idea of sacrifice itself seems precisely one of those religious notions especially prone to migrate into politics. Notions like ritual and cultic giving—sacrifice—bear a natural affinity for civic giving—for heroism or martyrdom, in short for all those examples of patriotic offering of oneself in "sacrifice" for the nation. Jay Winter has shown how the religious imagination excelled at producing what might otherwise be seen only as political entities—war monuments, myths about battle, ritual practices concerning the war dead, the rampant flourishing of supernatural or plainly occult beliefs and experiences. All these seemed thrown up by the religious imagination to handle the enormity of sacrificial mass death and the unbearable loss of life in the First World War.[18] Perhaps most notable of all, however, in the midst of all the ruction of modern mass warfare, the theme of sacrifice played at all levels. Common questions plaguing those involved in the war were ones such as whether the elders bore the blame for not stopping the sacrifice of the young?[19] Or was the sacrifice of the young worthwhile? Was it appreciated by those for whom it was offered?[20] Would the sacrificed dead have to return to set

9

things aright?[21] Thus, at least for our subject of sacrifice, the religious and political sectors of life are firmly bound together.[22]

At this point, however, we encounter a paradox. Although we quite correctly speak of nation in a political sense, recent literature on nationalism suggests that it has a deeply religious nature as well. This is to say that although the nation-state was devised in part to be distinct from religion, it cannot really be so. Why the nation-state becomes religious is not hard to understand. Whatever else they may be, nations are meaning-making entities of grand and transcendent sorts, creating an aura of sacredness about all their central doings. Not only do national borders mark boundaries of a sacred precinct as "taboo" to the intruder as do any temple's holy of holies, but the accessories of nationalism—its flags, monuments, anthems, and such—partake of the same transcendent glow of the nation as sacred being. In terms of national ritual, nationalism has taught us that "sacrifice" will routinely be required of individual citizens in one form or another. As such, in sacrifice the nation shows itself as the highest form of collectivity demanding human loyalty and one, notoriously, transcending palpable human individuality. Thus far at least, for all the efforts of universal cosmopolitan "humanity" to rally people to common causes, it has yet to outdo the nation in calling forth the loyalty of people and in getting them to lay down their lives for it. In its being then the locus of transcendent value and the stage upon which sacrificial rites are enacted, the nation *ipso facto* becomes religious.

A religious appreciation of nationalism is coming more and more to the fore. Recent studies such as Daniel Pick's exploration of the justification of mass slaughters in war concludes that appeals to instinct and biological or economic compulsion for mass murder do not suffice. Rather, Pick argues that we should instead seek ideological or cultural grounds for such extreme acts. The extremity of these acts directs Pick right to the domain of the main meaning-making forces of our day—religion and nationalism.[23] Similarly, Benedict Anderson has argued that the readiness of individuals to kill others and to sacrifice themselves can only be understood in terms of the religious nature of fellowship achieved by the nation-state.[24] People do not sacrifice themselves for "administrative units," such as the EEC, but for religious absolutes or nations like Islam or Christianity, on the one side, and Bosnia, Serbia, Ireland, and such, on the other. Thus, it is wise to pay attention to differences in language corresponding to differences in fundamental viewpoint. From an Israeli viewpoint, the independence struggle was fought for the imagined community of the "nation of Israel," and not for the "mandate of Palestine"—even though the two territories are virtually identical. In that struggle, the deaths of Jewish fighters counted as "sacrifices" and martyrdoms, not "terrorist atrocities," as the British insisted, who were arrayed against them. Similarly, from a contemporary Israeli view, which seeks to contain or deny Palestinian "nationality," those who die for Hamas are "murderers," "terrorists," and "madmen." But, seen from the viewpoint of those who want to make the imagined community of Palestine into a nation-state, these men are "martyrs" who have "sacrificed" themselves for "Palestine," Islam, and such. For them, these deaths are meaningful, and in this way "religious" deaths, not the random acts of madmen or visceral responses of an overly stimulated organism. For Palestinians, the West Bank and Gaza are not the mere "administrative units" that they are for Israel. They are part of the "imagined community" of Palestine in the same way the "British Mandate" was the imagined community of Israel for the Jewish independence fighters. The reason for this is that "administrative units" do not create meaning while, in a sense, religions and nations do nothing but create meaning—however gruesome it may be.[25]

The plan of this book is dictated by the way the Catholic notion of sacrifice played the protagonist's role in public matters that were prominent at key points in French history in the late nineteenth and early twentieth centuries. In the second chapter, I shall identify what I take to be the lineage of an original, periodically renewed, creatively reinterpreted, but ultimately dominant, discourse of sacrifice in France. In the next four chapters, I shall discuss four separate domains of French civic and religious life of the *fin-de-siècle* in which the conception of sacrifice played a discernible role, alternately dominant and contested. Chapter 3, for example, deals with the language of sacrifice prominent in the discourse of nationalism and war. Chapter 4 considers the rhetoric of sacrifice swirling round the Dreyfus Case. Chapter 5 explores appeals to sacrifice in the secular ideology of public education and a civic morals in the Third Republic. Chapter 6 shows how these civic, religious, and political issues were reflected in major efforts in French social thought, such as the theory of sacrifice central to the work of one of France's most eminent social thinkers, Émile Durkheim and his celebrated followers, Henri Hubert and Marcel Mauss.

2 CATHOLIC POLITICS, FRENCH SACRIFICE

Nous ennemis confus en restent là
Et nous aller chanter Alleluya!
Ah! ça ira, ça ira, ça ira, . . .

Suivant la maxime de l'Evangile
Ah! ça ira, ça ira, ça ira . . .

Le vrai catéchisme nous instruira,
Et l'affreux fanatisme s'éteindra . . .
Ah! ça ira, ça ira, ça ira . . .[1]

Episodes in the History of Sacrifice in France

In this chapter, I shall argue that a dominant set of ideas about sacrifice can be identified in the history of France, originating in French Catholic theology and spirituality. This set counts at least four episodes in its renewed interpretation of the sacrificial ideal, beginning in the seventeenth and extending at least to the late nineteenth and early twentieth centuries. I shall call these periods baroque, rococo, restoration, and intransigent/integrist.

Although I cannot find sufficient evidence to claim the existence of some ahistorical or "essential" French Catholic discourse of sacrifice, there is something that suggests a constant. This discourse would seem to take on a relatively constant character for many reasons. One reason is the way in which dogged and entrenched political grudges and religious animosities live on in France from one generation to another. As Eugen Weber put it, "in France, the dead live longer than in other places."[2] René Rémond, the great historian of the French "Right," has likewise marveled at the "continuity of thought" embodied in the way a symbol of sacrifice like the Sacred Heart of Jesus, first worn on the battle dress of the antirevolutionary rebels of the Vendée of 1790s, was taken up enthusiastically during the Fourth Republic by the "M. P. 13," a right-wing Catholic integrist movement.[3] Such persistence is made possible by the underlying material and social reality provided by the French Catholic Church. From the sixteenth to the twentieth century, the Church fought a protracted battle of reaction to the Reformation and then to its secularized republican offspring, well reflected, I am arguing, in the persistence of a Tridentine theology of the Eucharist that asserts the sacrificial and expiatory nature of Catholicism's central rite.

Yet along with continuity, an equal measure of change appears in French Catholic views of sacrifice. Indeed, the remarkable record of reinterpretation of the sacrificial ideal shows in turn how creative French Catholicism has been in adapting the notion of sacrifice to changing times. I shall argue in fact that one can distinguish styles of sacrificial discourse within the history of Roman Catholicism in France. These I call baroque, rococo, restoration, and intransigent/integrist conceptions, since each carries a characteristic style of sacrificial spirituality reminiscent of these general cultural distinctions.

First, "baroque" refers to the period of reactions to the Reformation in the very early seventeenth century, following the Council of Trent. This is also the period in which we can begin speaking of the high water mark of "royal religion," of organizations like the Oratory, the École Française de Spiritualité, and the Compagnie du Saint Sacrement. Second, comes the period of "rococo" sacrificial spirituality exemplified by the devotion to the Sacred Heart. Championed by the Jesuits from the later seventeenth century until their expulsion from France in 1764, devotion to the Sacred Heart continued even in their absence and during the French Revolution. This form of spirituality has been central to international Catholic piety at least up to the late nineteenth and early twentieth centuries. Third, I speak of "restoration" spirituality in the period after the French Revolution. What marks the sacrificial piety of this period is the new impetus given to it by the radical thought of Joseph de Maistre, especially the politicized character of his meditations on sacrifice and nation. Fourth, and finally, comes the period dating roughly from the first third of the nineteenth century to the early twentieth centuries. The period of intransigence and integrism is characterized by hardened dogmatic positions, reinforced by the Syllabus of Errors and the assertion of papal infallibility at the First Vatican Council. In terms of doctrine, therefore, the intransigents reasserted the teachings of the Council of Trent as they saw them applying to the French context.

In this stern attitude of orthodoxy and doctrinal uniformity, the right also saw in the example of de Maistre a model of their own political and religious opposition to all facets of liberalism, especially its individualism. Among these ideological weapons, as we will see, was de Maistre's conception of sacrifice, which informed intransigent attitudes to political policies in the Dreyfus case and the First World War. Wedded to this theological "intransigence" was a commitment to conform modern society to the Church's teachings, thus achieving an "integral" Catholicism. The monarchist dream lived on at least until the fall of General Georges Boulanger in 1891. Thus, while integrist hopes for a new "royal religion" gradually waned, they were resurrected by the realization that republican institutions could be manipulated to serve the purposes of those who had originally opposed them. In that case, as we will see, the deification of the nation achieved by the French Revolution could be co-opted in restoring a sense of the sacred to everyday life and with it an ethic of national sacrifice. Thus, along with a sacrificial constant, we should also expect flexibility in the conception of the sacrificial ideal throughout its entire history in France.

Sacrifice in France: Some Stipulations

Provoked by reactions to Protestant denial of the Eucharist as sacrifice, an entire Catholic theological literature on the nature of the Eucharist began to appear in early modern France and became fully developed in the seventeenth century. In its classic and most fully developed form, this literature was chiefly the product of the so-called École Française de Spiritualité, a theological school led by Pierre de Bérulle (1575–1629). Sacrifice, on this view, is stipulated to be both a total annihilation of a victim and an expiation for sin effected by that immolation. Although the changes wrought by the Second Vatican Council considerably lessened the influence of this conception of sacrifice among Catholics, it held sway from the time of the Council of Trent to the twentieth century. In 1912, writing in the official Catholic journal, *Revue du clergé français,* Jean Rivière reinforced the importance of the classic notion in attacking liberal Protestants for interpreting Jesus' death as sacrificial only in psychological terms. Rivière charged that this liberal interpretation is contrary to Catholic teaching and, to strands of Protestant orthodoxy as well. Even while denying the sacrificial nature of the Eucharist, the fathers of the Reformation nevertheless asserted "brutal theories of penal expiation" in connection with Jesus' death.[4] In recent times, opponents of the reforms of Vatican II, such as the renegade French bishop, Marcel Lefebvre, have reasserted the centrality of the sacrificial Eucharist with a sort of vengeance.[5]

Before exploring the details of this Catholic theology of the sacrificial

Eucharist, we should note that while this literature tends to be a mystical or "purely" theoretical, it is also linked closely with the social thought and national politics of its own time. This is so primarily because contemporaries just assumed that religion lived at the heart of social life and that its beliefs bore direct implications for the nature of the proper ordering of society. For Catholics, the Eucharist made ordinary citizens holy, and its character informed the lives and values of the faithful.[6] Recent historians have confirmed such connections across once seemingly unbridgeable boundaries by assigning an especially important role, for example, to the Eucharist "in reorganizing Catholic society and molding its saints of the post-Tridentine era."[7] The underlying assumption among Catholics of the post-Tridentine period seems to have been that the "reform of society depended on the Eucharist."[8] Religious values and doctrines held the key to the proper ordering of the body politic.

Fundamental to this theology of the Eucharist, for instance, one assumed a "hierarchical mode" of relationship between humanity and divinity, with the priesthood occupying the higher realms of hierarchy, ultimately mediating sanctity to ordinary humans.[9] This mode of relationship of clergy to laity was notorious among its critics for embodying an "esprit de domination."[10] Abject human sinfulness is posed against absolute divine power. Humanity needs to make a submissive, sacrificial return to the divine, institutionally mediated by the clergy. This theological position seems a straightforward species of the same discourse as certain social and political doctrines, such as the growing royal absolutism of the seventeenth century. Accordingly, in the French Golden Age, the "royal religion" of the Bourbons matched a theology of doctrinal absolutism with an ideology of Bourbon absolutism. This union was in part achieved through ritual identification of the French crown with the Eucharist. Thus, as Dale van Kley says, with "royal religion" the "French monarchy [was] . . . implicated in sacramental conceptions," even to the extent of the monarchy in particular being associated with the "consecrated host."[11] It is no mere coincidence that Calvin's attack on "religious" matters—the Catholic theory of the Eucharist and his critique of images, relics, and miracles—should have been seen in his time as "politically subversive."[12] Indeed, we see even more of this ritual identification of religion and politics as we look more closely at the doctrine of sacrifice worked out in this milieu and the personalities who labored in its behalf. Let me spell out what this notion of sacrifice stipulates and thus what will be presumed in French talk about sacrifice in both theological and political realms of discourse thereafter.

First, sacrifice is an offering to God, requiring total annihilation of a victim—quite often, but not necessarily, of oneself; second, sacrifice serves to expiate human sin, to appease the deity for human transgressions. As annihilation, sacrifice called for a total "giving up" of the individual self, rather than a prudent "giving of" (some portion of) individuals or their property. This is sacrifice in what may be recognized as the idealistic or altruistic mode of total giving of self for others or in the romantic mode of gallant offering of the self for the beloved. As such, sacrifice here carries a note of extremity, rather than a more modest connotation. It admits no room for a prudent "giving *of*" as sufficient to the notion. The normal sense of sacrifice is here total and uncompromising.

Second, as expiation, sacrificial death is thought to settle some cosmic score, to weigh in the balance of debts owed, and thereby to effect sure repayment, to appease the righteous wrath of the deity.[13] On this logic, transgressions can never merely be thought away, excused, or eliminated in some "spiritual" way. Even Christ's good intentions could alone never suffice in place of a real sacrificing death and resurrection. Because Adam's sin materially disturbed the relation between humanity and divinity, it must be removed by some sort of thoroughly incarnated process such as by a ritual, like sacrifice. Christ really had to take on flesh, live and die because human sin had really disturbed our relationship to God and put the cosmos out of joint.

That Catholics felt religious offense needed to be put right by deeds fits with what historians have suggested about the particular "bloodiness" of French history.[14] The history of France from St. Bartholomew's Day to the Revolutionary Terror, as well as the cheerful lyrics of the "Marseillaise" celebrating "les étendards sanglants," suggest that a certain symbolic charge attaches to blood—a sensibility familiar enough to anyone versed in Roman Catholic theology of the classic period or in later periods when, for instance, devotion to the Sacred Heart swept the nation. Thus, Natalie Zemon Davis argues that during the Wars of Religion, although Protestants and Roman Catholics were equally violent, their violence differed in kind. Whereas Protestants delighted in attacking the "material objects" beloved of Catholics, such as images and consecrated hosts, Catholics tended to savage the "persons" of their Protestant adversaries.[15] In such a time, when religious thinking both informed and dominated political action, I argue that these differences in styles of violence should be assumed to have religious causes. One might imagine that the severe Catholic spirituality that took shape in the sixteenth century, emphasizing images evoking death and the passion of Christ, had something to do with the way people behaved in other contexts.[16] I will argue that to understand both the quantity and style of mass violence in France—and thus sacrificial death—we will need to understand not only fundamental

Catholic beliefs about human nature but also, as I have been urging, the Roman Catholic theological interpretations of the Eucharist stemming from the period of the *réaction* to the Reformation.

In France, this widely assumed notion of sacrifice was worked out intellectually first and primarily by pious, some would even say "mystical," theologians, the foremost of whom was Pierre de Bérulle. In their hands, a Eucharistic theology regulating and informing Roman Catholic piety took shape from the middle sixteenth century, in effect implementing the reforms introduced by the Council of Trent. In Eucharistic theology, no notion is more important than that of sacrifice, since Catholics regarded the mass as a sacrifice and vital center of Catholic liturgical life.[17] As Henri Bremond writes in 1922:

> The center of the entire Catholic religion [*culte*] . . . is not the Eucharist distributed at the holy table. Our religion has the holy sacrifice of the mass as its center and chief source of vitality, renewing the immolation of Jesus Christ on the cross, along with the participation of the faithful in this very same sacrifice by means of holy communion.[18]

We will also find that Catholic sacrificial Eucharistic theology of the end of the century carried forward faithfully the doctrinal reforms worked out and codified at the Council of Trent and later given added impetus in French history in the seventeenth-century *réaction* to the Reformation. For these Catholics of the seventeenth century, the sacrificial dimension of the Eucharist, understood as the real physical passion, suffering, and death of Jesus, received an emphasis "it had not previously had."[19] What we may call Catholic baroque spirituality's conception of sacrifice broke with Aquinas's emphasis on sacrifice as the interior psychological act of the recognition of divine sovereignty.[20] When married to the practical spirituality of the "imitation" of Christ, this theology urges self-effacing self-sacrifice of the human individual. Such self-immolation in some way expiates for human sin by participating in what Roman Catholics thought Jesus accomplished by his death on Calvary.

For our purposes, five aspects of the sacrificial conception of the mass, developed by Bérulle and his school, need to be stressed.

First, Catholics felt that the death of Jesus on Calvary was a sacrifice with cosmic implications: it expiated all the sins of humanity—past, present, and to come. Despite appearances, it was not then in reality a judicial execution. Rather, Jesus as the Son of God sacrificed himself to the Father for the sake of making up the debt humanity had incurred, and would continue to incur, by its sinfulness. Jesus is thus seen as both the priest of

Sounds too existential for / std. piety.

fering the sacrifice of himself and the victim of that very sacrifice, because only a divine priest offering a perfectly holy victim could ever compensate the Father for the offenses of humanity.

Second, in his total immolation of self, Jesus holds nothing back in reserve. In his sacrificial death, he pours out his being in death for the sake of all humanity in an act of sacred annihilation. Ironically and mystically, in accepting annihilation he is raised from the dead and wins life everlasting for humanity.

Third, for Catholic theology, the mass both symbolically represents and mystically re-presents this sacrificial death and resurrection of Jesus. The sacrifice of Jesus is eternally present; every mass thereafter, as it were, perpetuates the sacrificial death and resurrection of Jesus. Thus, the mass is believed to be more than a symbolic commemoration of those past salvific historical events; it is fundamentally a mysterious "participation" in the reality of the historical moment of Jesus' sacrificial death and resurrection. Every mass, Catholics believe, makes otherwise past historical events present again for the faithful. As the pious Abbé Kerné put it in 1902, the mass is a "continuation of Calvary."[21] It is "not only the representation and memorial of the unique true sacrifice . . . it is identically the same."[22]

Fourth, at the center of the mass is the Eucharist, the sacrificial communion meal. In participating in this meal, the faithful believe themselves to be sitting alongside Jesus at his last supper sharing sacramental communion with him and of his divine substance. Through this participation in the sacrifice and substance of Jesus, the faithful are "made holy"—which is literally what "sacrifice" means.[23] Believers hold that in this way God imparts some of his holiness to humanity. Without this, adds Abbé Kerné, humanity should "recognize [its] nothingness and miserable [nature]."[24] Human holiness is thus "borrowed." It is neither produced by us nor derived from some supposed, but really nonexistent, innate goodness in human nature.[25] Even our human orientation to God—human religiousness—is also a product of gracious divine initiatives and not, as we will see later in our discussion, a trace of some innate human proclivity for religion such as in a primordial "natural religion."

Fifth and finally, the sacrifice of Jesus on Calvary is the only true sacrifice. Whether consciously or not, all other sacrifices, past, present, and to come, whether offered by Druids or Brahmins, with whatever intentions, are only, as Abbé Kerné informs us again, "imitations of true sacrifice." They are "an image, more or less exact, a memory, a recollection . . . a derivation of true sacrifice."[26] In this respect, Kerné does not damn the religious sacrifices of other cultures; he patronizes them. The sacrifices of the other religions are not "true," but they have something of the truth in

them.[27] In this way, believing Catholics inhabited a world of mystic correspondences, where ordinary time and space collapsed into the sacred
time of the sacred events of Christian salvation history. The focus of their
history became the focus for the histories of all others. At the center of
that history was a sacrifice.

"Royal Religion," Baroque Spirituality, and Bérulle's Oratory

These theological positions took their meaning and force in part from
their embodiment in society and its politics. It is therefore no coincidence that this theology of the Eucharist as annihilating and expiatory
sacrifice was championed by certain individuals who figured prominently
in the absolutist religio-politics of those days. A prime example of this
merging of sacrificial theologies of the Eucharist and absolutist politics
can be found in the leading French theologian of his time, Pierre de Bérulle
(1575–1629).[28] With Bérulle, the association of sacrificial religion and
the absolutist politics of the age reached perfection given that "the Church
of seventeenth-century France was above all Bérulle's Church."[29] Bérulle
mediated this influence as founder of the French version of one of the
most influential institutions of the French réaction to the Reformation,
the Oratorian congregation (1611) originally founded in the wake of the
Council of Trent by the Italian, Philip Neri. Through the Oratory, Bérulle
sought to renew Catholic education by revamping the ideology and training of priests and laity alike. Later to become a cardinal, Bérulle was a remarkable and in some ways ambivalent figure, mixing both a highly in-
teriorized religiosity with ambitions to a career at the highest levels of
statecraft. In the realm of spirituality, he created an influential self-immolating "mystical" spirituality centered about the self-sacrificing priestly figure of Jesus, a spirituality later to become what was known as the "École
Française de Spiritualité."[30] In his first publication, a tract entitled Bref
discours de l'abnégation intérieure (1597), he set the tone of his life's work
which put at its center an adoration of God, culminating in a total annihilation—"anéantissement"—of the devotee.[31] There, he called for "successive deprivations to the annihilation of the human self and the trans-
forming union with God."[32] Bérulle claimed that Christ's annihilating
sacrifice on Calvary becomes our own model. Our inner, spiritual "anéantissement" was to culminate in a total surrender to the Godhead, just as it
had for Jesus. [33]

What is particularly intriguing about the otherwise "mystical" Bérulle
is how fiercely political he was and thus, by extension, how political his Eucharistic theology of sacrifice was as well.[34] Far from being a withdrawn
mystic, he was one of the chief players in the French court politics of the

day. Cousin to Marie de Médici,[35] Henri IV's widow and regent to Louis XIII, Bérulle was a strong advocate of putting government powers of coercion at the disposal of the church.[36] Bérulle, for example, wished Protestantism to be proscribed entirely.[37] As a major rival to Cardinal Richelieu (1589–1642), Bérulle harbored ambitions to succeed him as the king's first minister.[38] But, by contrast with Bérulle, Richelieu showed himself the moderate. Despite the Cardinal's orthodoxy, he pursued policies of practical statecraft diametrically opposed to those of Bérulle and the so-called fiercely Catholic *dévot* party. He allied France with the Protestant powers against the hyper-Catholic Hapsburgs and refused to force the conversion of the Huguenots that Bérulle favored. Thus, perhaps sensing the danger to the peace of the realm represented by the potent mixture of Bérulle's theology and his politics, Richelieu took as much exception to the extremism of Bérulle's religious rigorism and mysticism as he did to his Catholic politics.[39] Does this picture of Bérulle match the profile of a quietist and mystic? If not, why should we assume Bérulle's sacrificial theology of the Eucharist does as well? Indeed, Bérulle proved himself not only a theologian of mystical devotion and spiritual severity. He also led an extreme political program of Bourbon "royal religion." This saw Bérulle's influence remaining powerful in both religious and political circles throughout the seventeenth century.

In the theological sphere, Bérulle's influence lived on institutionally in what came to be known as the "École Française de Spiritualité," or simply the "French School."[40] Notable among those articulating Bérulle's theology of interiority and priestly reform were members of the Oratory such as Charles de Condren and Jean-Jacques Olier.[41] Condren's theology of Eucharistic sacrifice was as annihilationist as Bérulle's. Some even say that Condren was "as Bérullian as Bérulle himself, and had been so long before meeting Bérulle."[42] Condren, for example, asserted that sacrifice is the first and foremost religious act and priestly function.[43] With the image in mind of Christ the heavenly priest continually offering sacrifice to the Father throughout eternity, Olier saw Christ's sacrifice as eternal.

> It cannot be doubted that there is sacrifice in heaven, because heaven is most of all the place of perfect religion. . . . By right, sacrifice should be offered there, and offered there unceasingly, because it is there that religion suffers no interruption.[44]

The idea of Christ's eternal sacrifice informed Olier's view of a reformed clergy: Christ's sacrifice was not only eternal itself, but eternally exemplary for the secular Roman priesthood and, by extension, for the faithful themselves. Indeed, later commentators have even called attention to the superiority of the Eucharist to Calvary: one might say, for example, that on Calvary only a single, temporally confined sacrifice was performed; in the daily offering of the Eucharistic sacrifice, Calvary is made perpetual. Thus, the core of this new spirituality consisted of seeing the whole of life as a living sacrifice. For the "French School," sacrifice consisted in an offering, its immolation and final "consummation" or acceptance by God.[45] In the process, it was the human individual who was annihilated. Condren's theory of sacrifice "requires destruction . . . [a] total destruction . . . as much as is completely possible." [46]

Condren's severe spirituality also seemed to be of a piece with the character of his wider life—in this case, his rearing, education, and political life. Indeed, the connections here between the child and the man are so obvious as to offer one of the better examples of the pertinence of contemporary feminist criticism of religion. Consider the bizarre details of the biographical sketch by Denis Amelote (1609–1679), a contemporary and devoted follower of Condren. Père Amelote tells us that young Charles's military father raised him as a soldier from infancy, inflicting upon him a "virile, military and somewhat savage education."[47] As soon as Charles had been weaned, his father refused to allow him to be held or carried about by women. Only soldiers were permitted to touch the young man; his days were filled with drilling and military exercises. Later as a youth, he "spontaneously" resisted any contact with women. Having been forced to attend a ball, he went into fever for eight consecutive days. Once a great beauty of the day warmly embraced him, kissing him dearly. Condren's reaction was horror: "the more she kissed him, the more he rubbed his cheeks."[48] He ran off in a rage. Fiddle music made him ill. But he loved the sound of the drum—not for its beauty, but because it was more heroic.[49] And thus too beauty repelled him—even his own. Although a handsome young man, he so detested beauty that he destroyed an especially flattering portrait of himself by shooting it with arrows.[50] Of all these incidents, his Oratorian companion offered such comments as "'Am I not right in saying that this blessed child from tender years partook of the fullness of Jesus Christ?'"[51] Later, after his ordination, his turn to spiritual writing and teaching continued this violent and self-hating trend of mind. In a collection of his maxims, we find Condren saying: "'I am a greater temptation to myself and injure myself more than the devil or the world can do; therefore I must hate myself more.'"[52]

By some standards, the key member of the Oratorian movement was Jean-Jacques Olier. Among Olier's accomplishments was the foundation of what would become the vanguard seminary of France, Saint-Sulpice.[53] In the seventeenth century, the Saint-Sulpicians were responsible for the reform of the secular French clergy according to the decrees of the Council of Trent in their creation of an ideology of priestly holiness inspired by the theology of sacrifice of the French School.[54] By joining the dual roles of theologian and administrator, Olier was positioned to establish a close connection between Saint-Sulpice, as a preeminent institution for the education and training of the French clergy, and the French School's theological vision of the priesthood.[55] Moreover, while dominating the education of secular French clergy for centuries, the influence of the French School was not confined to France alone. It spread far beyond, and came in time to dominate the thinking of the *réaction* about the nature of the priestly function among Roman Catholics of many nations.[56]

Baroque Spirituality and the Politics of the "Blessed Sacrament"

The sacrificial spirituality of Bérulle, Condren, and Olier matched up with their politics most visibly in an ostensibly religious movement known as the "Compagnie du Saint Sacrement." To best expose this connection, however, we will need to detour slightly by way of the Jesuits—key players as well in the sacrificial politics of "royal religion."

At the same time that the Oratory and the "French School" were shaping post-Tridentine Catholic piety along sacrificial lines, the Jesuits did something similar. Instead of reforming the spirituality of the local secular clergy, however, the Jesuits produced lay movements independent of the traditional parish and diocese. The Jesuits propagated a spirituality in many ways analogous to that encouraged by the French School through an array of lay organizations or sodalities, which they organized all across Western Europe. As dedicated as the French School in their primary devotion to the sacrificial Eucharist as defined by the Council of Trent, the pious members of these Jesuit-informed lay groups became known as *"dévots."*[57] Despite their differences, it ought to be noted, both Jesuits and partisans of the French School stood united in reasserting the Tridentine doctrine of the Eucharist as a representation of Jesus' sacrificial death on Calvary.

Nevertheless, some differences between the approaches of the French School and the Jesuits are worth noting because they witness to the vitality of Catholic determination to affirm the sacrificial nature of the Eucharist and the centrality of sacrifice as a spiritual trope. In part, because of their foundation as a missionary order, rather than as a movement to reform the interior lives of the secular clergy, the Jesuits frequently tended to emotional and public displays of piety. Their inclination to strategize and propagandize for the faith, led the Jesuits to sponsor public religious festivals and even conspicuous displays of piety such as in the practice of frequent communion and confession, or in the many sorts of public devotions encouraging support for the Eucharist as the center of Catholic religious life. Among the first of such bodies, organized by the Jesuits in 1554, was a Eucharistic sodality, the Society for the Veneration of the Holy Sacrament.

At the same time that the Jesuits sponsored public devotion to the sacrificial Eucharist, they also worked clandestinely to promote the Tridentine vision of the Eucharist. They thus encouraged the formation of secret societies pledged above all to promote the representation of Jesus' sacrificial expiating death and resurrection as articulated by Trent.[58] One such clandestine Eucharistic lay organization was the Company of the Most Blessed Sacrament. Founded in 1630 by Henri de Lévis, Duc de Ventadour, following Jesuit practice, it recruited its membership from among pious lay elites eager to blunt the Protestant advance. Witnesses to the importance of the Compagnie, even those often critical of the Jesuits, prominent leaders of the French School like Bérulle, Olier and Condren also counted among its members.[59] The character after which Molière fashioned Tartuffe may well have been sketched after the models provided by the pious *dévots* who flocked to the Compagnie du Saint Sacrement.[60]

On the surface, the Compagnie was a movement of rigorous personal moral reform and good works. As a charitable society, it founded hospitals, protected tradesmen's organizations, provided legal aid to the poor, and distributed alms to the needy.[61] The company cooperated closely with the charitable works of Vincent de Paul. Later it served a missionary role, both in Europe and overseas. But, at the same time that the Compagnie performed acts of charity, its membership organized into a series of secret cells spread across the country, in about fifty French towns, for the purpose of propagating the French School's reinvigorated sacrificial theology of the Eucharist. In this way, beyond cultivation of the inner life of the soul, the Compagnie was one of the chief social agents of the Catholic *réaction* to the Reformation, rallying the faithful to the Catholic faith during the height of the campaigns against the Protestants. A leading figure in the French School and also a member of the Company, Jean-Jacques Olier, for example, led public campaigns against the sale and display of so-called pornographic *tableaux* and sculptures in the open air market fairs held in Saint Germain des Prés.[62] At his instigation, the Company acted further as a "secret committee of public morality," which "attacked all manner of evil at any and all times."[63] Thus, in a style made famous by the Jesuits, the Compagnie was at once part of the great stream of intensified inward spirituality and also a social body practicing a sacralized politics.

In time, however, the "Compagnie du Saint Sacrement" grew too independent of royal control and invited dissolution. And so, despite its good services in behalf of the Counter-Reformation, despite its early devotion "without ambiguity" to the Crown,[64] despite its links with the queen mother under the regency,[65] and despite the possibility that Louis XIV himself would go over to the *parti dévot* late in life, Cardinal Mazarin, acting for the young king, disbanded the Compagnie in 1660.

Whether or not the Compagnie presented a real threat to the crown, its independence was sufficient to trigger repressive measures of Louis XIV. It is worth taking a few moments to understand the dynamic of the dissolution of the Compagnie du Saint Sacrement because it sheds light on the relation of religion and politics so important to our story. At first, the Compagnie showed an unreserved dedication to the Crown, going so far as to place the king on a level with the pope.[66] Nevertheless, as Louis XIV's disregard for Catholic, much less Christian, principles of governance later became manifest, the Compagnie drew back from the king. Alain Tallon believes that they sought to evade the conformist trends toward absolutism by adopting a policy of public prudence in affairs of state and by developing for themselves a notion of a king's fallibility.[67] Although they never advocated regicide or tyrannicide, the Compagnie turned to earlier models of French kingship—such as that of St. Louis— in order to maintain a consistency of viewpoint. In this way, despite their distance from Louis XIV, they maintained their militant Catholicism married to an equally fervent French nationalism. Indeed, Alain Tallon has argued that the Compagnie's dedication to the monarch did not at all arise from fear of royal power or mystic devotion to the person of the sovereign. Rather, it was part and parcel of their militant Catholicism, which Tallon says, is closely related to "profound nationalism."[68]

In line with the sense of the union of sacrificial religion and a kind of nationalist politics—absolutist or not—which we have already seen in the *dévot* religio-politics of a Bérulle and his confederates, the Compagnie's reservations about royal absolutism did not mean, however, that the Compagnie was any the less devoted to the union of religion and politics. As Benedict Anderson has argued, the readiness of individuals to sacrifice themselves can best be understood in terms of the religious nature of fellowship achieved by the nation-state.[69] That the Compagnie both celebrated sacrificial religion *and* militant nationalism testifies that the two realms in this case are really a single realm of religion and politics. In celebrating the memory of St. Louis, the model saintly monarch, for example, the Compagnie promoted the public policies of purging of prostitutes, Jews, blasphemers, and decadents from the realm.[70] While Louis XIV and the Compagnie disagreed about the all-important matter of the nature of sovereignty and the relative relation of spirit to governance, they nonetheless held politics and religion in close union. True to Trent's opposition to Machiavelli, the Compagnie wished to place religious morality and piety at the center of government.[71] They therefore abhorred Louis XIV's rule of *raison d'état* and personal absolutism in government, not because it mixed politics and religion but because it subjected religion to politics.[72] Perhaps most threatening to Louis, therefore, was the fact that the Compagnie did take its sacrificial religion seriously and sought to revolutionize French politics accordingly, while Louis, on the other hand, took his politics seriously and sought to manipulate religion pragmatically, even cynically, according to the needs of his royal policies.

Rococo Inventions: The Sacred Heart of Politics and the Jesuits

In the late seventeenth and early eighteenth centuries, the Jesuits gave new life to the "baroque" sacrificial spiritualities of the École Française de Spiritualité and the Compagnie du Saint Sacrement by promoting the ("rococo") cult of the Sacred Heart.[73] This cult encouraged devotion to (the heart of) Jesus under the species of his sacrificial suffering for the sins for humanity. As such, a passionate, vivid, albeit "bloody" imagery moved to the center of an essentially rococo religious imagination. Here was devotion to the "heart" of Jesus, which was sorely wounded for human offenses and which bled to redeem even those who had drawn first blood. Here, once more, was a spiritual movement bound intrinsically to Jesus as the perfect and total sacrificial offering for the expiation of the sins of humanity. Eventually, the cult of the Sacred Heart was to become a special mark of the Jesuit order and its commission of rolling back the Reformation.[74]

Despite antipathy between the Jesuits and the Oratory, devotion to the Sacred Heart received impetus from Bérulle's own involvement in the original emergence of the cult.[75] Bérulle had been at work on a kind of religious psychology of the heart years before the cult itself was to appear and fall into Jesuit hands. The heart, said Bérulle, was not only "the seat of affectivity" but also the "meeting place between a person and God."[76] This common ground of the heart provided a venue where both Christ and devotee could play their roles as sacrificial victims. The devotee not only meditated on Christ's expiating death and total immolation of himself before the Father, but also took the occasion to enter into Jesus' cosmic action by seeking a total identification with the suffering lord. We should also recall that Bérulle had already supplied the intellectual basis for an imagery of spiritual emptying or annihilation, realized so brilliantly in the cult of the Sacred Heart, in stressing the self-annihilating sacrificial Christ of the Eucharist. His theocentric teaching of the "abasement of the human self" over against divine majesty served the same ends.[77] Bérulle, however, ought not to be credited with starting the cult.

That honor goes to a pious Visitandinian nun, Marguerite-Marie Alacoque. In 1673, she reported violent and passionate visions of Jesus'
wounded heart all aflame with love for humanity, all intent on total human devotion.[78] Graphically depicted in terms of the tormented images
of self-sacrificing suffering, this sacrificial spirituality, supported by Bérulle's theology, provided the basis for a passionate Catholic reassertion
of sacrificial values.

But even here, in the midst of a ravishing spirituality, politics lurked.
Strong at court, the Jesuits sought to inform the cult of the Sacred Heart
with the ideal of obedience to the crown. In the time of rising absolutism,
the Sacred Heart was identified with the will to compel human "obedience."[79] By 1689, the image was so identified with the royal cause (and
thus with its absolutism) that the visionary Alacoque demanded that
Louis XIV add the Sacred Heart to the Bourbon family coat of arms. For
Alacoque, the political content of the devotion was indistinguishable—
as it should have been in those times—with its religious nature. Identification with the royalist cause grew stronger still when Queen Marie
(Leszczynska), wife of Louis XV and daughter of Stanislas Leszczynski,
whom Louis XIV had created Duke of Lorraine, became official sponsor
of devotion to the Sacred Heart in 1725.[80] By 1730 then, devotion to the
Sacred Heart became as much a part of the religious focus of the party of
the *dévots* as had been the dedication to the reserved sacrament championed by the Compagnie du Saint Sacrement. This witnesses to the fact
that in France in subsequent years, the cult would always bear an unmis-
takable "counter-revolutionary coloration" and constituted a definite
"political spirituality and theology."[81] The counter-revolutionaries of the
Vendeé accordingly proudly displayed the Sacred Heart emblem on their
clothing.[82] The Jansenists, apparently alone among Catholics, saw clearly,
from early on, the political consequences that so thorough an emphasis
on obedience would have on the realm. Given their opposition to anything that would increase the crown's appropriation of sacrality, they accordingly opposed the cult as long as they could, but without final success.[83]

Anticipating the coming chapters, I would simply conclude this discussion of the origins of the devotion to the Sacred Heart by noting its persistence as the leading emblem around which right-wing Catholic spirituality and politics rallied. Among the more familiar material monuments
to the politico-religious logic of the Sacred Heart is one that links, in a
truly spectacular way, the royal spirituality of the *dévots* of the seventeenth
and eighteenth centuries with the intransigent Catholic right wing of the
late nineteenth and early twentieth centuries. This is, of course, the
Basilique du Sacré Coeur in Paris. In 1915, the French bishops dedicated

the nation to the Sacred Heart and in 1917 vowed to celebrate its feast perpetually. Devotion to the "suffering Christ" of the Sacred Heart cult greatly increased during the First World War and was doubtless linked to the national travail induced by the great combat.[84] In the last years of the war, the most militant and intransigent Catholics campaigned to include the emblem of the Sacred Heart among the banners making up the "couleurs nationals"—an effort so bold that it energized the laïc forces in 1917 to a counter-offensive against the intransigent Catholics.[85] Thus, from the Jesuits of eighteenth century to the integrists and intransigents of the twentieth century, the Sacred Heart served as a focus for a complex of rightist politics and Eucharistic spirituality right into the twentieth century.

Thus, baroque and rococo religious movements such as the French School, the Company of the Blessed Sacrament, and the cult of the Sacred Heart pose for us a continuous set of cultural discourses and social formations that did their part in creating a certain political culture of national sacrifice typically seen as self-generating. Even though these movements were well in advance of the Revolution and its invention of "the nation," I want to argue that these apparently purely religious and spiritual movements can be seen as laying the foundation for what is conventionally called a secular ideology of sacrifice for the nation, which became prominent in the French Revolution. This supposedly unbridgeable gap between the sacred and the secular drastically narrows, for when it comes to sacrifice, there is little or no significant difference between the politicized royal religion of the prerevolutionary period and the sacralized politics of nationalism.[86] Thus, long before the Jacobins called for the magical rite of the sacrifice of Louis XVI to redeem the nation,[87] the *dévots* had assimilated the person of the Bourbon king to the Eucharistic body of Jesus.[88] Long before the Revolution, the devotees of the sacred heart, as we have just seen, had set a sacrificial spirituality at the center of Bourbon dynastic identity and national political salvation.[89] And, long before Michelet had tried to pass off Joan of Arc as a republican, national sacrifice for the "kingdom," and thus for the "nation," were already on the minds of patriots. Joan had already been venerated, for example, by Catholic royalists as the savior of the "king" and his sacred, Eucharistic, person.[90] With all that this projection of the savior role onto Joan implies as an imitation of the self-sacrificing Christ, the Catholic resonances could hardly be clearer. It is then much easier to imagine that one can uproot the national traditions of centuries than actually to eliminate what Georges Goyau called the "subconscious" Catholicism that "still survives in the soul of France."[91] All this inevitably leads us to take up the implications of the French Revolution for the discourse about sacrifice.

The Revolution and Sacrifice: Roman or Roman Catholic?

Catholic discourse about sacrifice has remained dominant in France despite notable efforts to reposition the nation with respect to its Catholic past. This was so, not only in the period when the Constitutional Church attempted to conform Catholic doctrine to the Revolution's ideals, but even thereafter in the radical "dechristianization" that began in September 1793. Not long after the Jesuits promoted the long-lived monarchist and Eucharistic cult of the Sacred Heart, the Constitutional Church was interpreting Catholic ideals of Jesus' self-sacrifice along nationalist revolutionary lines, which would shortly be succeeded by the Revolution's anti-Catholic ideal of national sacrifice for a national civil religion. Both these efforts only served to continue and reshape the basic Catholic model, which is one of the ironies of the story I have been trying to tell.

The Church split into two factions in 1790, when the revolutionary government demanded that Catholics swear loyalty to the Civil Constitution of the Clergy. Those pledging allegiance to the Constitution came to be known, naturally enough, as the "Constitutional" church, while those dissenting were called the "Refractory" church or clergy. In accepting the reforms of the Revolution, the so-called Constitutional Catholics created a theology in line with their new political situation. They made conspicuous efforts, for example, to celebrate social equality, among other revolutionary virtues.[92] The leader and one of the greatest thinkers of the Constitutional Church, Abbé Henri-Baptiste Grégoire, tells us that he sought to *"désolidariser"* Christianity from monarchy.[93] The Constitutional Church also launched a major hermeneutic industry to conceive of Jesus as a patriot in service to the Revolution.[94] In truth, they did not need to go very far down this path. As early as 1691, the great Gallican divine of the *ancien régime*, Bishop Jacques-Bénigne Bossuet (1627–1704) had already authoritatively articulated the theological and political ideal of Jesus as the "'good citizen.'"[95] During the early years of the Revolution, this theme was so pervasive that it often gave conspicuous aid and comfort to the revolutionaries at certain critical moments. Catholic funerals for those who died in the taking the Bastille or religious ceremonies blessing the banners of the Garde Nationale—all appealed to Jesus as patriot as "one of the principal motifs of the preaching" in those heady days.[96] It is also seldom realized that early on, the French Revolution was itself seen by Catholics as a divine providential act and that it was likened by them to Israel's escape from Egypt.[97]

It is perhaps not surprising that even the Constitutional Church drew upon certain select pre-existing images of Jesus from the *ancien régime*. In a condition of instability and strife, the image of the self-sacrificing Jesus embodied in the ideal of the patriotic Jesus was particularly adaptable to the tasks of building the republic and Revolution. Noteworthy, however, was how easily apparently counter-revolutionary aspects of the *ancien régime*'s conception of Jesus formed the basis of the Constitutional Church's revolutionary spirituality. In particular connection with the sacrificial imagery of the Paschal lamb and its transformation into Jesus' self-effacing sacrifice on Calvary, the Constitutional Church passionately reaffirmed the image of the submissive and "obedient" (unto death) Jesus.[98] Thus, with the image of Jesus submitting to power[99]—and not rebelling against it—annihilating sacrifice once more rose to the surface of French religio-political consciousness, but this time in service to the "nation," not the monarch. From the pages of his *A la Piété patriotique: Discours apologétique sur la constitution du clergé* (1791), the Constitutional *curé* of Évry-sur-Seine, François Mille, tell us that "'It is from the Gospels themselves that I will never stop showing you that the bad citizen is not a true Christian, since the adoration which it prescribes to us regarding the divine author is tightly linked to the submission that it imposes on us with respect to the powers of this world.'"[100] Thus, the Constitutional Church adapted Jesus to the Revolution, even while it maintained the same theological structures as those employed by the *ancien régime* in behalf of divine monarchy. Jesus, and thus the faithful of the Revolution who imitated him, were circumscribed by the same sacrificial discourse employed by the Church of the Golden Age and its theologians of annihilating self-sacrifice.

The Constitutional Church was not long-lived, despite its patriotic eagerness in reading Jesus along lines conducive to the aims of the Revolution. It was in effect swept aside in 1793 by the campaign of dechristianization. The leaders of the Revolution felt that they could safely begin French history anew by replacing Catholic symbols with religio-political ones of their own devising. Thus, devotion to the Goddess of Reason replaced the solemnities honoring the Blessed Virgin in the cathedral of the Notre Dame; the Supreme Being tried to nudge the God of Abraham, Isaac, and Joseph off center stage, and festivals of fecundity and citizenship filled the Revolution's new calendar as full as the feast days of Catholic saints had populated the old. Catholic Christianity's central rite—the Eucharistic sacrifice—seemed likewise destined for a lofty place in the piety of the radical Revolution.

Despite its ferocity, real questions remain as to the real success of the Revolution's program of dechristianization.[101] On this score, Simon Schama concluded that of "all the failures of the French Revolution, none would be so inevitable and dismal as the campaign of 'dechristianization.'"[102] In this vein, it is ironic that the dechristianizers seemed to follow a Christian script even in pursuing their policies of dechristianization. Willy-nilly, for example, they fell back upon the same self-effacing sacrificial structures that had informed the Catholic traditions they sought to replace. Patrice Higonnet notes that the "Jacobin's thirst for harmonizing sacrifice ran deep."[103] Standard appeals to the duties of citizenship, for example, were made in terms no less bloody than the language of Calvary. The severe Saint-Just, discoursing on the relation of ardent love of country in relation to its laws as constituting a real *"patrie"* spoke in words as chilling as anything coming from the mouths of Condren or Olier:

> Where there are no laws, there is no nation [*patrie*]. And, that is why people who live under a despotism don't really enjoy nationhood [*patrie*]—except in the sense that they despise or hate other nations.
>
> But, just because laws exist, does not mean that there is nationhood [*patrie*] either—except in the sense that there is some sort of common good. But, in this common good, there is a deep truth—the very pride of liberty and virtue. It is only out of the common good that men rise up for whom the love of laws is like heavenly fire, and in whom runs blood which thrills at combat, and who sacrifice [dévouant] themselves in cold blood to both danger and death.[104]

More, therefore, than sweet *fraternité* or cordial "harmonizing" guided the Jacobins, at least in the assertion of sacrificial values. The Jacobins notoriously "saved their enthusiasm for selflessly and even suicidally heroic individuals. They idealized those moral souls who chose or accepted a patriotic death that transformed individualism into communitarian wholeness." Higonnet tells us further that even Robespierre "explained that he would gladly sacrifice his life to the nation and the future. 'Should I be the victim of some miserable cabal, I will at least die with a name that will be dear to posterity.'"[105] As if such words did not strain enough in the direction of the religious discourse of sacrificial transcendence, Higonnet tells us that so strong was revolutionary "yearning for a universalizing society where the one and the many would come together" that people literally "rhapsodized" about the possibility "that self-becoming and self-sacrifice were overlapping values."[106] A veritable political kingdom of heaven would come into being on this revolutionized earth. So, despite its reputation as a major proponent of a secularizing and fissiparous individualism, the left wing of the French Revolution, at least, displays a self-effacing annihilationism in the service of community (church) worthy of the Oratorian fathers.[107]

But imitation, however, in all likelihood, unconscious in the case of Catholicism, did not end with attempts to trade on Catholic notions. Aware that they needed to break free of Catholicism's stranglehold on their imaginations and, at the same time, find historical legitimacy for the republic, the Revolution anchored its sacrificial ideology in remote historical periods, independent of the Christian past.[108] The French Revolution found this historical precedent in the ancient Roman republic. Simon Schama, in fact, refers to nothing less than the "Roman fetishism of the Revolution" in pursuit of a transcendent model of a radiant republican past, entirely cutting out the Christian past.[109]

This modeling of the revolutionary France upon so ancient a template as republican Rome was made possible by the standard secondary school education in the classics prevalent among the elites and bourgeoisie. Many of the leaders of the Revolution, for example, had been schooled in selected classics of the ancient world at the Jesuit *collèges*, where mastering classical languages and texts constituted much of the educational process. In this way, the leaders of the Revolution had already been exposed to an alternative non-Christian model of social life.

Among the moral lessons learned from reading the Roman classics were such republican social values as equality and justice. These emerged typically in expressions of distaste for empire in favor of the Roman Republic. Interestingly, these transcendent ethical values of the Revolution survived efforts made to suppress them by the Jesuits and Oratorians, who dominated teaching in the *collèges* where the classics were read.[110] They typically railed against the evils of egalitarianism as a source of social disharmony and confusion. The effect of their attempts to discredit republican values, however, seems to have been the opposite of what the teaching orders intended. Instead of inspiring loyalty to the monarchy and its system of social ranking, the teaching orders provoked the future revolutionaries to overthrow them.[111] Along these lines, Camille Desmoulins relates how he conceived a republican future for France by reflecting on the egalitarianism of the ancient world.

> The memory of those triumphal chariots of the Romans, where a man of high rank was given to understand by a slave at his side that he was, after all, only a citizen; here, on the contrary, the profound sentiment of their pride, of their scorn for the nation; that extravagant idea which I thought I read in their faces, that it was to God and to their swords, and not to us that they owed their elevation to a position of honor; the comparison of their individual insignificance with that inflated grandeur . . . all these pictures filled me with an indescribable indignation, and my hatred of royalty brought on a fever, the only one I have ever had.[112]

But higher still on the Revolution's list of civic values rooted in Roman examples—especially as the Revolution came more and more to see itself threatened by external enemies—was the readiness of heroic citizens to "sacrifice" for the newly conceived nation.[113] We, in fact, know that the future revolutionaries drew upon the lofty examples of the "neo-Roman ideal of patriotic sacrifice," exemplified prominently by the figure(s) of Brutus.[114] The Jacobins, for example, "felt emphatically that classical figures had prefigured the great men of their own times."[115] "Brutus" occupied a particular place of honor here for the revolutionaries. For the revolutionaries, the proper name, Brutus, applied chiefly to Lucius Junius Brutus (c. 500 BCE), who slew the tyrant king Tarquin in order to establish the first Roman republic, but also, to a lesser extent, to his better known descendent, Marcus Brutus, who joined in assassinating Julius Caesar (85–42 BCE), ostensibly to save the Republic.[116] Perhaps the most favored text for republican patriots was Plutarch who records the lives of both in great detail and in a spirit of moral engagement, carrying a message of devotion to nation.[117] In both cases, the self-sacrificing acts of "Brutus," whether to establish the first Roman republic in 508 BCE or to attempt to save its successor from the rise of Julius Caesar, the moral lesson of sacrifice for the community is the same. The links between the two were even felt in Roman times. On the occasion of the rise of Julius Caesar, Plutarch tells us that the Roman republicans tried to rouse Marcus Brutus to action against Caesar by recalling his ancestor of five hundred years before! "The tribunal upon which he [Marcus Brutus] sat as praetor," says Plutarch, "began to be covered day after day with writings which read, 'Brutus, are you asleep?' or 'You are no true Brutus.'"[118] In its turn, the Revolution sanctified loyalty to the nation by celebrating the blow of both Brutuses, but mostly of Lucius Junius, against their own monarchs, just as the Romans of Caesar's time rallied republican spirits against actual or potential tyrants by symbolically associating Tarquin with Julius Caesar. Indeed, Edith Flamarion has shown how some of the success of the Brutus myth resulted from the "confusion" of these different historical Brutuses in the sense of a symbolic "identification" of them as one expressive "Brutus."[119] Voltaire, for example, published his play about Lucius Junius, *Brutus,* in 1730 followed immediately in 1731 by one about Marcus Brutus, *La Mort de César.*[120] In a fit of revolutionary indoctrination, the Committee of Public Safety decreed that both the "Brutus" plays were to be performed *weekly* by all the theaters in Paris![121] Admiration for the great ancestor of the "noblest Roman of them all" even called forth the creation on the 22 September 1793 of the "Feast of Brutus" in memory of Lucius Junius.[122] The deployment of the myth of Brutus was furthermore secured by "his" memorialization in the plastic arts, especially in officially sponsored sculpture. A decree of 27 August 1792 required that all public buildings and associations should be adorned with a bust of Brutus. This resulted in literally "millions" of images being manufactured and put into place all over the nation.[123]

In the sacrificial drama, both Brutuses were cast as victims—as men sacrificed or sacrificing themselves and their families. In the risks taken and losses incurred for the republic and nation, both Brutuses suffered greatly for the nation. Their sacrifices were not therefore immolations of "kings" like Tarquin or Caesar, but sacrifices of themselves. In these figures of revolutionary ardor, the Christian commandment not to kill was deliberately offended by the duty to kill for the sake of liberty.[124] Of Voltaire's two Brutus plays, it has been said by scholars of the period, that no one emerging from one of these productions would hesitate, along with the Brutuses, to "stab the villain who might attempt to enslave his country."[125] This will provide a telling contrast to Joseph de Maistre's view of Louis XVI's death as a great sacrifice performed unwittingly by those who saw their act as a simple criminal execution or act of revolutionary self-preservation. Brutus thus served as a Christ-like republican image of willingness to accept his own total sacrifice by putting himself and his family at risk of death for the nation.[126]

Someone like Charlotte Corday, the upper-class, convent-educated assassin of Jean Paul Marat, for instance, shows how potent this image of the self-sacrificing Brutus could be. As a "Plutarchian Republican,"[127] whose head brimmed with the republican ideals taught by the great biographer, Corday did not hesitate to speak in *self*-sacrificial language appropriate to Brutus in order to justify her murder of Marat. "'I have never lacked energy'" for the deed, she told her inquisitors, since she saw her murder of Marat modeled on Brutus's deed. She always felt that she would be counted as one of those "'who put their own interests to one side and know how to sacrifice themselves for the nation.'"[128] Although he does not tell us which Brutus, he has in mind, Patrice Higonnet argued that like "Brutus" Corday "wanted to kill Marat so as to reconcile all Frenchmen, at the cost of her own life."[129] What is important for an appreciation of the social depth of the image of Brutus as sacrifice for the nation was the fact that the symbolism of Corday's deed went beyond her own private sense of self. Its symbolism was transparent at the time to keen observers like the German devotee of Rousseau, Adam Lux. He names Corday's gesture precisely in the "sacrificial sense" of the assertion of the common good over individual interests, which is the essence of the Brutuses of both Plutarch and the Revolution. Saint-Just, for example, mirrored Lux's vision of Corday's act as a sacrifice for the community modeled on Brutus.[130] We would do well to recall how Shakespeare's Mark Antony declares of Lucius Junius's successor in the business of self-sacrifice for the noble values of the republic what all republicans thought about both these self-sacrificing Brutuses:

> All the conspirators, save only he
> Did that they did in envy of great Caesar;
> He only, in a general honest thought,
> And common good to all, made one of them.
> (Act 5, scene 5)

In his republican patriotism, the Marcus Brutus of Voltaire does not really differ. Although Voltaire casts Brutus as the natural son of Caesar, it is Brutus's love for the collectivity, for the republic, that enables him even to overcome the pressures of his familial obligations and strike down Caesar. Shortly before the assassination, Brutus discloses his heretofore unknown paternity:

> I shall appall you with a horrid secret.
> I owe Rome his death, to you, to your descendants,
> To the happiness of mortals; and I have chosen the hour,
> the place, the weapon, the very moment that Rome wishes him to die:
> The honor of delivering the first blow is placed in my hands;
> Everything is ready: but know now that Brutus is his son!
> (Act 3, scene 2)[131]

One final caveat. While not diminishing the extent to which the Revolution's conceptions of civic duty and patriotic sacrifice owed direct and unmediated debts to classic Roman models, one must bear in mind at least three factors that force us to consider the persistence of the "cultural references" related to Catholicism.

First, as we have had occasion to note, through the eighteenth century until their expulsion by Louis XV in 1763, education in the classics rested chiefly with the Jesuits.[132] After the expulsion of the Jesuits, the Oratorians assumed the role of chief teaching religious order.[133] Barbaroux, Brevet de Beaujour, Courtois, Le Bon, Robespierre, Desmoulins, Saint-Just, and Danton, for example, were all schooled in the classics by the Oratorians.[134] Some of these key figures in the Revolution, like Robespierre, had also been schooled earlier by the Jesuits before entering the Oratorian *collèges*.[135] Thus, education in the literature and history of Rome was in large part sifted through the same masterly hands as had articulated the classic Catholic theologies of sacrifice we have had occasion to review.[136] As we have seen, one of the main features of both Oratorian and Jesuit theologies during the same period was their articulation of a spirituality of sacrifice, for example, as it had been developed by the Jesuits in the cult of the Sacred Heart. Further, we also know that the classical authors, such as Plutarch and Livy, were taught to illustrate ethical lessons useful for moral guidance in the everyday world.[137] Such values as social duty and patriotism were among the moral lessons of great power emerging from the Roman material as it was shaped by the hands of the religious teaching orders.[138] Read as a source for a veritable secular republican "Lives of the Saints," Plutarch's *Lives* was among the most popular of all classic works read by the young students in the *collèges*, showing us how the Church's ability to mediate the classics often meant its ability to use them for its own purposes of theological information. Once more our source is Camille Desmoulins. He tells us, for example, that he was greatly impressed by how his instructor, the Abbé Royou, glorified Brutus for his dutiful and sacrificial giving up of himself and his relatives for the salvation of Rome.[139] Why then should we doubt that other Jesuits or Oratorians used their advantages in the classroom to influence their young charges to accept a "Catholic" sacrificial reading of tales of Roman civic duty and heroic self-sacrifice?

Second, despite attempts by the Revolution to obliterate the "cultural references" of Catholic France, all too many examples reveal, as I have argued, that instead of effacing Catholic ideas, the Revolution reinterpreted and continued them. This arguably remains true as well of those values that one might be tempted to identify as exclusively "Roman." Is not the passion for justice so prominent in the ethical readings of the Roman classics, just as prominent in the biblical teachings preached by the Church—from the prophets of the Hebrew bible right through to Jesus? Where did the ideal of egalitarianism get its rationale, despite hierarchy, save in those same, sometimes internally conflicted, Catholic teachings, especially as emergent in Jansenism?[140] Was not the secular belief that reason and fraternity would inevitably prevail only a modern streamlined version of the doctrine of divine providence?[141] François Furet even writes of the Terror as having "refashioned, in a revolutionary mode, the divine right of public authority."[142] If these Catholic notions should survive in revolutionized form, why not "sacrifice"—either mistaken as Roman in origin or misattributed to the originality of the revolutionary consciousness?

Third, unlike notions of patriotic duty easily linked to Roman examples, some of the notions of sacrifice current during the French Revolution lack Roman antecedents entirely. These notions, in fact, turn out to be classically Catholic, as we will see. To mention only two, which form the core of Catholic ideas of sacrifice, one may cite sacrifice as expiation and as total immolation.[143] When Danton thought that the mass executions ordered by the Revolution would serve to "'appease'" the people, he must have had Catholic notions of Christ's expiating death at least subconsciously in mind.[144] One must conclude then that even during the French Revolution, the grip of the Catholic ideal of sacrifice maintained a remarkable strength.

Prelude to Restoration: Michelet, "Catholic" Malgré Lui

Adding further weight to the case for Catholic influence even in the midst of revolutionary attempts to root out the Church's influence was the way in which Catholic models continued to resurface later among some of the Revolution's staunchest supporters. Concerted republican efforts by figures like Michelet to create "a viable national mythology" of sacrifice to replace the old Catholic model simply ended in rehearsing the Catholic idea all over again. The Passion story of Jesus, the saintly myth of Joan of Arc, the transcendent reality of the martyred France and of the holy "People"—all these had irresistible and "profound attraction" for this determined de-Christianizer. So too, recent students of French sacrificial ideology note that a revolutionary of the generation of 1848, poet Alphonse de Lamartine, came to the same realization of the persistence of Roman Catholicism's deep structures. In his portrayal of Joan of Arc, Lamartine "had hoped for national myths that would somehow be devoid of the supernatural and the irrational." Yet, this proved to be a vain "wish that underestimated the emotional continuity of monarchist mythology, Catholic theology, and the Revolutionary myth of fraternity, a wish that failed to recognize the persistence, on the left as well as on the right, of intense anti-modernist trends."[145]

An excellent example, therefore, of this ironic turn in the course of French political and religious history can be found in the work of Jules Michelet.[146] A staunch republican, Michelet deliberately set out to overturn the royalist cult of noble sacrificial martyrdom, which had grown up around the execution of Louis XVI.[147] Rather than adopting a commitment to the Bourbon dynasty or to the sacred person of the Most Christian King, Michelet centered his loyalties instead on the nation, typically cast as "the People." For Michelet, the French Revolution defined the moment in which the People realized their special identity and destiny, and its lessons became the guidelines for the pursuit of national and, indeed, all human life. Embracing absolute transcendence while displacing God in one move, Michelet felt that nothing commanded human worship more than the nation. Conor Cruise O'Brien draws the ironic conclusion of this new nationalism articulated by Michelet:

> What is new in the French Revolution is not nationalism itself but the severance of the ties that had joined nationalism to the super-

natural from time immemorial. That severance was symbolized by the decapitation of Louis XVI. Henceforward, there was nothing above the Nation. The Nation itself became God.[148]

Ironies of ironies, however, in trying to articulate his post-religious vision, Michelet fell back upon older models. More and more, he conceived "French nationhood in Catholic and mystical terms."[149] All of French history, for example, comes to replace the Bible, since French history alone comprehends a sacred text of universal meaning.[150] As for sacrifice, that central rite of Catholics, Michelet claimed that "sacrifice reigned supreme: indeed sacrifice was his political ideal," even if it was "sacrifice for the nation."[151] Carrying this logic further, we are not surprised to find Michelet celebrating the French Revolution as the school in which the People learned sacrifice.[152] French nationhood as a whole, viewed through the lens of sacrifice and martyrdom, revealed that France was at once "an innocent and divine victim and savior."[153]

Susan Dunn concludes from this that we ought to see Michelet as inadvertently carrying on the Catholic theological lines articulated by royalist Bishop Bossuet,[154] famous for, among other things, reinvigorating the doctrine of the divinity of the French king as Louis XIV's personal tutor.[155] But while Dunn is surely correct in her analysis of the ironies of Michelet's neoreligious deification of the People, I think the historical depth and length of her work can be increased. In particular, I want to move this discussion of the religio-politics of the French discourse of sacrifice into the late nineteenth and early twentieth centuries, while also filling in the substance of the theological background that Bossuet, and thus Michelet, inherit. It is that distant source of Michelet's sacrificial thinking, by way of Bossuet and several others, which I shall show is resolutely Catholic. Let me now turn to identifying the nature of this understanding of sacrifice and then move on to consider its historical sources.

Sacrifice in the Restoration: Joseph de Maistre

If Michelet supplied unintentional evidence of the entrenchment of Catholic ideas of sacrifice in French political and religious culture, the restoration thinker, Joseph de Maistre (1753–1821) gave open and enthusiastic testimony. A vigorous monarchist and slashing critic of the Enlightenment and French Revolution, de Maistre championed the cause of Catholic ultramontanism and a restored monarchy. De Maistre's status as a traditional "Catholic" thinker has been contested because of his distance from classic Thomist thought, but his identification with Catholic interests is beyond dispute.[156] Although he never set foot in "France," proper, the Savoyard de Maistre was a great student of its literature and philosophy. Most of all, he was an equally great observer of the travails of the French nation and its institutions as it passed through revolution. Born of a noble family in Chambéry, Savoy, de Maistre began his intellectual life as a student of law in Turin. At the same time, he turned his hand to writing on topical subjects. Among these are works on the French Revolution, political sovereignty, the pope, science, Protestantism, and refutations of the political and social philosophies of Rousseau and Francis Bacon.[157] After a period as chief judicial officer of Sardinia, he served for fourteen years as Sardinian ambassador to the court of Czar Alexander II in St. Petersburg. It was there he began work in 1809 on the most fully developed rendition of his theory of sacrifice, *Eclaircissement sur les sacrifices*.[158] The thrust of this work was to fashion an ideology in which sacrifice would play a central role in an overall theory of history and society.[159]

De Maistre's conception of political sacrifice recalled much, but not all, of the Eucharistic theology of the École Française de Spiritualité. For both, sacrifice involves bloody annihilation and achieves expiation for sin.[160] Humanity has been subject to "radical degradation" by sin. De Maistre's innovation was, in effect, to apply sacrificial theology of the "École Française de Spiritualité explicitly to the political realms and to emphasize the religious ideas that were already there. In order to expiate human sin and degradation, a pure and innocent victim must be offered to redeem the guilty. The merits of the innocent, transferred by bloody sacrifice of the innocent, are laid on the altar and substituted for the sins of guilty.[161] Notable in de Maistre's conception of sacrifice, and at the same time aligning him with the Oratorians, is the severity and mystique of his views.[162] Not only did he hold the standard expiatory thesis of Catholic teaching—that actual killing and shedding of blood are essential to socially redeeming sacrifice—but he also argued that the guilty can only be redeemed by the sacrificial death of the innocent. De Maistre considered the execution of Louis XVI, for instance, a literal ritual "sacrifice" expiating the evils of the Revolution.

De Maistre's work marks a new episode in thinking about sacrifice. He unites the religious nature of politics with the political nature of religion.[163] He does so by adapting a theory of sacrifice, close to the classic Catholic theology of the sacrificial Eucharist, to the politics of his time. This synthesis of religion and politics was powerful because it reinterpreted Roman Catholic theology while looking forward at the same time. It continued baroque and rococo Roman Catholic spiritualities of the Compagnie du Saint Sacrement and the Sacred Heart of Jesus, all the while creating an analogous vision adapted to the post-Revolutionary age.[164] Thus, despite de Maistre's affection for monarchy, the notion of "nation" was triumphant. If a Roman Catholic theology of sacrifice was to survive, it had to adapt to the reality of the ascent of the nation-state. De Maistre thus restocked the intellectual armory of the Catholic right in its battles against the continuing legacy of the Revolution right up to the twentieth century.

De Maistre's Absolutist "Throne" and Sacrificial "Altar"

For de Maistre, sacrifice was a universal human institution. All human cultures, he asserted, believed in a universal guilt and the need for ceremonies of sacrifice to repair the broken relation between humanity and divinity. It was only by means of sacrifice that societies could assure the vitality of the body politic.

> One especially finds that all nations agree on the marvelous efficacy of the voluntary sacrifice of the innocent who sacrifices himself to the divinity as a propitiatory victim. Men have always attached an infinite price to the submission of the just person who accepts these sufferings.[165]

In the same vein, de Maistre applauds "the most favorable changes" in nations which "are brought about almost always by the bloody catastrophes in which an innocent is a victim."[166]

In political terms, this, in effect, meant accepting the religio-political principle of *raison d'état* —as it was realized under the novel conditions of life in (a preferably monarchic) nation-state.[167] De Maistre thus in effect posits a "'religion of state,'" and is not shy about spelling this out. "Government is," says de Maistre,

> a veritable religion: it has its dogmas, its mysteries, its ministers. To submit it to the discussion of each individual is to annihilate it. It only lives by the national reason, that is to say, by political faith, which is a symbol.[168]

As religious, the state then of necessity requires patriotism, which de Maistre believes entails "'individual abnegation.'"[169] De Maistre thus reasserted the principles underlying the "royal religion" of the sixteenth and seventeenth centuries, in assuming a religion of "immanence."[170] Political and religious discourses merge into a common discourse of political sacrifice.

Anticipating Maurras and the integrists, de Maistre meant to argue for submission of the individual to the will of the monarch or state; in religious terms, this meant submission to the magisterial will of the church as demanded by the intransigents. When the two realms were thought to inhere in each other, as they were in the "royal religion"—the "religion of immanence" of the Golden Age—or for various integralist movements of the late nineteenth and early twentieth century, the result is totalitarianism. In this light, we can well understand why the intransigents and integrists of the late nineteenth and early twentieth centuries would be especially faithful to Trent, given that it celebrated the annihilating "consummation" of the individual in baroque spiritualities like that of the "École Française de Spiritualité." In doing so, Trent rehearsed the authoritarian convictions that have done much to define those analogously related parties of the French "right."[171]

In this commitment to the necessity of annihilating sacrifice as the heart of social order, de Maistre has been seen by liberal political theorists like Sir Isaiah Berlin as a precursor of fascism.[172] Indeed, as we will see, Charles Maurras, founder of the proto-fascist Action Française was a devoted student of de Maistre's writings. But I shall argue that while this judgment may be on the whole true, it is also possible to see in de Maistre an appreciation of the hard truths of social life sometimes glossed over by liberalism. In this regard, we will see how a communitarian liberal such as Émile Durkheim held a good number of views reminiscent of de Maistre. Foremost here, for the purposes of this book, is Durkheim's belief in the necessity of sacrifice for the existence of society. Tellingly, although repelled by the logic of de Maistre's convictions, even a liberal like Berlin saw a depth in de Maistre's conceptions about sacrifice and society that he would not gainsay. Without sacrifice, says Berlin interpreting de Maistre, society could not exist. "Men must give, not merely lend, themselves. Society is not a bank, a limited liability company formed by individuals who look on one another with suspicious eyes—fearful of being taken in, dumped, exploited."[173] This is so for de Maistre because society is not an "artificial association based on calculation of self-interest . . . but rests at least as much on . . . the impulse to immolate oneself on the sacred altar without hope of return."[174] So, even passionate liberal critics of de Maistre must give this troublesome philosopher his due. Although it is not necessary to my argument, since I admit that attitudes toward sacrifice can arise independently of "influences," perhaps Durkheim owes de Maistre his due as well?

In the conclusion of this book, I shall show that de Maistre is hardly alone in believing in the necessity of sacrifice. His theory of sacrifice, however repugnant it may strike some at first reading, spurred an endless string of discourse, such as we will find in the social sciences. For example, even the liberal, republican Durkheimians shared de Maistre's adherence to the precontractual nature of society, as well as de Maistre's view that society required sacrifice. The Durkheimians turned away from the harshest interpretation of this requirement by undercutting the conceptual underpinnings of this received notion of sacrifice. Like the good liberals they were, the Durkheimians articulated a "bourgeois" theory of sacrifice contrasted to the expiatory, annihilationist, and absolutist character of de Maistre's theory. Marking out this territory of the bourgeois, for the Durkheimians, sacrifice should be seen as a prudent "giving of," not the total "giving up" advanced by the Catholic right.

Yet we should not forget that however one may judge de Maistre in his own time, in the late nineteenth and early twentieth centuries, his thought would serve protofascists with far more fidelity than would classic conservatives. De Maistre thus fed the ideological needs of a generation of intransigent and integrist thinkers—whether Catholic or not—such as Charles Maurras, Louis Veuillot, and others.[175] Of particular note for the current study, we will see that de Maistre emerged conspicuously on the side of those seeking "sacrifice" of Dreyfus for *raisons d'etat*. Writing with official Church approval, Abbé Bouquerel urged in 1912 that sacrifice speaks of a need to "appease" God and "expiate" our crimes. Explicitly naming de Maistre, but arguably bending his ideas close to Catholic notions of expiatory sacrifice, Bouquerel repeats the very words of his eighteenth-century master in recognizing sacrifice as the only way of making amends and setting affairs in the social order aright with the almighty. "Man recognizes his culpability, offers a life to repair the outrage he has committed. Not able to immolate himself, he substitutes a victim, and this victim is destroyed, burnt, consumed by way of an expiating reparation."[176]

Pure and Inevitable

Before leaving de Maistre, I want to call attention to the further significance of his placing the immolation of the innocent at the center of his thought about sacrifice. In doing so, de Maistre developed the fundamental ideas of purity and inevitability in the logic of sacrifice even beyond what earlier thinkers had dared to do. Of course, the purity of the sacrificial victim and the inevitability of its immolation were already contained in the classic Catholic theologies of sacrifice and Eucharist. But, as we will see, de Maistre gives them new poignancy and theoretical import.

One of the key elements in the classic Catholic theology of sacrifice was the requirement for Jesus to be victim at the center of the act. But why Jesus? First of all, if we consider sacrifice as an expiation, as payment of a debt, only Jesus as God had the requisite cosmic "heft" or value to atone for the sinfulness of all humanity. Only Jesus carried a sufficient mass of holiness and goodness to put into the balance against the counterweight of the accumulated sin of humanity. But second and certainly just as important, Jesus' innocence guaranteed his absolute purity and thus his perfection as victim to be offered. Only the perfectly innocent victim could hope to be pure enough to be acceptable before God in the cosmic sacrifice to be offered. Thus, Jesus' sacrificial death—the death of a supreme innocent, since incapable of sin—rather than being an additional injustice in the already flawed arrangement of the cosmos—is seen by the religious logic of sacrifice as the only guarantee of relief from the cosmic deficit that burdened humanity. Real and effective sacrifice requires a pure victim, in effect a victim innocent of the crimes being expiated.

As for inevitability, the passion narratives of the Gospels, together with the theological rationales of Jesus' death, tell us that Jesus had to die. In a way, his death is a fated death. Against all utilitarian, pleasure-maximizing, and pain-minimizing logic, Jesus submits to his executioners, even though as God, he could at any time have revealed himself in his glory to the consternation of all. The logic of Jesus' passion in the Catholic conception of his death is thus suffused with an air of inevitability settling over him, the ideal paschal lamb; he is close-mouthed and submissive to his Father's will unto his own destruction. Throughout the gospel narrative of Jesus' passion, the background voice of the narrator again and again reminds the reader how things, often tiny things, occur because they had been foretold. Jesus does this and that to fulfill what has already been foretold by the prophets. His sacrificial death is inevitable because cosmically ordained prophecies must be fulfilled.

Especially in John's gospel one hears the constant refrain that certain events occur "in order that the Scriptures be fulfilled." Now while it is unremarkable that this should refer to major incidents in Jesus' passion, such as his betrayal by one who has supped with him (John 13:19), many seemingly small and insignificant events are likewise said to occur to fulfill the minutiae of prophecy. Thus, an air of determinism and inevitability attend Jesus' delivery to sacrifice on Calvary. Thus, John 12:15–16 tells us Jesus will enter Jerusalem on a donkey in order that scriptural prophecy be fulfilled. John 15:24–25 relates similarly that Jesus was hated for no other reason than that it was foretold in the scriptures. John 19:24–25 claims that even the trivial details of the casting of lots and division of Jesus' clothing among the Roman soldiers attending his crucifixion are items foretold in the scriptures and done in order that these prophecies be fulfilled. Or consider the air of inevitable predetermination of events likewise implied in John 19:34–37, where the evangelist tells us that in lancing Jesus' side so that no bone of his was broken, the Roman soldiers had unwittingly also fallen into the web of inevitability in which Jesus' passion and sacrificial death are embedded.

What is significant about this air of inevitability is how it places the otherwise trivial particulars of Jesus' final days into a larger, indeed cosmic, plan. Are the evangelists saying something as trite as that just because some of the prophets wrote as they did that Jesus therefore could not have falsified their texts? After all what does Jesus owe these scribblers? As the omnipotent Lord and creator of the universe, he could have simply abrogated the contract at any time. After all, for other monotheists, such as the Muslims, it is indeed the ability of Allah to abrogate contracts that is precisely a measure of his godliness. Something else is afoot in the gospel narrative, and as well in the minds of the Catholic intransigents. Jesus' death hews closely to a script. Indeed, it may well follow something like the script of a ritual sacrifice, a scheme that has been carefully scripted as indeed many rituals are. The life (and death) of the savior imitates the art of ritual, not the other way around. Things must be done just so, in order that the efficacy of the ritual act be guaranteed—in order that the cosmic scheme not be upset. As such, the justice of the death of Jesus is irrelevant. The logic of his death is not the logic of justice, but that of a ritual sacrifice. This syndrome of ritual inevitability, often found in sacrifices,[177] makes rational in religious terms the otherwise irrational way Jesus surrenders to his attackers so that "all things may be fulfilled."

Adhering to this logic of purity and inevitability, de Maistre comments on the execution of Louis XVI in a way that rehearses the same themes that Catholic theology had reserved for Jesus. Quoting from the 1799 work of a German author, Johann Jung-Stilling, writing on the death of Louis XVI, de Maistre records its conviction of the king's Christlike death:

> King Louis XVI matured in his long captivity and he had become a *perfect bouquet*. When he mounted the scaffold, he lifted his eyes to heaven and said like his redeemer: *Lord, forgive my people.* Tell me, my dear reader, if a man can speak like this without being penetrated by the spirit of Jesus Christ![178]

This appreciation of Louis's innocence is echoed in de Maistre's account of the final days of the Revolution's prize victim. There, de Maistre records how the king's jailers, ever eager to degrade him, denied him even the use of a shaving razor. Against this, the king's faithful servant urged him to present himself to the National Convention unkempt and bearded to enlist their sympathy. But the king refused to use this tactic to arouse interest in his fate. De Maistre then adds: "So what must have been happening in this heart, so pure, so submissive, so prepared? The august martyr seemed to fear escaping the sacrifice or making the victim less perfect. What acceptance? And what must this acceptance have been worth?"[179]

So de Maistre finds his sacrificed king, like Jesus, the picture of purity and resignation to his inevitable death. De Maistre brings theology down to the hard earth of regicidal politics.

Lambs and Goats

Another key sacrificial figure called forth by the thought of de Maistre and made famous recently by the work of René Girard is the "scapegoat." Christians are typically ready see Jesus as the sweet, pure and innocent "lamb led to slaughter." Except for René Girard,[180] however, quite a bit less is said about Jesus as the wretched, cantankerous, and impure "scapegoat" of biblical fame. The image of the scapegoat originates in the Jewish practice of ritually expelling a goat, symbolically laden with the sins of the community, from the protective confines of the city into certain death in the desert wilderness. The goat, wretched, cantankerous, and impure, is sacrificed for the sake of the sins of the community by removing its transgressions far outside its borders. The sins of the human community are thus transferred to the goat, which serves to remove them from the community. Of course, as the real sinners, do not members of the community merit "death" for their wretched sinfulness, their cantankerous refusal to abide by God's law, and their consequent impurity? But, by the magic of sacrificial ritual, by suffering death in the wilderness, the goat substitutes for the "death" that should really have fallen upon the human community.

By this logic of the scapegoat, as we will see, the "sacrifice" of Dreyfus was justified in part by Catholic intransigents and integralists. Norman Ravitch's reading of Maurras's intentions, echoing the biblical phrase, that it is "'expedient that one man should die for the people'" tells us all we need to know about the identity and kind of thinking of the Catholic intransigents with whom we have been concerned. Behind what so often seem irrational features of the judicial process and representation of Captain Dreyfus himself, we will find that Dreyfus is not only a prisoner on Devils' Island but is also confined by the logic of Catholic notions of the scapegoating ritual sacrifice. This is another way then of reinforcing the thesis of the hegemony of a rightist Catholic conception of sacrifice in the political life of France.

Securing this link to the "right" is the notion of inevitability. Even more deeply informing this belief in ritual inevitability is cosmic inevitability, so well in evidence, for example, in the Aztec case. Interestingly enough, cosmic inevitability is also a part of the French Catholic and right-wing mentality as well. As René Rémond observes, even in the late nineteenth and early twentieth centuries the old characteristic of the right—"submission to the natural order"—animates the right-wing world view.[181] Now, while the fatalist aspect of right-wing ideology is certainly in part the result of being pitted so sharply against the classically voluntarist spirit of the Enlightenment, Rémond is suggesting that its roots reach down much deeper into the Catholic bedrock of France. In indicating the link between the Catholic right and the classic Catholic sacrificial theology of the Eucharist, along with its Maistrean variant, I submit that I have reached that "bedrock."

After de Maistre: Intransigence, Sacrifice, and the Novel

Given that the theme of sacrifice figured prominently in baroque and rococo theological traditions, in Jacobin justifications for the execution of Louis XVI,[182] in the Restoration thinking of Joseph de Maistre, and notably in Michelet's interpretation of Joan of Arc as sacrificing herself for the nation,[183] it should not be surprising that sacrifice should also figure in the turbulent end of the nineteenth century. There, this discourse was deployed in the extravagant growth of sacrificial rhetoric in intransigent and integrist Catholic circles.

A major voice in this effort to establish an integral Catholic social order—and a dominant power in the Catholic world in late nineteenth-century France—was the Assumptionist order. Through their publication, *La Croix,* the Assumptionists led this effort rhetorically by appealing to the dominant language of sacrifice of "Catholic" France.[184] "Assumptionist" Catholicism, as it was called, viewed the world as an arena in which human suffering, ultimately to the extent of sacrificial death, was expiation or compensation for human misdeeds.[185] Like de Maistre,[186] they argued that the balance between good and evil had been upset by the many transgressions of the French of the modern era.[187] Maistre, along with intellectual heirs like Louis Veuillot provided the intellectual underpinnings and energy for much of this "Assumptionist" Catholicism. Whether it be the result of the godless Revolution, the liberal anticlericalism of the Third Republic, the moral license and religious indifference of the bourgeoisie, or in the waning years of the nineteenth century the slow but sure progress toward the separation of church and state realized in 1906, these intransigent "Assumptionist" Catholics felt that reparations to God were due.[188] Countering this mass of transgression, they argued that the faithful should place their own vicarious penitential suffering on the scales of cosmic justice. As mere individuals, ordinary folk could make up for the grievous irreverence inflicted upon God by "vicarious suffering or mystical substitution." The idea of vicarious suffering as self-sacrifice "assumed an importance out of all proportion to the other doctrines of the

Church. . . . God so arranges the world that the sins may be balanced by expiatory sacrifices."[189]

The theme of expiatory sacrifice likewise filled the pages of French literature as the most popular theme of Catholic writers of several generations such as Bernanos, Léon Bloy, and many others.[190] Initially introduced in Barbery d'Aurevilly's *Un Prêtre marié* (1865), the term "expiatory suffering" first gained its great currency in that time.[191] In the estimate of historian Richard Griffiths, this novel created the impression of the wholesale practice of sacrificing the self for others.[192] In like manner, other famous French Catholic authors, such as Paul Claudel in his play of 1896, *Le Repos du septième jour* portrayed its lead character as suffering for others as a "symbolic portrayal of Christ's original sacrifice for man."[193] In the same vein, *L'Immolé*, a novel by Emile Baumann, was said to well reflect the "interests of the Catholics of his day" in sacrifice.[194] It recounted the tale of a man "who offers up his whole life as a sacrifice" based on the model of Jesus.[195] One might also add to this chorus the voice of Ernest Psichari, who invoked the name and doctrines of Joseph de Maistre for the utility of sacrificial asceticism, which gained indulgences—even when the asceticism was excessive. Psichari argued like de Maistre that people can suffer vicariously for others. De Maistre claimed that the Catholic practice of "indulgences" "showed that 'not only can a person enjoy its specific merits, but by virtue of divine justice, these satisfactions can also be extended to strangers by him.'" Psichari agreed heartily. Moreover, the redemption thus won conformed to the principles of the efficacy of the suffering of the innocent laid down classically by de Maistre. Says Psichari of his great inspiration: "'The Redemption says de Maistre once again, is "only a great indulgence accorded to the human species by the infinite merits of the innocent, par excellence, immolated willingly for it.'"[196]

The power of intransigent sacrificial rhetoric is impressive to the degree it also moved Catholic writers and political figures usually not identified with right-wing politics. Take Charles Péguy as an example. While he deplored the harshness of these rightist Catholic writers of his time, he nonetheless posed his Joan of Arc as a victim suffering for the souls of the damned. For Péguy, such a rendering of Joan fit naturally with the common assumption that the doctrine of sacrificial suffering was central to the Catholic belief of his time.[197] Equally surprising as well, the anarchists of the *fin-de-siècle* paid bizarre tribute to the power of the integral Catholic symbolism of expiatory sacrifice. In order to give what might be seen as meaningless deaths a cosmic significance, the anarchist movement put together a mythology of the "expiatory" sacrificial death of the activist drawn from Catholic precedents.[198] In 1882, anarchist writers, Elisée Reclus and Carlo Cafiero, for example, published an influential pamphlet,

"God and the State." There, they said, along with de Maistre and, with slight variants, along with the long tradition of French Catholic Eucharistic theology, that religion is founded on sacrifice, on the eternal immolation of humans to an angry God.[199] Often likening the judicial executions of agents like Ravachol to Jesus' death at the hands of Pilate, the anarchists skillfully calculated that tapping into the deeply entrenched Catholic discourse of sacrifice would well serve the interests of their political program.[200] People would know what they meant.

Finally, not least among the better known French thinkers of the late nineteenth and early twentieth centuries who carried on the spirit of sacrificial severity was Georges Sorel, the father of radical syndicalism. A somewhat perverse Catholic, Sorel thought religion and politics shared an inner core and therefore the two could be spoken of in the same breath, so to speak.[201] Political and religious modernisms for Sorel were but two instances of the same fundamental phenomenon, subject to the same analysis. Thus for Sorel, the self-sacrifice of the early Christian martyrs captured something essential in Christianity, which had been lost by the liberal and modernist theological programs of his day. Liberals could not even countenance the "sacrifice of the intellect" characteristic of real Christian faith, such as that required to believe in miracles. What intransigent Roman Catholicism and socialism shared in common were absolute assent to key doctrines, comprehensive views of history, the rigorous use of reason, and last but not least, the sense that "the greatest sacrifices" would be demanded from them.[202] Finally, in this parade of variants and shifting contexts, a significant "relative continuity" of meaning and purpose of sacrifice typical of the "right-wing" Catholic movements emerges across the centuries.[203]

Sacrificial Annihilation for Catholic Modernists Too

Attesting to the depth of these classic expressions of sacrificial piety is their persistence among Catholics opposed to the intransigents and integrists. Even there, a sacrificial annihilationist and expiatory ideology seemed well entrenched and unchallenged. Alfred Loisy, for example, France's chief Catholic "Modernist" and the bane of the intransigent party among French Catholics, echoed the views of his religious opposites. Specifically, Loisy repeated such views concerning the value of the individual in relation to sacrifice! As Loisy frankly put it, "sacrifice remains the religious act *par excellence*—all the more religious to the extent it is more consciously and voluntarily consented to."[204] Despite his intellectual liberalism, Loisy's religion was just as irrational as that of the intransigents. Religion was "la mystique"[205]—an "expression of this unseen, indefinable mystery"[206]—a "system of mystical relations established between men and things."[207] Even Loisy's conception of religious humanism—his cult of humanity—carried one beyond humanity to the universal and supreme—"'to that domain of the unknown, which is the profoundest sense of the universal.'"[208] With *mystique* so much part of his view of religion, it is not surprising that Loisy should prefer an equally extreme view of sacrifice as the total surrender of the individual, as the total "giving up" of the self—as we will see in greater detail—in wartime to the nation. The absolute character of "la mystique" is mirrored in the equally absolute devotion of the individual to the nation, with nothing held back in the name of individual privilege.

Ironically, however, one of the stronger testimonies to the entrenched character of the intransigent Roman Catholic theology of sacrifice is to be found in Loisy's reflections about sacrifice *after* the war. Amazingly, even "after the massacre,"[209] as Loisy call it, Loisy's absolute commitment to the equally absolute norm of "giving up" oneself to the nation seems unshaken. In his 1923 *La Morale humaine,* Loisy sums up with what can only be called a hymn to total self-sacrifice—one as annihilationist to individual citizens over against the nation as anything coming from the intransigent camp. Speaking first of the war dead, whom Loisy believes are "the happiest" [sic], he observed, against the sentiment of the time, which Jay Winter has so well documented,[210] that they "perished in the tempest with the conviction of serving a great cause and having won it. They have at least gained something for themselves."[211] From what we know of the epidemic fear and depression of the common soldier, "happiness" was the last thing filling their pathetic hearts. But Loisy goes on and addresses the state of the survivors. He thus seems equally blinded by sacrificial theology, and strikes an equally mistaken note. In a time of growing cynicism, Loisy tells them that their

> duty is to consecrate themselves to the service of the society to which they belong, in order to assure the future of humanity. . . . And after all is said and done, this service amounts to giving things up.[212]

Incredibly, he persists in a call to further sacrifice:

> It is in sacrifice that the secret of happiness lies. Sacrifice, which seems to be the negation of happiness, is on the contrary, its condition and reality. It is its condition, because, in one way or another, the sacrifice of individuals is required for the equilibrium and preservation of society, for the common good, for the establishment and maintenance of concord. It is the reality of happiness because voluntary sacrifice is, for those who do it, something different than

a rending / 291 / or renunciation, a sort of suicide that is imposed without compensation. It is above all and essentially an act of love in an act of faith: as love, it is the transcendent and moral truth of life—supreme contentment. This is indeed true of all sacrifices, large and small; they never count for nought. Even if they count for nought, they would be of no small use to society, of no small satisfaction for those who made them. But because sacrifice counts for something, because it always counts for a lot, and on occasion, for everything, sacrifice is, for that reason, useful; its author feels it to be a spiritual joy, and society, sees it as a spiritual advantage. [213]

While Loisy may be the last man in France to feel this way, that a major thinker of the post-war period, long disaffiliated from official church teachings and institutions, should publish such claims, witnesses to the deployment and strength of the assumptions about the concept of sacrifice assumed by intransigent and integrist Roman Catholics.

Reading someone as estranged from official Catholicism as Loisy supports the view that the intransigent and integrist Catholic view of sacrifice as annihilation and expiation continues across time in the national mentality. Indeed, in Loisy's case, this may well be so, although we saw that the continuity thesis encountered some difficulty in the case of de Maistre's relation to Roman Catholicism. To the extent that the continuity thesis is true, then later so-called secular calls to patriotism would arguably be derivable from and maintained by a peculiar kind of Catholic theology, as articulated in the theology of the Eucharist as sacrifice. While it is not necessary to my thesis so to argue, it can be appreciated how well ingrained this Catholic theology was, so much so that, in instances at any rate, it became the point of reference for all thinking about sacrifice ever after. It even served as the point of departure for attempts to revise or eliminate it.

Intransigence and Its Social Bases

In the period just before World War One then, one must imagine an accumulated history of discourse about sacrifice, built up largely by the labors of dominant segments of French Roman Catholicism, who earlier in the nineteenth century had identified themselves as "intransigents."[214] In the period from 1870 to 1900, sacrificial discourse became the mark of this intransigent Catholicism. Commenting in 1912 on the current scene of socialist agitation, Georges Sorel claimed that radical socialism and intransigent Roman Catholicism really served the same moralities: they required "certain immolations, efforts, sacrifices on the part of society's members . . . [certain loyalties to the] transcendent, immutable, absolute."[215] Perhaps Georges Goyau was even correct when he claimed in 1918 that a continuously existent intransigent, "subconscious" Catholicism was the very thing which "incites" the French "to sacrifice."[216] If so, then although Catholicism in France has never been one uniform thing, in the late nineteenth and early twentieth centuries, it became so on the issue of sacrifice and carried the same message of annihilation and expiation.[217]

A series of material and social conditions had fed the rise of this intransigent Roman Catholicism, raising it to prominence within the French church.[218] With the restoration of Louis XVIII to the throne in 1814 and the reign of Charles X that followed, religious and political victories became one, victories, however uneasy, of "Ultraroyalism,"[219] of "political and social conservatism . . . completed by religious conservatism."[220] Later in the century, despite the attempts at reconciliation with liberal political and religious values sought by the Catholic liberals, the First Vatican council and its 1864 Syllabus of Errors put its official seal on the work of the intransigents.

None of this should cause us to underestimate the efforts of Catholic liberalism of the nineteenth century. Montalambert, Lamennais, and Lacordaire[221] continued to exert intellectual influence in public matters. A so-called "Orleanist" Catholicism showed vitality throughout.[222] And, at century's end, republican Catholics seemed vindicated by Leo XIII's *"ralliement"* to the Third Republic. Yet, in the balance of religious forces, Catholic liberals were outmatched by the intransigents.[223] Within the Church and the nation, the right still prevailed. This was so even though in the early decades of the twentieth century the intransigents were seemingly becoming more and more "isolated."[224] Similarly, Michel Despland's argument that rightist shows of strength, such as devotions to the Sacred Heart at Marie-Marguerite Alacoque's base in Paray-le-Monial, were in large part concocted by elites in an "atmosphere of panic," would need to be balanced by advances along the religio-political front made by the Catholic Revival of 1905–1914 and other movements of Catholic intransigence.[225] Thus, right on the heels of the *"ralliement,"* the voices of intransigent Catholicism grew shriller and louder in some domains of discourse, even as they bent toward accepting the Third Republic. Although Denys Cochin, one prominent Catholic intransigent member of the Union Sacré government, was dismissed during the war, the influence of the intransigents within the Union Sacré government persisted throughout. One must recall that swiftly after the war, the Catholic right won control of the national assembly in the parliamentary elections in 1919 under the banner of the Bloc National. For all its complexities and ambiguities, Vichy too bore many of the marks of the culture that intransigent and integrist Catholics valued. A dominant "rightist" party thus had emerged within the French church in the late nineteenth and early twentieth centuries. It was they who carried the message of a national theology of sacrifice whose roots were firmly planted in the sixteenth and seventeenth centuries.[226] It is from this intransigent Catholicism, historical baggage in hand, that the discourse of sacrifice in France of the late nineteenth and early twentieth centuries came. Part of our story concerns the ways this intransigent Roman Catholic hegemony over the meaning of sacrifice was contested (or reinforced) by other religious communities, primarily the Liberal Protestants, by "secular" thinkers known as Free Thinkers or "laïcs," and finally by the leading school of social thinkers of twentieth-century France: Émile Durkheim and his followers in the Durkheimian school from Hubert and Mauss to Georges Bataille. When we see how, in terms of its own logic and institutions, intransigent Roman Catholic theology was profoundly committed to a certain view of sacrifice, we will better be able to understand why sacrifice was such a powerful and contentious notion. In the present day, we will also follow this same lead to help better understand the theoretical work on sacrifice by René Girard. Thus, in terms of struggling over control of this symbolism, we will see that this entrenched French national ideology or theology of sacrifice could only be engaged in the terms laid down by these Catholic intransigents. I believe that most French thinkers had no other choice but to address the issues turning round sacrifice in the principal language that had first and continually articulated it—intransigent Roman Catholic theology.[227] They, even like theorists of today such as René Girard, simply took these Catholic notions for granted and engaged the issues concerning sacrifice largely in terms of them.

curious observation

What else might one expect, really?

3

CONTESTING THE NATIONAL
RITES OF SACRIFICE

The self-sacrifice of individuals for the sake of the community, suffering made glorious—those two things which are the basic elements of the profession of arms—respond to both our moral and aesthetic concepts. The noblest teachings of philosophy and religion have found no higher ideals.

—Charles de Gaulle[1]

Sacrifice and the Literature of Disenchantment

These days, when we dredge up images of the First World War, we are likely to dwell on the cruelty and futility of the unending carnage suffered by its "ignorant armies clashing by night" or conjure up images of men cowering in their bunkers under incessant artillery barrages or feel horror at the misery of life in the mud-filled trenches. Finally, we may think of the wave of revulsion for massive total war that swept over its participants as they fell into exhaustion. We, therefore, may not think at all of notions like "sacrifice," which had in part informed the mentalities of the combatants at the beginnings of the war and which have preoccupied me in this book. Or, if we do consider sacrifice, we will tend to regard it as foolish, as indeed it came to be regarded once the war bogged down. "Sacrifice" is just a euphemism for the meaningless deaths and exploitation of the war's naively idealistic but, finally, hapless victims.

Such a mood was well captured at the very time the First World War turned sour in the great works of literature issuing from those speaking to us in their encounters with death at the front. Of German authors, one thinks of Erich Maria Remarque. In Anglophone literature, we may recall names like Wilfred Owen, Siegfried Sassoon, and the like.[2] On the French side, as well, a list of potent authors in many ways pioneered this genre of disillusionment, especially disillusion with the ideals dominating the entry into the war and its early years.[3] Theirs might be called an "antiliterature" of sacrifice, a literature in which sacrifice is just "monstrous."[4] Here, one recalls the graphic literary works relating the war's horrors written in wartime. Henri Barbusse's *Feu,* Henry Bourdeaux's *Les Derniers jours de Fort de Vaux,* Georges Duhamel's *Civilisation: 1914–1917* and his *Vie des martyrs: 1914–1917.*[5] Each in its own way bears on the themes of this book in doing its share to convey at last the reality of what a frightful and revolting thing "sacrifice" in wartime meant. Disgust and disillusionment with "sacrifice" is everywhere in this writing. Thus, a common *poilu* in Henri Barbusse's *Feu* complains of the hypocrisy of talk about sacrifice. He protests the uncomprehending nature of what "sacrifice" meant to the man at the front:

> But military glory—it isn't even true for us common soldiers. It's for some, but outside those elect, the soldier's glory is a lie, like every other fine-looking thing in war. In reality, the soldier's sacrifice is obscurely concealed. The multitudes that make up the waves of attack have no reward. They run to hurl themselves into a nothing. You cannot even heap up their names, their frightful inglorious poor little names of nobodies.[6]

From Barbusse's *Feu* as well comes another reminder of how the fortunes of sacrifice fell after the war stalemated. The squadron featured in the novel are enjoying a brief respite from life on the front and are on leave for a few days in Paris. Wearing proudly their Croix de Guerre, they are seen by some curious civilians in a café where they are taking refreshment. We know how the soldiers are sickened by the stench of sacrifice and revolted by its rhetoric. The civilians, on the other hand, privileged and remote from the war, still live in the fool's paradise promised by the heroic sacrificial rhetoric of the pre-war period. Seeing the soldiers at their small table, and eager to know about the war, the civilians make conversation. They ask about how rough things are. They quiz them on their exploits. They congratulate the soldiers on their "physical and moral endurance," trying ever so skillfully to coax the details of some great adventure from them. These queries only meet with self-effacing shrugs and modest admissions of the "misery" of life at the front. But stepping forward in a self-important manner, a lady in the group of civilians presses the men. "'I know,'" she says, there are compensations! How superb a charge must be, eh? All those masses of men advancing like they do in a holiday procession, and the trumpets playing a rousing air in the fields! And the dear little soldiers that can't be held back and shouting, "Vive la France!" and even laughing as they die! Ah! we others, we're not in honour's way like you are.

Stunned, the soldiers can scarcely utter a word in response. Where does one begin with the likes of these? Muffling their anger, Barbusse tells us that they just "furtively . . . stole away."[7]

A Literature of Sacrifice and Enchantment

I shall argue in this chapter that the force of this disillusionment with sacrifice can only be appreciated against the background of at least a generation's worth of cultural formations—including a whole literature—extolling sacrifice, which immediately preceded it. Historians speak of a French "nationalist revival" of extraordinary intensity during the decades before the First World War. So strong were the sentiments driving this mobilization of the nation that Eugen Weber observes that by 1914, all French political parties were "nationalist" in the sense of supporting drastic military preparations against Germany.[8] Although the language differed, the message was always the same: France risked present national danger in the face of German power; the losses of 1870 must be avenged. In response to this perceived national crisis, a consensus formed round the need to repair the national morale and to adopt an ethic suited to the needs of national revival and survival.[9]

So intense was the new nationalism of the *fin-de-siècle* that it subordinated French individualism to "collectivity."[10] In attacking the deplorable state of national morale, intellectuals were chided for their "egoism" and "lazy melancholy." Workers were scolded for their small-minded localism, for their "lack of enthusiasm for collective causes,"[11] as articulated by the elites. Further, only a "force," spiritual or mystical in nature, could "heal society and intellectual nihilism."[12] It was assumed that religion, or something at least called "religion," would bind citizens into common service to the nation, as it had always done, and at the same time inculcate a spirit of "national unity" and "morale."[13] Reflecting the efficacy of this collectivist patriotic religiosity upon ordinary citizens, one of the chief characters in Adrien Bertrand's great wartime novel, *L'Appel du sol*, calls war a "sanctification."[14] Less romantically, seasoned as he is with his trademark stoicism, Vaissette, the principal Free Thinker anticlerical in the novel, waxes religious in describing the disappearance of bourgeois individuality inside the national war effort. He explains things as best he can to a confused comrade:

> The day that you put on that uniform, while the bells of all the villages of France and the drums of all the town criers announced the general mobilization, you were at that very moment given totally over to the nation. She owns you; she owns you completely. We don't think things over anymore: it would be futile. We are cogs in an enormous machine. We aren't even ourselves any more. The country has absconded with your soul. Now, do you get it?[15]

As the consensus grew that sacred French soil must be recovered from those occupying it, so too did the belief that this effort would require the blood of sacrificed French soldiers.[16] An ethic of sacrifice comfortably at home among French Catholics spoke eloquently to this program of national unity and the suppression of unruly individualism. Claudel's words "'Lord, deliver me from myself,'" captured much of the mood of antiindividualism typical of the nationalist Catholics.[17] So too did the declarations from Claudel's plays, such as *L'Annonce fait à Marie*, in which we hear a lead character articulate a chilling ethic of sacrifice:

> It is not a question of living, but of dying. Not a question of building the cross, but hanging from it and giving what we have joyfully. That is what is meant by joy and freedom, by grace and eternal youth. The blood of an old man on the sacrificial cloth next to that of a young man makes as red a spot and as fresh as that of the first year lamb.[18]

Nationalist Catholics, such as Claudel, were unusually "fascinated by suffering, and especially in the surpassing of their common humanity which it allowed." Their viewpoint issued in expressions of a plain "desire to sacrifice," in imitation of Christ. For the Catholic nationalists, "death was a gift to God in exchange for the gift of life." On the front, they sought to be "active martyrs, conscious of their sacrifice." J. D'Arnoux's novel *Les Sept colonnes de l'héroisme* reflects such sentiments in declaring that "'the soldiers of Verdun . . . [were] victims on an altar, like Christ on the cross, the altar of the world.'"[19] War was for them an "immense Good Friday," a lesson taught in what has been called their "École Doloriste."[20] The blood of masses of sacrificed French soldiers would bring renewed life. It would refresh the nation as spring rain would renew the good French earth for the benefit of all.[21]

As for taming individualism, the Catholic parties felt that Catholic ideals served national ends particularly well. It was no surprise that the extreme nationalist Maurice Barrès claimed that in these times of national crisis (1914) "all of France becomes a national cathedral."[22] This call to national devotion opened the door to talk about sacrifice and thus to long-entrenched traditions of sacrificial discourse articulated by the Church since the seventeenth century. In Adrien Bertrand's classic novel of First World War, *L'Appel du sol*, Vaissette's opposite, Captain Antoine de Quéré, a figure representing the ideals of intransigent Catholicism, thrills at the changes the war will force on the unruly nation. He indeed "glories in this war" because it supports the beliefs of intransigent Catholicism and integral nationalism that politics should be governed by antiliberal Catholic social and religious values. For Captain de Quéré, the war is really a blessing, and "essential for our country." The war is essential precisely because individualism has run amok in France. "In our country, everything has been liberty, disorder and anarchy"—all the things the Catholic "party of order" abhorred. "But now," Captain de Quéré goes on, "both the way we are conducting the war and the attitude adopted by the government will show the necessity of rigor, discipline and authority."[23] The war was indeed a dream come true for intransigent Catholic spirits such as these (fig. 8).

On the face of it, the Revolutionary tradition produced the same result. Although it seemed unambiguously to have reversed the Catholic ranking of the collective over the individual by asserting as holy and inviolable the rights of (the individual) person in the Declaration of the Rights of Man and Citizen, in reality, the Revolution was at war with itself over the matter of individualism. By asserting the infallibility of the General Will and the duty of all citizens to submit to it unconditionally, Rousseau, in effect, created a republican form of the *ancien regime*'s Divine Right of Kings and gave new strength to the principle of *raison d'état*.[24] Robespierre, among others, followed Rousseau's absolutizing of the General Will, and held aloft the transcendent ideal of the nation as superior to any individual will.[25] As Adrien Dansette, the great historian of French religious history, expressed it, even in Robespierre's attempt to replace Catholic ideas of God with his new religion of the Supreme Being, Robespierre at best reproduced the Christian God. At worst, the

real deity was still composed of the principles that the Revolution claimed to incarnate. The constitutional cult had strictly subordinated the spiritual to the temporal. It made no distinction between what was God's and what was Caesar's because, as in the world of antiquity, Caesar or the State was God. That was what Robespierre meant when he demanded that the revolutionary tribunal should punish "those who have blasphemed against the Republic."[26]

Thus, in the wake of the defeat of 1870, when certain Catholic nationalists reconciled Roman Catholic and republican thinking, old resemblances emerged in explicit form. When the nation was perceived to be at risk from Imperial Germany or its suspected agents such as Dreyfus, we find the military agents of Third Republic, such as Foch, recapitulating Roman Catholic arguments in favor of the sacrificial imperative. These would seem for all the world indistinguishable from their Enlightenment and Jacobin counterparts, mostly because in a strange way they were not.

As I shall argue, these hidden correspondences have their own sources in fundamental dynamic exigencies of social and national life, and do not necessarily rely on influences passing from one source to another, such as from Catholicism to republican nationalism—however convenient and often true it is to speak in this way. Even during the French Revolution itself, royalist political thinkers were able to use the very words of someone like Rousseau to justify counter-revolutionary policies and principles. Royalist Abbé Augustin de Barruel appropriated Rousseau's rejection of the priority of representation, later taken up by Jacobins, in support of royalist claims.[27] Royalist Abbé Sabatier de Castres cited Rousseau as well in defense of his views on the rights and responsibilities of the sovereign and subjects. These thinkers, in effect, argued in a style much like that of Jacobin totalitarian readings of Rousseau. They claimed that the sovereign, like the General Will, was the true representative of the people.[28] One of the most influential royalist journalists, Abbé Thomas Marie Royou, used Rousseau to argue that "individuals in a state of nature, realizing the inadequacy of their abilities, had surrendered all their rights to society as a whole." This surrender was "absolute, unlimited, irrevocable, and perpetual." Thenceforth, in an anticipation of the rhetoric of nationalist sacrifice, individual interests had to suffer if necessary for the welfare of all.[29]

Slow to Sacrifice

But, at first, the traditional religious communities of the nation were either slow to catch this new patriotic spirit or inept at doing so.[30] In particular, Catholicism, the tradition best equipped theologically and historically to legitimize a national ideology of sacrifice, was then deeply alienated from the anticlerical Third Republic. By contrast, French Protestants were in no position to provide a national sacrificial ideology, either. Even though they tried to mount a campaign to declare Protestantism "the" religion of France, they consisted of no more than 1½ percent of the nation's population. In terms of ideology, French Protestants were also hampered by traditional objections to sacrificial religion, which stood in the way of their offering an unambiguous ideology of national sacrifice.[31] Did not Protestant individualism make them opportunists, "jealous" of their own personal lives and treasure, and thus unfit to promote sacrificial visions,[32] Paul Sabatier, the popular Protestant author wondered aloud?[33] A Protestant, in his view, was only "able to give himself up to his individual task" and unable to raise his consciousness to the level required by the national crisis.[34] As far as French Jews were concerned, although Jews could lay claim to a history of ancient nationalism and its sacrificial traditions, they were only one-half of one percent of the French population. Like the Protestants, Jews had played down their own traditions of sacrificial religion, which had been put on hold until the coming of the Messiah. Thus, even though French Jewish theologians and philologists, like James Darmesteter, claimed that Judaism too could just as well qualify as the national religion, his brand of "reformed" Judaism could not provide the sacrificial ideology needed to legitimize the demands of the nationalist revival.[35]

In time, nationalist fervor of the Third Republic dictated that this sought-after "'religion de la patrie'"[36] would be nothing less than nationalism itself. "After 1870," said Paul Sabatier, "patriotism became the religion of France."[37] The so-called Free Thinkers or "laïcs" who led this movement doubted that the religious traditions could be retooled to provide the spiritual legitimacy France's coming war with Germany would require. They therefore fell back upon the sacrificial discourse of the French Revolution and its celebrants, like Michelet, and proclaimed the new religion or "morality" with its vivifying sacrificial rites.[38] One is not surprised to learn, therefore, that even under the anticlerical Third Republic, the army sought to inculcate "'in the heart of their men the great ideas of sacrifice and devotion to the patrie.'"[39]

Furthermore under the Third Republic, public education served a critical civic function in socializing the young into service to the *patrie.* Every student in the state's primary and secondary schools memorized patriotic themes set forth in the *manuels scolaires,* edited and sometimes composed by Ernest Lavisse, the influential Sorbonne historian. Typical of the sacrificial slant of these handbooks of national religion, leading questions were put to France's youngest citizens: "'Who are, in your opinion, the greatest martyrs for our *Patrie?'*" In this way, Lavisse sought to achieve a republican appropriation of the Catholic rhetoric of sacrifice by subsuming prerevolutionary Catholic traditions of heroism and sacrifice to a republican discourse, which had previously sought to sever historical relations with the Catholic past.

Given the central place of sacrifice in the logic of nationalism itself and given the sacrificial character of central Catholic values embodied in the Eucharist, it is no accident that Lavisse selected sacrificial virtues for emphasis. Indeed, for him, sacrificial virtues captured the heights of French civic virtue. The "history of France," Lavisse said, "culminates in hero-ism."[40] Sacrifice captured the essence of the "eternal France," which La-visse sought to mobilize for battle. Perhaps most important of all in se-lecting a value at once elemental for both the Catholics, who constituted the bulk of the "right," and the traditions of the French Revolution, where Lavisse saw sacrifice as essential, Lavisse achieved a remarkable ideologi-cal reconciliation.[41] As we will also see further, this reconciliation of the mythologies of revolution and Church was deployed throughout the pri-mary and secondary educational systems, but also, as we might expect, into the other national institutions of France.

An additional level of influence was more subtle. While sometimes Catholic thought was deliberately exploited by an otherwise secular, even anticlerical, government for political ends, at other times, because of its long history in the life of the nation, French Catholic sacrificial thought made unconscious inroads into the ways people thought about sacrifice. Sometimes the influence operated at both levels simultaneously. From 1870, the secular, even anticlerical, republican government "fortified the patriotic conscience of the nation"—exploited Catholic ideas and social-ization—"already completed to a degree by the Church"[42]—resident al-ready in the national psyche. Even segments of the extreme, nominally secular left, such as the anarchists, show how deeply buried Catholic ideas could resurrect later in a transformed condition. Anarchist visions were, for example, often articulated in the same religious language as the forces of "intransigence," all the better to trade on the familiar sensibility and vocabulary of Catholic religiosity.[43]

Even excommunicated Catholic thinkers like Albert Loisy seemed to have joined this consensus, forming around a national religion of patrio-tism proclaiming sacrifice as its chief rite.[44] In this period of national cri-sis, Loisy felt that what really moved the French was patriotism, not Catholicism.[45] Even if Catholicism could rise to the challenge of the na-tionalist crisis, it was useless to urge most French people to "return" to Catholicism. Loisy felt that most French people did not wish to "return" anyway.[46] In these days, Loisy felt that the only viable religion for the French was the religion of the "native land."[47] As

> nonbelievers find themselves animated by a feeling for France, a
> feeling far more profound than our ordinary run-of-the-mill public
> morality, [so also] among the believers it was more profound than
> the ordinary run-of-the-mill Catholic morality. . . . This feeling for
> French humanity . . . is our common religion.[48]

As for sacrifice, Loisy never stopped believing that it remained the chief rite of the religion of the nation. In an essay addressed to the survivors shortly after World War One, Loisy affirmed the cardinal role of sacrifice in the religion of patriotism. Here, Loisy declared that "the sacrifice of individuals is required for the equilibrium and preservation of society, for the common good, for the establishment and maintenance of concord."[49] Despite the disastrous massacres of the war, sacrifice remained at the center of national life.

Thus, at the century's end, laïc French nationalists of all stripes were prepared to harvest the fruits of an entire tradition of religio-nationalist thinking. While Catholics remained hostile to the republic and Protestants and Jews remained too small in numbers, the laïc republicans laid claim to a tradition of sacrificial rhetoric, dating at least, in their minds, from the Revolution and carried on into the end of the century. Amplified by the likes of Michelet, the laïc neorevolutionary deification of the "people" made national values ultimate and worthy of a sacrificial "giving up" of the individual self. Did not Renan after all teach that the nation was a "cultural race" and sacrifice was the essential national rite?[50] Taking additional cues from Comte's positivist religion of humanity, the laïc partisans of the religion of patriotism pledged that sacrificial virtues such as altruism would increase in proportion as a Comtean new religion of humanity grew.[51] Reflecting these universal human values, embodied in the revolutionary tradition, the devotees of the religion of patriotism urged a spirit of collective solidarity based on "humanitarian ardour" and "mutual love."[52] The chief symbol in the arsenal of this new religious campaign, much on the minds and in the hearts of "nationalists," was sacrifice.

Who Owns Sacrifice? A Catholic Religion of Patriotism

While the republicans gathered their ideological forces around a religion of patriotism, the Catholics slowly began to take notice and react. In declaring a national ethic of sacrifice, the republic in effect threatened to displace God and Church from the center of French spiritual life, as Loisy indeed wished. The nation in effect would steal from the Church the symbol of sacrifice and, in doing so, subsume the Church to the interests of the nation. In response, intransigent Catholics took advantage of the rise of this religion of nationalism to reestablish the patriotic credentials of Catholicism in this period of crisis. The result was, however, a model of the law of unintended consequences: the secular republic was compromised by religion and religion finally co-opted by the secular republic.

Given that the doctrine of sacrifice preached by the religion of patriotism recalled the spirit of total giving of the self, embedded in the Eucharistic theology of the seventeenth century, reviving Catholic patriotism was not a difficult task.[53] By virtue of its unique position in the centuries-old historical and cultural formation of the nation itself, Catholicism unwittingly supplied the religion of patriotism with much of its content and structure.[54] This seems what Georges Goyau referred to in 1918 among the French as the "sacerdotal spirit," that morality "which welcomes death as an achievement of resemblance to Christ."[55] Reaffirming the Catholic priorities of ordinary French soldiers, Maurice Barrès contemplates the sacrifices of a young soldier fighting out of a spirit of ritual devotion to the ancient sacred woodlands of the French frontier: "For this young soldier there exists no imaginary conflict between the cult of Nature and heroic Christianity. Self-immolation, the spirit of sacrifice, has seemed to us irreconcilable with this enchantress. How easily he subordinates great Pan to the Son of God crucified!"[56] What Goyau does not say, but what affirmation by the likes of integral Catholics like Maurice Barrès affirms, is that this "sacerdotal spirit" of national sacrifice is mostly the work of the intransigent Catholics.[57] In equally spiritual tones, Micheline Tison-Braun observes how a "nationalist mystique" was embodied in a "magical nationalism" of the *"terre sacré"* of the French nation. This "mystique," which Tison-Braun also feels was a "psychosis,"[58] nonetheless had overwhelming power. "Insidiously, [it] encouraged a belief in the magical power of sacrifice, as if some tribal deity, well sated with the blood of its victims, guaranteed supremacy to its people in return for their submissiveness."[59]

Over against the competition mounted by the likes of Lavisse, the Church launched a series of counterattacks. It deliberately tried to co-opt the republic's ideal of civic heroism by identifying it with the old Catholic ideal of martyrdom. For the Catholics, the task was not difficult. Given that the cult of the martyrs and Christian heroes was already strong in France, the church launched a campaign of its own to intensify the cult of martyrdom.[60] In 1886, Abbé Profillet published a book of the lives of six hundred saints called *Les Saints militaires*. Within a few years, this work expanded to six volumes and finally counted 3,000 hero-saints.[61] The church lost no opportunity popularizing the deaths of missionaries in the recently expanded colonial domains, marking them both as heroes and martyrs. Clergy killed by the Commune were also added to the venerable list of martyrs to the faith.

In the process of merging republican and Christian discourses, even would-be royalists, like most of the intransigent Catholics of the day, finally came round to the idea of embracing the Third Republic's nationalism. They did so, not out of some sudden conversion to republican values, but because they seemed to be fighting a battle they could win. Compromise offered them, in effect, an opportunity for affirming their own Catholic integral ideals and Catholic religious piety from within the national covenant. Compromise enabled the intransigents to create an opening for themselves in the politics of the republic, where before they had been shunted aside to its margins. In the years to follow, they exploited the nationalist crisis by contesting a series of elections throughout the life of the Third Republic. Notably in 1919, they won a parliamentary majority under the banner of a political entity called the "Bloc National."

One of the most "concrete" expressions of the Catholic exploitation of the nationalist mood came in 1915 when the French bishops used the occasion of the dedication of the Basilique du Sacré Coeur to pledge the nation to that well-recognized symbol of counter-revolution and sacrificial expiation, the Sacred Heart of Jesus.[62] At the urging of the French hierarchy, the pope canonized Joan of Arc in the same year and shortly thereafter, by unanimous vote and without debate of any sort, the National Assembly declared the feast of St. Joan of Arc a national holiday.[63] Patriotic "religious dramas" were revived in the towns.[64] A movement to canonize Napoleon gained support and promised to be an event that "would achieve absolutely that union of patriotic and religious sentimentality to which the Church in France directs its activities."[65]

So complete was Catholic success in co-opting nationalist feeling that only a rump of the more extreme anticlericals in the government resisted these affiliations of Church and State. Naturally enough, the anticlericals viewed Catholic symbols, such as Joan of Arc and the public Catholic solemnities connected with her, as a dangerous blurring of religious and political discourses. They typically found ways to absent themselves from such religio-political solemnities, or, when they were able to control events, they replaced symbols such as Joan of Arc with those from the revolutionary tradition, such as Marianne.[66] So uncompromising was this resistance that the laïcs resolutely refused participation in war-related solemn occasions at major Catholic venues such as the Sacré Coeur. Whatever else this behavior may indicate, it testifies to the success of the Catholics in deploying Catholic symbolism in nationalist discourse and thereby influencing its significance.

On the propaganda front, the Church deployed a French Catholic discourse of national religious exceptionalism, with roots traceable to the Wars of Religion. In pastoral letters, the First World War was seen as a "holy war" against Protestant Germany, a "just war."[67] In a letter from the front, the seminarian, Yves de Joannis, a cannonier in an artillery regiment, but a Catholic theologian still, vented his fury upon the

> Luthero-Kantian colossus of Germany which imperils both France
> and the Church. I am not able to stop myself from risking hostile en-

emy fire or from directing my cannon to combat this false philosophy, this false interpretation of scripture, and this politics so full of
error and arrogance, which seeks to enslave the world. Nor can I resist attacking those who would lie about our race, our history, our
traditions and our faith. And just think of it, rather than rereading
Bossuet, our great classic authors or St. Thomas Aquinas, there are
those among us who delight instead in reading Kant, Schelling,
Nietzsche or Schopenhauer![68]

Counterreformation battles against the Protestants were thus updated
and fought all over again in symbolic form: "Catholic" France was now pitted against "Lutheran" Germany. "Germany, that 'daughter of Odin,'
now faced the armed might of the Eldest Daughter of the Church. The
cause of the France and the Church were one."[69]

Inadvertently aiding this effort of the Church to capture the nationalist imagination of the republic, the leaders of the Third Republic were
quick to appeal to these same religious collective memories by trading on
the very same religious metaphors of sacrifice now being broadcast widely
by the Church. So-called secular political efforts were so much saturated
by Catholic ideas that even in the resolutely anticlerical Third Republic,
religion "constituted the reinforcing structure of patriotism."[70] Summing
up this remarkable transformation, historian Jean-Marie Mayeur judged
the state of play between Catholicism and French nationalism in these
words: "No matter how little and how seldom nationalism had been 'clerical,' it now took on a Catholic coloration: the religion of the patrie, army,
and the cults of the dead led to religion or even restored religion."[71] This
encompassing of the national cause within Catholic conceptions sometimes appears in vivid form in the literature of the period. Bertrand's *Appel du sol* (1916) casts Captain Antoine de Quéré, the novel's model of intransigent Catholicism, in the role of articulating a formula for merging
patriotic war effort with his Catholicism. "If I die," he says, "I shall die a
modern Christian. But I shall not die *for* Christianity. Rather, I shall die
for my country."[72] As a result, de Quéré and, one must assume, those like
him, believed that what might appear to be a mere political struggle was
actually a religious crusade. He sees in the troops under his command the
"very men-at-arms of Saint Louis," and thinks that "it is the destiny of
France to be an example of Christian *noblesse* and to be the missionary for
the ideas of Louvois and Joseph de Maistre."[73]

For its part, the Church's consecration of patriotic values led to significant changes in its policies and relations to the Third Republic. The Republic directed that the clergy should be expected to do front-line service. The Church posed no objection. At the front, the common clergy

performed with courage and gained respect from a broad segment of the population. Even in their routine duties at home, the roles played by the Catholic clergy began to raise them in the esteem of the nation. Not even their critics could gainsay the value of the role of local priests in conveying news of casualties and war deaths to affected parties.[74]

In terms of practical policies concerning the war and preparations for war, the Church moved from a divided policy to one wholeheartedly in service to the nation. Pope Benedict had been in the process of trying to mediate a highly publicized early end to hostilities. Significant sectors of French public opinion saw this proposed peace as favoring Germany. At the time, the then intransigent bishops opposed the mobilization of the clergy as chaplains, stretcher-bearers, and the like on the grounds that such tasks were inconsistent with Vatican directives.[75] Vatican policy together with Catholic antipathy to the Third Republic fueled rampant rumors of Catholic treason.[76] Episcopal resistance to the mobilization of the clergy fueled charges from left-wing organs of the press like *L'Humanité* that priests were simply seeking to excuse themselves from service to the nation.[77] But all this changed. Georges Goyau reported how during the war "the Abbé Perreyre desired that priests should look upon death as though it was their last mass, offering themselves as a sacrifice as they had offered Christ every day."[78] In the spirit of this remarkable religious discourse, French Catholic policies changed accordingly. Besides the cultic solemnities devoted to the spirit of national militance, Catholic attitudes became increasingly bellicose. Even Pope Benedict's attempts to broker a peace with Germany were overwhelmingly cast aside by French Catholic opinion in favor of a "French peace." In general, French Catholics were hostile to papal attempts to mediate between the combatants. The pursuit of all out-victory ruled the day.[79] Jean-Marie Mayeur notes, *"Imperceptibly, nationalism rehabilitated Catholicism."*[80] Perhaps just as imperceptibly, nationalism had compromised the Church's prophetic role to the service of the nation.[81]

Innocents on the Battlefields of the Lord

From the 1870s through the early twentieth century, although deployed from different ideological centers, a grim nationalist religion of sacrifice flourished in several Catholic contexts. As the impact of the war was first felt, the explicit public policy statements of the Church hierarchy took a marked turn toward talk of sacrifice and expiation. Typically made in *lettres pastorales* read in all churches throughout a given diocese, these letters interpreted the war in the sacrificial mode beloved of the intransigent

Catholics. The Church thus deployed its substantial reserves of rhetoric to ennoble militance, suffering, ritual violence, and sacrifice in behalf of the war effort. Although an early consensus among the clergy held that war was at best "permitted," while not being encouraged by God, this mood was now decisively changed. An early and emblematic, pastoral letter of early 1915 issued from Monsignor Guérard, bishop of the diocese of Coutance. For Monsignor Guérard, it was the duty of "believers to implore God for victory, but in praying for it to humble oneself for it, atoning for it."[82] Jacques Fontana argues that this particular pastoral letter set the tone for the entire important genre, revealing "a state of mind in its ideas as much as in its style." Subsequent pastoral letters issuing from other dioceses thus went on to develop the same themes of the war linked to expiating sacrifice for the nation.[83]

Prominent among these new themes were theological justifications of the war, which were related to the discourse on sacrifice as it had developed since the seventeenth century. In the new sacrificial vein, the war became a tool for evangelizing and conversion—a veritable "voice of God," in which the faithful learned their "'duties to God.'" Chief among these duties was the need to take part in the cosmic drama of atoning or expiating for sin by sacrificial suffering—either voluntarily or not.[84] As Richard Griffiths observes, the Catholic of this age conceived of war as having important purposes, the first and foremost of which was "individual purification, by which the country itself will be made more perfect."[85] Zev Sternhell also notes something of a precedent in Renan's view in "La Reforme intellectuelle," that the entire nineteenth century would be seen as "'the expiation for the Revolution'"![86] In those cases where the World War was seen as "chastisement" and "expiation," they were applied only to those guilty of "egoism," greed and "forgetfulness of God."[87] Indeed, the Abbé Servant declared the war a "consequence of human egoism," a result of a world that had turned its back on God. Bishop Gauthey of Besançon remarked how war exposes the "menace" of "egoism."[88] Supporting such views, even Pope Benedict XV taught that wars in general might be punishments for human sinfulness.[89]

It was those who had erred in these respects especially who especially needed to "sacrifice"—and thus to endure real physical suffering and death in order to repair the breach between man and God. Witness in this regard how late nineteenth-century religious enthusiasms such as pilgrimage to the little Calvary of La Salette or devotion to the Sacred Heart rehearse these themes of expiation through suffering, modeled upon Jesus' death on the cross.[90] Compare by contrast how, like characters from a Dostoevsky novel, the Russians believed that salvation would come by

enduring suffering experienced in battle.[91] In this new patriotic and expiatory sacrificial mood, war was a divine effort at the "correction" of
French morals and piety, indeed a "chastisement," even if not generally a
vengeful one.[92] Suffering was part of sacrificial expiation, a moment in
the cosmic scheme of exchange between penitent humanity and a forgiv-
ing, but demanding, God. Although suffering was seen as "one of the
great laws of human life," it was not to be endured for its own sake. Rather,
the French bishops saw suffering as a way of bringing errant humanity to
heel. Suffering "atones and perfects, winning many merits."[93] Cardinal-
Archbishop Luçon of Reims elaborated, saying that "in allowing the war,
God wanted to stop France 'from sliding down the slippery slope to perdi-
tion, upon which she was headed.'"[94] Indeed, as was to prove so prescient,
the Vicar of Rouen promised his congregation that the war would teach
the French a "'lesson in the spirit of sacrifice.'"[95]

Although the theologians might have preferred that the guilty alone
sacrifice in atonement for their sins, the innocent were clearly implicated as victims of sacrifice as well. Such unfortunate things simply could
not be avoided amid the confusion and tumult of war. Thus, the Catholic
theologians needed to make religious sense of the sufferings of these
innocents—much as de Maistre had done. At the level of the ordinary
soldier, the poor *poilu* was, for example, cast as "'enduring an enforced
Lent.'" Typically, the soldier was likened to Christ, the ultimate Christian
model of an innocent sacrificial victim atoning for humanity. Just as Jesus's self-immolation expiated the sins of humanity, the individual self-
sacrifices of common soldiers were also seen as an *expiation* for sins committed by France in modern times. [96] Historian Paul Gerbod notes that
the defense of such heroic values was

> rooted in one dominant idea: the grandeur and power of a nation
> such as France is founded upon the heroism and spirit of sacrifice of
> each and everyone. Heroism is not only something egoistic and per-
> sonally satisfying, but is an exceptional kind of gift of the self for the
> common good.[97]

The bishop of Nantes reportedly put it this way: "The troops are cold just
like Our Lord was when he shivered in the stable; they are hungry the way
Our Lord was in the desert, and thirsty as He was on the cross; they are
struck, torn apart and murdered as was Christ throughout His passion."[98]
Prominent among the patriotic voices from the official Church were the
newly conscripted clergy.[99] After passage of the law of 1905, requiring
clergy to serve in the military, their voices took on a special authority not
granted them beforehand. Discoursing on the meaning of the death of a
priest in wartime, the Dominican, Ambroise Soudé says,

What is the death of a priest? Something ignored, no doubt—just like his life. But, about such a death, we really only know what it means in the eyes of God. There, it purchases France's salvation. . . . God has created both priests and soldiers for us. We priests, we die as soldiers if the *patrie* wishes it. We'll be the first. Our life, already employed in ministering, will also be good for death. We would then be twice as useful for France. And no, this sacrifice will not be too so distressing, since it is an inexorable law of positive science. It is a deed which declares a history and which cries out for devotion. In this way, we start taking all of the ideals of France to heart.[100]

In a similar spirit of sacrifice, an anonymous "Abbé X.," a priest of the diocese of Paris, reflects on his role in the war:

I leave tomorrow. And, what will tomorrow bring? I'll make a total sacrifice of my life, because I have the presentiment that the end approaches. Yet, I offer this life of mine of my own free will for my God and *patrie*.

I am a priest, and desire nothing more. Tomorrow, if it should come to pass, I will lift up my arms in absolution or blessing. And, tomorrow, if God wills it, I shall be with Him. Let this life of privations and hardships be offered in expiation for my sins![101]

"Abbé S," a priest from the diocese of Arras, reflects particularly on his role as a sacrificial victim—one he finds especially ennobling:

From the time I was sent in, I saw myself as abandoned, a mere victim. . . . But now, by the grace of God, I felt that to be a victim on the field of duty is to die at one with Our Lord, to be a priest indeed from that moment henceforth in union with the Celestial Lamb in light and glory, and to be really joined with the souls of the beloved. What an ideal! With this, the horrors of the campaign, the sufferings of death, the threat of atrocities as well—all vanish in light of such a prospect! [102]

Remarkably, even as the glorious optimistic glow of the first days of the war faded, soldier-priests continued to resort to heroic Catholic sacrificial notions. One such was Abbé Guillard, an infantry sergeant, who lay dying in early September 1914. Guillard was shot clean through the thigh and went down. Tellingly, for this generation of intransigent Catholics, his first thoughts were of the uncanny resemblance of his wound with that of his "dear savior Jesus on the cross." Guillard, it seems, was as he tells us, "truly nailed to his own cross, being unable to move his leg even a millimeter." Despite this, Guillard affirms his good spirits. He concludes that "with my crucifix before me, I pray and wait upon the will of the good Lord." More than that he reminds his readers of how much his life was englobed in the sacrificial ideal. "You know that before I took my leave, I had already dedicated my life to sacrifice. Ever since yesterday, I have renewed this pledge several times, and once more I renewed it again along with everything it pleases the good Lord either to add or to cut out."[103] However reluctantly, even the renowned philosopher and theologian, Cardinal Mercier of once "neutral" Belgium had to chime in on the theme of the sacrificing soldier, following the invasion of his country by the Germans.

> In the strict theological sense of the word, the soldier is not a "martyr," for he dies with weapons in hand unlike the martyr who loses his life to the violence of his executioners without defending it.
>
> But if you ask me what I think about the eternal salvation of the brave who consciously give up their lives to defend the honor of their country, and to avenge the violation of justice, I do not hesitate to answer that, without doubt, Christ will crown such military valor, and that a death, accepted as a Christian, guarantees the soldier the salvation of his soul.
>
> We do not have, said Our Lord, a better way of practicing charity than by giving up our lives for those we love: "Greater love has no man than he give up his own life for his friends."
>
> The soldier who dies to save his brothers, to protect their homes and altars of the *patrie*, performs this high form of charity.
>
> The moral value of this sacrifice would not always pass muster under minute analysis, as I would have it. But, is it necessary to believe that God asks of the brave soldier enduring the fire of combat to master the methodological precision of the moralist or theologian? We admire the heroism of the soldier. Would not God accept him with love?[104]

De Maistre's War

Catholic ideas about sacrifice, especially as transformed by Joseph de Maistre and reinterpreted by Catholic thinkers of the late nineteenth and early twentieth century, seem to have shaped the way commentators regarded and represented the war. Although it was generally agreed that the soldiers who went to the front were innocent of France's wrongdoings, their innocence only heightened the sacrificial character of the situation. It was as if de Maistre had turned up in the midst of the debate about the meaning of the war, and had told the French once more that they were all sinners and that therefore the innocent were immolated for the sake of the redemption of the guilty. Bloodshed redeems the evil that enters human life, only if the victim is innocent. Evil must be extirpated.[105] Thus, de Maistre tells us what Olier or Condren never did, even in their most self-negating moods:

> One especially finds that all nations agree on the marvelous efficacy of the voluntary sacrifice of the innocent who sacrifices himself to the divinity as a propitiatory victim. Men have always attached an infinite price to the submission of the just person who accepts these sufferings.[106]

For the Catholic intransigents, their belief in the efficacy of the sacrifice of the innocent claimed a rational, albeit cosmic, justification. The basis for this belief rested on the view that in order for a sacrifice to be acceptable it must be pure and somehow "written into" the inevitable architecture of the cosmos. For de Maistre, sacrificing the innocent made sense because only the innocent could be pure enough to receive a divine welcome and thus to effect expiation. Furthermore, only if an innocent were encompassed within a cosmic drama of inevitable fate could such a mere individual serve the purposes of the expiation of the collective. Resorting to the example of the judicial sacrifice of Louis XVI, de Maistre waxes eloquent about the martyred king's purity and involvement in a cosmic process that could not be derailed, delayed, or sidestepped. Indeed, the victims somehow prove their moral superiority over their sacrificers by a dignified acceptance of their death, as if realizing all the while that they will prevail in the cosmic view of things. "This heart," says de Maistre, recalling the innocence of the doomed king, was "so pure, so submissive, so prepared." And, like Jesus led to his own prophetic slaughter, the "august martyr seemed to fear escaping the sacrifice or making the victim less perfect."[107]

Lay Catholics also joined in the production of this Maistrean patriotic literature. The work of the intransigent Catholic thinker Louis Veuillot is an especially clear example of de Maistre's impact. His rousing *La Guerre et l'homme de guerre* dates from 1870.[108] There, Veuillot sought to strike a blow for a militantly patriotic Catholicism while refuting *philosophe* charges of religious "fanaticism," stemming from Enlightenment critiques of the Wars of Religion. Against Voltaire's charges that Catholicism was essentially bloodthirsty and prone to warfare, Veuillot threw up the even bloodier record of massacre and violence among the ancient Romans so beloved of *philosophes* like Voltaire. "Pagans massacred Christians; the legions massacred each other; one half of the world is armed in order to massacre the other half. . . . War, feuds, revolutions, conquests, crimes . . . existed before Christianity. And they continue to exist thereafter as well." Not until the reign of the newly converted Constantine had massacres of Christians and other blood sports been stopped. [109]

Yet, Veuillot preaches anything but pacifism. Neither the gospel nor the traditions of the Church and its great teachers, such as Bellarmine and church councils, supported pacifism. The Catholic is only enjoined to avoid "unjust" violence.[110] Indeed, the role of the Church is to harness violence, to encase it in a system of moral rules. The Christian needs to choose among *kinds* of violence, not about whether violence can be part of a Christian life. Take sacrifice, for instance, Veuillot asks us. The "belief that God's anger might be appeased by the sufferings which other creatures underwent as substitutes for the truly culpable," is "in principle reasonable."[111] However, in Veuillot's view, the fundamentally good primordial religious and moral insight in sacrifice became an "abominable superstition" as it more and more developed into human sacrifice, reaching its nadir in the infant sacrifices of Baal-Moloch and Carthage.[112] Ultimate proof of the way the sacrificial ideal became thus "distorted" is the fact that each of the nations practicing such hideous rites has been effaced from the earth. It was thus left for Christianity to purify the world of violence and sacrifice so that violence would be contained by morality. Thus, while Christians might make war, even wars of "conquest," such wars should never become wars of "extermination"—wars without moral limits.

Monarchists like Veuillot felt that Christianity assisted in controlling violence in society overall by legitimizing monarchy, by "investing royal authority and the very person of kings with a sacred character."[113] But this controlling influence of the sacred over the otherwise profane does not end with the monarchy. It is a rule for society at large. In Veuillot's view, as with intransigent Catholics in general, the profane must be totally informed by the sacred, right down to the level of the ordinary citizen. Profane activities were to be suffused with sacred purpose. Veuillot provides us with a wonderful account of this infusion of the sacred into the profane in his stirring account of the military as a kind of religious order like the priesthood. The military literally led the Church militant. *La Guerre et l'homme de guerre* concludes with a chapter-length discussion of the many ways priests are really soldiers, and soldiers really priests. "What is a solider?" asks Veuillot.

> He is a monk by virtue of his orderliness, sobriety and asceticism, by the manner in which he surrenders his will to his superior. For a Christian, there is no other station in life more closely approaching that of the monk's than the soldier's.

As for the priest, Veuillot asks,

> What is a priest—above all the monk—that is to say, a priest raised to that height of lofty abnegation, which comprises human virtue? He is a soldier, par excellence, the one posted where it is the most difficult, the one sent where there is the most danger, the one cast away onto frigid polar regions, into equatorial deserts, or onto the savannas of America—he whom one tells to go fight the savages, heretics and unbelievers. Yet he goes, and he even dies there. And even if he dies from weariness or torture, even if he has been flogged, consumed by fire, or wolfed down with relish, others hastening to assume his place, others stirred by the same ambitions, in the end, raise the cross on the ruins of these bloody pulpits or on the ashes of these pyres. Like a soldier, atop the debris of an enemy fortress and on the corpses of his fallen brothers, he plants his conqueror's standard.[114]

Veuillot then closes with an appeal to reclaim the ideal of France as a Christian nation, embodying the intransigent Catholic model of the state guided and informed by Catholic values. For it is only by virtue of the moral and religious discipline issuing from religious faith that bold fighters arise.

> I have faith in those Christians who know how to be in God's militia at the same time as they are in the militia of this world. They won't be the last to join an assault on a Russian fortress. Nor will they hold back in the assault against an antireligious madness that wants to separate France from her Christian nature. Over against this invasion of the brutal passions and barbaric minds who once more menace Christ's empire, the priest and the soldier join hands with one another—just as they did in the time of Clovis, Charlemagne, and St. Louis. And, in the wake of this union, France will become in the eyes of God what it should be: "a brave people, and a people of brave men" (Joseph de Maistre).[115]

We will see later how this spirit of martial devotion, taken up by the increasingly Catholic officer corps, may have shaped French attitudes about war and its pursuit generations later.

Since, in the eyes of intransigent Catholics like Veuillot, soldiers were innocent sacred beings, the sacrifice of the lives of soldiers during the First World War was deemed perfect. Like priests in all their purity celebrating a Eucharist with implications far beyond the manipulation of mere bread and wine, soldiers acted as pure agents in a sacramental, sacrificial drama with inevitable cosmic consequences. Of the soldiers he met near the front, Barrès asks rhetorically, "How can I make you see the unforgettable purity of their gaze as they scan the horizon, seeking, not their own destiny, but the destiny of their country."[116] Those conveying a sense of the war in literary form, also report the same acceptance of the inevitable "sacrifice" that they faced—even after the first enthusiasms for reckless attack have subsided. Henry Bourdeaux's 1916 novel of the heroic resistance to the fall of Fort de Vaux (near Verdun), *Les Derniers jours de Fort de Vaux,* reports that the troops stoically "submit" (*accepter*) to the war.[117]

A partisan of the stab-in-the-back theory of France's fortunes during the war, Loïs Dabbadie further exemplified this complex of Maistrean religious and political attitudes. Dabbadie was especially obsessed by the sacrificial victimization of ordinary soldiers. He accused the French high command and government of having failed to prepare properly for the war.

> Like ancient Israelites listening to the priests of Baal, the French have become the slaves of German and Jewish Freemasonry, which preaches atheistic pride. Handed over by this secret society and disarmed by it, they in effect atone for its stupid ingratitude. So, France escapes miraculously from the Teutonic yoke only because its warriors were champions of Christian civilization.[118]

Dabbadie felt these selfless heroes tragically foresaw their own desperate fates; yet carried on nonetheless: "Far from being gullible or full of illusions, on the contrary, they knew that this frightfully unfair battle would require self-denial to the point of sacrifice."[119] Indeed Dabbadie believed the simple soldier's "strength of soul"[120] held the key to victory. As if to reinforce prewar propaganda themes, Dabbadie reaffirms the ideology of sacrificial heroism in warfare: "Without sufficiency in materiel, victory can only be won by the stoical spirit and the spirit of sacrifice pushed to its utmost limits."[121]

It is worth recalling here how these sentiments about war death rehearse what we have seen from thinkers as far afield in time and space as the "École Française de Spiritualité" and Joseph de Maistre. In 1920, Geoffroy de Grandmaison's collection of correspondence and personal tributes to a victim of the First World War, Captain Pierre de Saint-Jouan, replays these themes with uncanny precision.[122] The link between Christ's priestly sacrificial death and nationalism is made explicit by our author. After quoting the following stanza of some verse by a wartime poet, Déroulède, Grandmaison goes on:

"Forward! Too bad for the fallen,
Death, it is naught. Long live the grave
when the country comes out of it alive"

Thus, the consolations of patriotism make a name illustrious at the same time as patriotism saves the nation's independence. This is the whole of the sanctifying and generous doctrine of the immolation, which is at once the ground of the world's law and the foundation of our beliefs, since the time of the sacrifice on Calvary—which has itself conquered death by death.[123]

De Maistre's views are then brought forward explicitly to the *fin-de-siècle* and linked to the ideology of sacrifice first articulated by him:

However, in the veins of Saint-Jouan flows blood too French not to relish the honor of sacrifice, too Christian not to understand the value, the beauty of heroic duty and to adore the paternal hand of God even when it chooses to strike. They do not doubt for an instant that death in combat only carries great privileges, and along with Joseph de Maistre they believe that "the victims of this dreadful judgment have not shed their blood in vain."[124]

Confirming this association of Catholic sacrificial theology and sacrificial violence from afar, we can also identify what seems the very same ideology of sacrifice behind Irish independence tactics. Padraic Pearse, leader of the Easter Rising 1916 was devoted to Calvary, to "Christ Crucified." His politics was directed by what can only be called a clear sacrificial religious vision. For him, the Rising was not "a military operation, but . . . a deliberate blood sacrifice."[125]

In their turn, the French nation's Catholic faithful, whether innocent or not, should approximate as much as possible the atoning work of the saintly French soldier at the front. "'For their part, Christians should impose sacrifices upon themselves. No one should to remain unconcerned,'" as the bishop of Laval declared in a pastoral letter of early 1915.[126] True to type was the argument of Bishop Gouraud of Nice, who promised that if the faithful endured the trials of life, they would be "raised to the rank of sacrifice and . . . bestow a true nobility upon life"— in war time as well as peace.[127] Sermons everywhere across the nation resounded explicitly with "the insistence on the Christian duty of sacrifice [and] the regenerative value of suffering."[128] The Church thus saw sacrifice everywhere, not merely limited to the guilty who needed to atone for the sins that had brought the war to the nation.

Another level of influence merits some treatment in depth. Typically operating at the unconscious level, but arguably more consequential, Catholic sacrificial thought contributed to forming the mindset of the strategic theorists of the French military as well as the mentality of the common foot soldier.

The Religion of Sacrificial Slaughter

Offensive thinking dominated the military thinking of all combatants during the First World War. But even though all parties to the War were committed to an offensive strategy, especially in the early years of the war before the stalemate of trench warfare settled in, the French version of the offensive strategy was especially piquant. What interests me here is of course the extreme French variant of the offensive strategy called the "attaque à l'outrance." Lieutenant-Colonel Louis de Grandmaison, proponent of the offensive strategy, made something of a mystique of the new plan for fighting modern war, even though he claimed to have devised it from close observation of fighting as far flung as the Boer War and the Japanese incursion into Manchuria.[129] One is drawn to the conclusion that the new strategy was rooted more in pre-existing values than in sober induction, especially after savoring the spiritualist—and therefore possibly Catholic—flavor of Grandmaison's vision. While this may well be a military man's version of everything from the radical philosophical Idealism of the day to the popular influence of Bergson's élan vital, it also reflects the influence of a Catholic spiritual formation, with its emphasis upon otherworldly. Thus, Grandmaison reproaches his peers for their playing down of spiritual factors in war.

> At the beginning of each of our military regulations, the importance of moral forces is affirmed in so many eloquent phrases. But in general, our worship of them does not transcend the level of traditional perfunctory invocation. So, after finishing with this ritual, destined, it seems, to pay back some kind, but remote, divinity, we believe ourselves justified never to think about them any more.[130]

Grandmaison then goes on to declare straightforwardly the "preponderant" role of values and motivation in his new vision of warfare: "It is a seriously wrong, as often is done, to want to study the methods of instruction and the processes of combat somewhat impersonally and independent of the 'moral' nature of the combatant—just as it would also be senseless to construct a machine without taking account of the engine which would drive it."[131] Or even more romantically, Grandmaison quotes some unnamed authority and announces that the "'human heart is the point of departure in everything concerning war.'"[132] By letting loose this "heart" and "force" in the form of an orderly offensive strategy, France would be sure to win the day. Thus, Grandmaison left little doubt about how war was to be fought. Not only is to "attack is to advance,"[133] but to "win is to advance"[134] as well.

Not everyone was as convinced as Grandmaison, however. In his memoirs, former Allied commander in Chief, Marshal Foch regretted this reliance on the extreme offensive strategy because it "led our soldiers into so many blind and sterile attacks." In Foch's judgment, "Our war doctrine was . . . too summary, limited as it was for all ranks to one magnificent formula: the offensive."[135] Some even judged this stratify the "least rational" of all.[136] The policy of unleashing Gallic furor wasted swarms of men in futile assaults on well-entrenched German lines. In maximizing the heroic, sacrificial, and even metaphysical values that informed the strategy of *attaque à outrance,* the French command virtually ensured the massive slaughter of its own infantry, at least in the early stages of the First World War. Indeed, in 1913, Joffre admitted as much. The results he sought in pushing the strategy of the offensive could "'only be obtained at the price of bloody sacrifices.'"[137] Of heroism, there thus seemed to be no end—even in the demoralizing stagnation of defensive warfare in the trenches. In Bourdeaux's *Les Derniers jours de Fort de Vaux,* we meet the humble stretcher-bearer, Vanier. He is singled out because he gained his "stripes" by taking on a fighting role when ordinary soldiers had lost courage. His example speaks volumes about the power—or at least the representation—of sacrificial attitudes among the French troops. Bordeaux concludes his little story of battlefield bravery by lauding Vanier's "heroic courage and self-sacrifice" (*dévouement*). Just as Vanier was about to go "over the top," he declared: "I don't want to be a prisoner; I'd sooner be killed."[138]

Many explanations have been given for such conduct. Marshall Joffre, commander in chief of French forces in the early years of the war, for example, goes on at length in his memoirs to recount his own experiences with the origins of the French offensive strategy. He even offers an explanation of sorts. Several factors were at play. First, following the old adage to the effect that generals always fight the present war as if it were the previous one, the Prussian defeat of the French defensive strategy in 1871 encouraged French strategists to take the opposite position. Yet this tendency does not explain why the offensive strategy gained ascendance only after 1885. But Joffre has an answer to this. The timing of the rise of the offensive strategy, Joffre argued secondly, came swiftly when the French learned that the Germans had developed a high-explosive shell capable of piercing the walls of the defensive fortifications the French had built along their border with Germany.[139]

But, if we are to believe his reservations about the offensive strategy written years later in his memoirs, Joffre was alarmed early on by the early advocacy of an offensive strategy by its chief proponent Lieutenant-Colonel Louis de Grandmaison in 1908.[140] Of Grandmaison's lectures, Joffre noted that "their brilliance made them all the more dangerous."[141] Thus, it is interesting that Joffre supplements his material and military account of the rise of the offensive strategy with the intriguing beginnings of a moral analysis. Even though he would become commander of an army in the field directed by such a strategy, Joffre complained years later in his memoirs about the "unreasoning character which the passion for the offensive strategy took" and, with evident contempt, how it became "the fashion in high places."[142] Nonetheless, Joffre was a "good soldier" and worked to prepare the army "intellectually and morally to" implement the offensive strategy. He saw it his duty to "create a solid doctrine" and to "impose it upon officers and men." Perhaps, in those years before the war, Joffre came to agree with a deputy of the National Assembly, whom he quotes in his memoirs: "'offense alone is suited to the temperament of our soldiers'"?[143]

Aside from these few words, no explanation for the adoption of this extreme form of offensive has mined the history of religion in France. Without by any means claiming that French Catholic culture bears sole or perhaps even major responsibility for the values of making war in the twentieth century, is it possible that France's centuries-old religious culture should have had no consequences for informing the French national culture of warfare? Natalie Zemon Davis has argued, for instance, that French Catholics and Protestants warred against each in distinctive ways. French Catholics preferred to massacre Protestants, while French Protestants took special delight in defacing Catholic symbols, icons, images and the like.[144] If this is true of French Catholics and Protestants, why could not something similar be true of the modern French Catholics at large? Violence may have styles of its own. Even during its self-consciously anti-Christian period, Simon Schama says that the French Revolution's "uninhibited warfare and demonic destruction" of its foes exemplified how the "revolutionary temperament" was "still trapped in the body of royal government."[145] The first killings after the fall of the Bastille were, for example, regarded by their perpetrators as sacrifices of retribution, "punitive sacrifices," indeed examples of a "revolutionary sacrament."[146] Patrice Higonnet emphasizes how the Jacobins, such as Robespierre, "idealized" fellow citizens "who chose or accepted a patriotic death that transformed individualism into communitarian wholeness." Robespierre himself volunteered that he would eagerly "sacrifice his life to the nation and the future," should it become necessary.[147] For commentators of our own time, such as Higonnet, this indicates a near-religious or neoreligious "yearning for a universalizing society where the one and the many would come together." In Higonnet's view, the devotees of the Revolution had dedicated themselves to the dogma "that self-becoming and self-sacrifice were overlapping values."[148]

Daniel Pick's study of the rationalization of slaughter in the First World War argues against the standard issue Marxist materialist view that the slaughters of the war followed naturally from the workings of capitalism in crisis. On the contrary, Pick argues, profit-maximizing bourgeois societies seek instead the "frictionless" conditions of peace, the better to do business, undisturbed by threats of mass dislocation and destruction. War may benefit a few arms merchants and military vendors, but it also disrupts the much vaster flow of peacetime commerce.[149] Nor does Pick see war as an instinctual outburst of violence driven by our biological needs. Empirical surveys reveal more fear and general reluctance among the combatants than eagerness to fight.[150] Indeed, although French adoption of Clausewitz's theories of massed infantry attack explains certain aspects of the massive slaughters of the early years of World War One, Pick believes that no science of warfare can be wheeled in to explain battlefield slaughters.[151] Instead, he sees many discourses conspiring to encourage and legitimate the slaughters of World War One. Where then might one start?

Could Bergson's concept of *"élan vital"* have served as an ideological agent that legitimated the doctrine of attack? Given the broad popularity of the philosopher, there is no reason to question this possible connection. Bergsonian thought had a particular resonance among Catholics in France and since the army high command was heavily Catholic *élan vital* may well for something.[152] However, as Joffre tells us, there was more to the strategy of the offensive than Bergsonian energy. Essential in the idea of the offensive is also the ideal of "'bloody sacrifices.'"[153] To attack is to open oneself to risk and loss, most critically to loss of life. To advance a strategy of the offensive is to accept, however tacitly, the need for individual soldiers to prepare themselves for probable sacrifice.

Knowing this, can we ignore the place of Catholic socialization about sacrifice among the military command and its theoreticians? Evidence of *fin-de-siècle* Catholicism's positive encouragement of the ultimate act of giving one's life in a patriotic war, comes from Roger Martin du Gard's great 1914 novel of the pre-war period, *Jean Barois*. Here, an avowedly Catholic, although perhaps also Bergsonian, doctrine of action gets full play. In a passionate exchange between Barois and two young intransigent Catholic youths, one of them—Tillet—testifies to the power of Catholicism in his life. "The Catholic religion provides exactly what we require . . . the Church exalts our zest for action. . . . What we need today is a faith capable of inspiring us to action and heightening our energies."[154] Gliding easily from action to duty, Tillet concludes his declaration of new Catholic faith to Barois, ever skeptical of religious certitudes: "we know what we were doing when we elected for the idea of duty, the duty ready to one's hand."[155] What such duty might involve is altogether clear in the bellicose nationalism of Barois's two guests. Deriding the skepticism and rationalism of Barois and his ilk, Tillet's mate, de Grenneville, lashes out:

> Your generation, Monsieur Barois, unlike ours was satisfied with abstract theories, which not only failed to inspire it with the desire to do things, but did much to—to sterilize it. Self-complacently. Well, that sterile, navel-gazing contemplation may be good enough for Orientals, but, let me tell you, contemporary France, the France that has been through the Agadir crisis, and lives under the German threat, has no use for it! . . . No, Monsieur Barois, that generation of yours was not a fighting generation.[156]

Can we also pass over even more explicit and salient declarations that Catholicism shaped attitudes toward sacrifice in wartime—even when those words come to us in literary forms such as the realistic novels of the First World War? Here, once more Adrien Bertrand's *L'Appel du sol* provides a telling source of reflection on war and religion by the predominantly Catholic officer corps. Captain de Quéré, the spokesman for intransigent Catholicism in the novel, shows no reluctance recognizing that, in his words, "my religion makes sacrifice and resignation easier for me."[157] Indeed, fallen soldiers defending their *patrie* are really "martyrs."[158] Captain de Quéré explains this in recognizably orthodox Catholic style by appealing to the transcendental cosmic scale of life as seen by the pious Catholic. Like the martyrs of Roman times, so also for soldiers of that day: "If it seems easy for me to die, I believe it is because I know that a reward awaits me—eternity."[159]

Perhaps better than anyone else, Marshal Ferdinand Foch, a devout Catholic, reveals the formative influence of these intransigent Catholic ideas of sacrifice. His words are especially impressive after noting his putatively early reservations about the offensive strategy. Educated under the Jesuits, Foch was devoted to the thought of Joseph de Maistre and his view of the sacredness of war and its essentially religious nature. In his memoirs, he recalls how his "patriotism" was "stimulated to a burning glow" by one of his priest-instructors at school.[160] Asked why he attacked in the midst of what seemed like overwhelming German forces in the battle of the Marne, Foch replied: "'Why? I don't know. Largely, because of my men; a little, because I had the will. And then . . . God was there.'"[161] Making explicit his conscious devotion to de Maistre, Foch agrees with him that wars are both won and lost because of spiritual or "moral" factors. Foch even cites de Maistre's discussion of war in the *Soireés de Saint-Petersbourg*, using it to show that the moral origins of the offensive strategy, which might be mistakenly assigned to Bergson, are actually to be found in the thought of de Maistre.[162] To complete the picture of his dedication to de Maistre's thinking about sacrifice, Foch announced a theme now familiar to readers of this book as part of the intellectual stock in trade of the intransigent Catholic theory of sacrifice, namely that "war was appointed by divine ordinance as the perpetual ordeal and expiation for man's sin."[163] The case of so prominent a leader of French military strategy as Foch reveals that when the French elites articulated the ideal of sacrifice in warfare, some of them occupied their minds with an ideal sacrifice drawn from the theological materials supplied by official and unofficial Catholic teaching. Thus, the discourse about sacrifice upheld the common good of society and church over the autonomous value of the individual.

Similarly, how can we imagine that the ordinary soldier was free of the effects of "Catholic" socialization—either explicitly so or in the "secular" form they took after the French Revolution transformed them?[164] These Catholic ideas of sacrifice, transformed by the French Revolution into so-called secular ideals of civic devotion, seem to have shaped the mentalities of the common troops no matter how anticlerical many of them may have been. Noncommissioned officers like the anticlerical Sergeant Vaissette, of peasant stock, as described by Bertrand in his *L'Appel du sol*, loves France because of Robespierre, Rousseau, and Marat, rather than for the likes of de Quéré's heroes, Bossuet, Fenelon and Pascal.[165] He himself says he has a kind of "religion"—namely the religion of "humanity," the "religion of the *patrie*."[166] The French Revolution's devotees of the pre-Christian Roman republican world and figures like the Stoics or Lucretius show him how to live (and die) for his nation.[167] Impassivity and acceptance in the face of death and the "indifference" of nature mark the superior man.[168] That is to say that war teaches Vaissette, as he tells us, the very Catholic-looking "virtues of sacrifice, enthusiasm and submission."[169] Finally, as if realizing this historical kinship between the explicitly and implicitly Catholic sentiments of sacrifice, Vaissette himself declares that in the end, both he and Captain de Quéré are dedicated in equal measure to "submitting to the call of the *patrie*."[170] By uniting the country in a common patriotic sacrifice, the war changed many things in France. It reconciled, at least for the while, the oppositions that had torn the nation apart in modern memory.

It seems then that both the offensive strategy of the elites, as well as the common attitudes of the *poilus,* the kind of thinking evident in the Catholic sacrificial mentality we have seen in the realms of Eucharistic theology as well as in its secularized form, as originally articulated by the French Revolution. I am arguing not only that ideas have consequences, but that certain discrete religious ideas about sacrifice, embodied as they are in French Catholic institutions, culture, and theological thinking—from Bérulle to Joseph de Maistre to Robespierre—may well have paved the way for certain military policies and values that prevailed during the First World War.

I am thus assuming that in the case of war and national interest, little of these Catholic notions will stray very far from the reality of nationalism. They in fact may well reinforce one another. As Pick argues, nationalist discourse at least begins to explain things that are refractory to mechanistic and materialist approaches,[171] primarily because nationalism has the "aura of religion about it."[172] Like religion, nationalism raises people above themselves and their immediate interests, and legitimates their sure encounter with death. The transcendent religious quality of nationalism makes sense of why even the visceral fear and loathing of war can be suppressed, at least for a time. Nationalism as a kind of religion spins its own vast web of enchantment; it bestows upon war the magic of a "revelation." Patriotic love of the territory of France, for example, exhibits many of the features of traditional religion. During the First World War, we find expressions of the remnants of a romantic religion of nature and sacred place merging seamlessly with elements of Catholicism's "long cultural development" in France.[173] One is reminded again of Barrès's young soldier who had pledged to liberate French territory near the Meuse, which was now held by the Germans after the annexation of Alsace and Lorraine, for whom "there exists no imaginary conflict between the cult of Nature and heroic Christianity!"[174] In France, going to war for the nation in 1914 was both a religious and a political act: it was a "consecration."[175] Thus, intransigent Catholic, Maurice Barrès, observed how expeditious sacrificial death in war creates the nation: "And so, while they are making the France of tomorrow, France herself is being made in them. Already this miracle is manifest on the surface of their lives, in their words, in their acts. O blessed augury!"[176] Barrès confirms what Renan articulated so clearly in 1882: sacrifice makes the nation; nationalism necessarily requires sacrifice.[177]

A fortiori, if nationalism participates in the religious through its necessary involvement in sacrifice, *fin-de-siècle* French nationalism did so in the extreme. Again, Maurice Barrès is our guide. From his reportage of the sentiments expressed to him in letters from the front, he observes: "The spirit of religion pervades this whole younger generation. They are not all equally sustained by it; certainly they are not all of the same creed, but history, in speaking of them, will use the words of Léo Latil: 'In this war the spiritual element dominates all.' "[178] Thus, while ordinary French citizens were little attracted to abstract patriotic ideals stirred up by the "laïc" propaganda of the Third Republic, they clung to deeper sources of national feeling.[179] Stéphane Audoin-Rouzeau has recently argued that even in secular France, "the roots of national sentiment go deep"[180]—deeper than the rousing efforts of the Third Republic that were aimed at establishing the kind of patriotism needed for waging war. The Third Republic "only completed the 'task' begun many years previously."[181] The "national sentiment" evident in the years of the war "was . . . already complete, and must be seen as part of a long cultural development."[182] But how deep?

If the (ultimately) virulently anticlerical French Revolution is anything to go by, these roots seem to push well beneath the modern surface of French history. For even during that dechristianizing era, Catholicism provided, for one and all, that "vast frame of cultural references"[183] that anchored political discourse. To the extent that Roman Catholic theological thought about sacrifice shaped some of the "long cultural development" of the nation and therefore its warfare,[184] we would expect to find it in the trenches. In this, we are not to be disappointed. At the level of the common soldier, while one meets frequent complaining about the war, all embrace the sacrificial construction of the soldier's roles in it. Further, while it is also true that the common *poilus* "could not stomach" the "high diction" of "sacrifice" preached at them by policy makers and the officer corps, they nonetheless constructed their experience as one of being placed within an arena of sacrifice.[185] This meant that while they may not have bought into the grand expiatory schemes of cosmic sacrifice of the theologians or the proud national appeals to abstract duty promoted by the military high command, they still assumed that their duties to the nation were essentially religious—in particular—sacrificial.[186] Although one must beware of taking the claims of Catholic integralists, like Maurice Barrès, uncritically, he nevertheless testifies that among the troops from whom he had heard during the war, there was a distinct "acceptance of sacrifice, the consciousness of a great Presence at one's side—we come across these again and again."[187] What front-line fighters feared most of all was not sacrifice itself but that their sacrifices would go for naught— that their sacrifices would not be "recognized or appreciated" by the nation.[188] Thus, despite whatever differences obtained between the common soldiers and the elites, in their different ways the both saw themselves as actors in a cosmic sacrificial drama.

Eucharistic Theology and Military Strategy

Although there is a danger in making too much of the contribution of religious socialization to military thinking, elements of a Catholic theology
of sacrifice, both Bérullean and Maistrean, from baroque to restoration,
seem to have worked their way, consciously or not, into the minds of the
major theoreticians of the offensive strategy—especially insofar as these
theorists identified with Catholicism. It seemed, if anything, a commonplace in the literature of the First World War to recognize the Catholic
pedigree of sacrificial discourse. A fine example comes from Bertrand's
L'Appel du sol (1916) in such emblematically Catholic characters as Captain de Quéré. There, he is described in a manner reminiscent of the
seventeenth-century Roman Catholic Eucharistic mystics. We are told that
Captain de Quéré was originally meant for the priesthood, but took up a
career in the army instead. In the same breath, we are also told that he was
someone "only loving the poets of the seventeenth century and the Latin
authors,"[189] and as someone with an "ardent sympathy" for the Jesuits.[190]
Indeed, he is said in a way to live in the past of the Catholic Golden Age
and certainly to hope at least to "revive its spirit" in the present day.[191] For
him, France is the nation still ruled by Louis XIV. As a result of this desire
to inform modern France with these old Catholic ideals, Captain de
Quéré strikes one as "dogmatic. Things are absolute for him, with everything clear and uniform in both science and in faith." Tellingly, these intransigent Catholic values bespeak certain social and, finally, military values, making de Quéré "violent, authoritarian, and head-strong, with his
mystical eyes envisaging a society and order of things modeled on the desires of his own soul."[192] He is a kind of fanatic French and Catholic patriot who

> neither fears for himself, because he has prepared himself well with
> spiritual mortifications, nor fears for the nation because he has no
> doubt about the result of her battles. He believes in the invincibility
> of French weaponry, and in the purification of the nation's blem-
> ishes under the discipline of combat and by shedding her blood.
> And, above all other nations, he believes in her redemptive mission.
> *Ad majorem Dei gloriam!*[193]

As for the real elites, although the defeat of 1870 created a deep-seated
desire among the French to revenge their losses, the adoption of the offensive strategy was not a foregone conclusion. It had to be argued and
contested. The policy of *offensive à outrance* was the culmination of a generation of argument among military theorists. Chief among those shaping the strategy of the offensive was the elite military theorist, Ardant du

Picq (1821–1870). Du Picq's ideas shaped the thought of the future Marshall Foch and inspired his lectures given while director of the École Supérieure de la Guerre. Colonel Grandmaison, another champion of the offensive strategy during the First World War, also owed intellectual debts to du Picq.[194] Credited with having developed this offensive strategy out of his own devotion to the "heroic ethic," Ardant du Picq taught the importance of the "moral factor in war."[195] Du Picq typically spoke in the idiom of an anti-individualist Catholicism, ever ready to subordinate the bourgeois individual to the collectivity. Du Picq thus prized what I have been calling "sacrifice," since he abhorred the "*esprit capitaliste* which made [soldiers] . . . parsimonious with their own lives and their good positions."[196] Among the troops, there was need for a kind of "passionate unity, comradeship, and even amity among themselves which overshadows the individuality and animates every soldier with collectivistic or group "'passion . . . religious fanaticism, national pride, a love for glory.'"[197] After a while, du Picq finally taught a more flexible concept of offensive war than his successor in the advocacy of the offensive strategy, Grandmaison.[198] Yet, thinking like his arguably contributed to the concerted campaign for the offensive strategy led by men of the right in opposition to attempts by Jaurès and others for a strictly defensive war against the anticipated German assault.

At the risk of pressing the case too strongly here in favor of the seeing only Catholic ideas of sacrifice at work in shaping the articulation of French military strategy, it is nonetheless interesting to note that at the time of the First World War the high command tended overwhelmingly to be Catholic and monarchist. The same is, of course, not true of the army as a whole, composed as it was of the entire mix of French ideological tendencies. It is, however, a fact that the army elites saw their military careers in explicitly Catholic religious terms. For them, as for Louis Veuillot, membership in the army was a kind of sacred vocation, equivalent to belonging to a "celibate religious order"[199] (fig. 8). Thus, at least among the Catholic military elites, we may anticipate how sacrificial Catholic religious ideology predisposed the high command to embrace sacrifice in warfare.[200] For the elites, war was an heroic sacred rite directed by them as its "celibate" priesthood. The values of the officer corps thus fit well those inculcated by Catholic Eucharistic preaching about sacrifice.[201] First, was the value placed by that theology upon absolute or annihilationist *self*-sacrifice. *Individuals*, therefore, in imitation of Jesus' perfect self-immolating sacrifice of self, should be prepared to suffer death or lesser penalties, either in reality or vicariously, *deliberately*. Here, it may be well to recall the statement of Captain de Quéré in *L'Appel du sol* that his "religion makes sacrifice and resignation easier for" him,[202] or Joffre's conviction that "'bloody sacrifices'" would be necessary in the war.[203] Whereas Jesus sacrificed himself for the salvation of all humanity in a sacrifice of himself to God the father, the common soldier would sacrifice himself by laying down his life for the sake of the national group, for *raison d'état.*

Civic Sacrifice and Franco-Jewish Patriotism

So powerful seems to have been the underlying mix of Catholic and French Revolutionary patriotic rhetoric that the tiny French Jewish community (50,000 or so) seemed little different from the Catholics in their susceptibility to patriotic pressures. The pull of nationalism on French Jews was strong, if for different reasons, since each religious community had patriotic credentials that could and would be questioned. Since they had been longtime opponents of the Third Republic, Catholics needed to reassure the bulk of the nation of their patriotic loyalty. Ever since the defeat of 1871, Protestants too were sometimes under suspicion for nursing affection for the home of the Reformation across the Rhine. And during a period of intensifying anti-Semitism, the Jews were especially easy to target as subversive force, a foreign body within the French body politic.[204] After all, although Protestants were often associated with Germany or Britain, the Jews were the only religious community within France with a history of separate nationhood. No other community was subject to these often unstated pressures as much as the Jews.[205]

Thus French Jews had for some time seen it as their duty to "give of" or "give up" themselves to the interests of the nation.[206] But what strikes one about French Jews of the *fin-de-siècle* was how thoroughly a severe sacrificial imagery informed their civic piety. In truth, Jewish civic sacrificial notions are scarcely distinguishable from what we will meet shortly in the annihilationist political literature connected to the Catholic Eucharistic theology of the *"réaction."* Thus, the sacrificial traditions of ancient Israel, made real in stories of limitless devotion like that of Abraham's intention to sacrifice Isaac, became exemplary for modern French Jews facing the coming war with Germany. Let us see then how closely Jewish attitudes conformed to the standard nationalist line.

So closely did representatives of Franco-Judaism identify the two communities that Jewish exhortations to patriotism were commonly justified by citing Jewish equivalents for symbols of French national identity— sometimes, one imagines, straining the credulity of even the most convinced assimilationist. In 1890, Rabbi Armand Bloch commended devotion to Joan of Arc to French Jews at the dedication ceremony for her newly installed statue. This statue had, in fact, been erected on the property of a Nancy synagogue as a Jewish tribute to French patriotism.[207] The irony of this situation notwithstanding, Bloch urged Jews to be comfortable with her presence among them. After all she was much like Esther and Judith and other heroic Jewish women of the bible. Moving back toward a more nationalist position, Bloch argues that no conflict of faiths occurred here, since Joan was really not the property of any traditional religion, but the symbol of France herself. After all, said Bloch to his coreligionists, "she was a French woman, and we are all French here!"[208]

During the War: France or Humanity?

Even before the war, Jews had happily adapted themselves to the conditions of French patriotism. Much as in the Catholic tradition, religious metaphors of ritual sacrifice were also sharpened for service in the coming war. In a pre-war Rosh Hashana sermon, "L'esprit du sacrifice," Grand Rabbi Jacques Henry Dreyfuss argued that the sacrifice of Isaac proves something about Jewish character: it is "doubtless a deed which is most edifying and moving—the most renowned manifestation of the piety that personifies the founder of our race."[209] When Grand Rabbi Dreyfuss then turned to inquire about the essence of this piety, he answered by naming a series of *civic* virtues: service to "others," which only has the "commonweal" in mind. This piety consists in patriotic virtues of "heroism," "devotion," even "devotion pushed to its extreme limits."[210]

As the conflict raged, sacrificial rhetoric kept up. In an editorial in the influential liberal Jewish newspaper *Archives israélites*, "Kippour et l'esprit du sacrifice," its editor Hyppolite Prague declared that as good French citizens, the Jews of France were "electrified" by the "cause."[211] On Yom Kippur 1916, the *Archives* declared proudly that the "spirit of sacrifice is an innate virtue *chez* Israel."[212] Jews would therefore wholeheartedly fight to defend France said another editorial, "Le Soldat Juif," in 1915.[213] In taking an active role in the army, French Jews also drew on the warrior history of ancient Israel. Jews would defend France in the way their ancestors defended Jerusalem.[214] In a later piece, the editor of the *Archives* proudly pointed out how Jewish soldiers displayed the "spirit of the Macchabees" in elite fighting units such as the Zouaves, where they numbered some 60 percent of the total.[215] In 1916, the *Archives israélites* called the victory in the Battle of the Marne as much a providential act as was the deliverance of the Israelites as narrated in the book of Esther.[216] Not even the gloom of a continued and increasingly inconclusive war dampened the rhetoric of sacrificial devotion in the Jewish community. Thus two years into the war, *Archives* reaffirms Jewish sacrificial attitudes:

It is because we love God that we consent to the sacrifices which make up the prescriptions of his cult, (because we love God that we submit ourselves) to his laws. . . . It is because we are French, [because] we love our *patrie,* that we consent to all these painful sacrifices of blood and self-interest, in the long run in order to safeguard the existence of France and to ensure her triumph.[217]

Readiness to Sacrifice the Individual for the Nation

In their readiness to urge civic sacrifice and to employ sacrificial imagery in its service, French Jews took positions about the expendability of the human individual reminiscent of the Catholics. In this, they differed, as we will see, from liberal Protestant spokespersons like Raoul Allier. There is, for example, no Jewish equivalent to Allier's hesitance in using sacrificial language to describe the death of individuals in the war. There is no Jewish equivalent as well to what we will see of Allier's brazen distortion of the text to invent Abraham's "hesitation" to sacrifice Isaac, just to save some small shred of the Reformation's belief in the sacredness of the individual. In 1890, Rabbi Jacques Henry Dreyfuss wrote that as a Jew he sought "devotion pushed to its extreme limits."[218] Dreyfuss makes clear the anti-individualist and even annihilationist meaning of his appeals to sacrifice: "Without going outside ourselves, we are constantly impelled by the spirit of sacrifice, and under pain of moral decline, we fight to immolate ourselves without cease."[219]

At best, some Jewish thinkers tried to assert a Jewish distinctiveness in matters of war and violence. Unlike both their Catholic countrymen and the German adversary, a 1915 editorial in the *Archives israélites* was quick to assert, Jews did not believe that "war was a divine institution, such as de Maistre and Moltke have said."[220] The ineluctable rise of the nationalist and military tide also put cherished aspects of European Jewish culture, such as socialist internationalism and pacifism, into question.[221] An internationalist and religious liberal like Salomon Reinach, for example, was distressed by the rise of chauvinism attendant upon the war. The cosmopolitanism, which he labored to encourage, was sure to suffer in the wake of increased intolerance among the world religions. Resurgent nationalism coincided, observed Reinach, with outbreaks of the occult and "superstitions" such as the belief in guardian angels and diviners. Reinach even links the rise of the prestige of military virtues and authority with the Catholic revival's regressive assertion of religious authority and hierarchy. Militarism and revanchist Catholicism were two sides of the same coin.[222] Yet, however astute Reinach may have been, his was a minority voice within both France and the Jewish community. But then again, Reinach was out of step with the course of history in other matters. Loyal to the fading secular internationalism of assimilated Jewry, he also opposed the nascent Zionist movement. He dismissed Zionism in what for him were among the strongest possible terms as "a new religion founded on the idea of a native land."[223]

But aside from such reservations, Jewish interests in the war were collective, both in behalf of France and the Jewish community taken as a whole. So, when French Jews did respond to the call of nationalism, they did so enthusiastically, bringing to bear the anti-individualist resources of their religious tradition, prominent among them the sacrificial past of ancient Jewish religion. Like intransigent Catholics, patriotic Jews justified—spoke *about*—death and service in war in terms drawn from—speaking *with*—the ritual sacrifice of ancient Israel. And, like the Catholics, Jewish opinion did not make special provisions for the sacredness of the individual.

Anti-Semitism in the "External" Context: "No-Win" Game

The willingness of the Jewish community to offer themselves for the nation took remarkable turns. Renewed pogroms in Russia, for example, created an especially painful situation for French Jews, many of whom had only recently fled Russia to escape the anti-Semitic campaigns of the 1880s. Normally, French Jews would have been vocal about these egregious anti-Semitic acts. But with the Franco-Russian alliance a linchpin of national foreign policy, French Jews felt constrained to keep silent in the face of renewed Russian pogroms.[224] In the Dreyfus Affair, some observers took a cynical view of this willingness to "sacrifice" one of their own for the nation; it was only a tactic to protect the interests of the Jewish community. Charles Péguy, no anti-Semite himself, claims early Jewish reaction to Dreyfus's plight was apathy or worse. For Péguy, this signaled the willingness of French Jews to turn their backs on Dreyfus, to see him "sacrificed" in order to divert public ire away from the interests of the larger community. "They would only ask," observes Péguy bitterly, "to sacrifice Dreyfus in order to ward off the storm."[225]

Similarly, despite what we have seen about Jewish patriotic enthusiasm, French Jews had been accused of wishing to avoid *any* losses of Jewish life during World War One. Jews were all too willing, anti-Semitic slanders went, to "sacrifice" *others*, and to save themselves from the dangers of death in battle. Heeding this charge, the Durkheimian Robert Hertz made a remarkable declaration about his willingness to sacrifice himself in behalf of France in order to prove the devotion of French Jewry. Hertz "had the presentiment," a contemporary report said, that he would not return. But this presentiment changed into a determination to become a sacrifice. Jewish by origin and French by all the thoughts of his mind and strivings of his moral being, he reckoned that the blood of the men of his race and of his own conscience would be usefully shed to liberate their children from all reproaches of egoism, particularist interest, and indifference in the eyes of a suspicious France.[226]

Hertz was not unique in this attitude. Reflecting identical sentiments, the Jewish poet André Spire declared in 1917 that French Jews "went to battle with the pure spirit of sacrifice";[227] they fought for France with such "ardor and daring" in order to defend "the honor of the name 'Jew.'"[228]

Thus by 1900, the upshot of this patriotic propaganda in the midst of German belligerence showed real effects among all religious communities. A veritable and "irresistible process of heroization" in France,[229] which culminated in an "heroic contagion," infected the broad sweep of French opinion. The cinema, sport, pulp literature, and popular culture at large were marked by this mood. And, just three years short of the outbreak of the Great War, despite pacifist critiques, people were saying that sacrifice in war was glorious and that "'heroes are once again in fashion.'"[230]

From Protestant Pacifism to Protestant Nationalism

One possible means of confirming my thesis of the Catholic nature of sacrificial theory at the turn of the century would be to compare it to Protestant views of sacrificial death in war. What we find is that the national crisis of the *fin-de-siècle* did not call forth exactly the same reactions from Protestants as from among Catholics, even if they eventually followed the Catholics down the path of intransigent nationalism.

The Protestants took a somewhat different route than the Catholics in coming to terms with the looming war. If suspicions of treason and sympathy for the Germans dogged Catholic attempts to rehabilitate themselves with the voices of public opinion, the Protestants were hardly less disadvantaged. Even among the laïcs, age-old "Catholic" prejudices persisted against Protestants: "Catholic" France was now pitted against "Lutheran" Germany, thus making accusations common that Protestants were "foreigners" or "virtual foreigners."[231] These charges persisted despite the fact that Protestants were disproportionately overrepresented in the officer corps of the military. One of the greatest army chiefs, General Nivelle was Protestant, as was Admiral Gauchet. In fact, the French fleet in place in 1914 owed its existence largely to the work of the Protestant Admiral Jauréguiberry.[232] Making matters worse for the Protestants was the way public opinion was to some degree manipulated by certain Catholic "publicists" who accused Protestantism unjustly of having been responsible for German nationalism.[233] In the *fin-de-siècle*, these Protestant "foreigners" were well represented in the anticlerical government of the Third Republic, so hated by the Catholic intransigents—even though the number of prominent Protestants in government was far less than in the 1870s and 1880s.[234] Providing further fuel for the suspicions of the intransigent Catholic nationalists, before 1914 official Protestant policy toward the war was diffident at best. This was mostly because a "small but active . . . leftish and relatively pacifist" minority prevented the Protestant war party from prevailing for some time within the official Protestant organizations, thus raising suspicions among nationalists of treasonous Protestant intentions.[235] This minority felt that any war at all—especially the offensive and aggressive war for which the nationalists lusted—would be the disaster it soon proved to be. In the end, the "pacifist" party lost, and had to accept—however reluctantly—the policy of a defensive war like that advocated by Jean Jaurès.[236]

But finally, along with the mass of the nation, French Protestant opinion changed radically with the German invasion of Belgium and its subsequent atrocities. As if trying to prove their patriotism to French public opinion, even the "pacifists" joined in common condemnation of German responsibility for the war[237]—although true to their antibellicose inclinations, even after the invasion of Belgium, Protestant leaders sought to head off an even greater conflict by pleading with both sides for a "humane war."[238] Frustrated by their failure to win German Protestant support to mitigate the violence of the war, the French Protestants finally insisted that their German coreligionists "recognize the 'crimes' of their government, and in particular those concerning Belgium."[239] Furthermore, after the invasion of Belgium, French Protestants fought back against any and all attacks on their patriotism, indeed against their new-found nationalism. The Protestant press rebutted attacks—chiefly coming from the Catholic press—on a regular basis, even turning Pope Benedict's reputation for favoring Germany against their attackers.[240] Such well-intentioned, but perhaps naïve, attempts to broker peace by Swedish Lutheran bishop Nathan Soderblom were dismissed by the French Protestant leadership as "'German propaganda.'"[241] In the end, in fact, Protestant opinion had "hardened" against the idea of peaceful compromise or resolution to the war. Their position became, for the most part, indistinguishable from that of other nationalist parties. In the surprising words of a nineteen-year-old Protestant theological student, now at the front (admittedly from the conservative theological stronghold on Montaubon) comes a remarkable declaration: "My thoughts turn to the France of tomorrow—to the divine France which is bound to be. I could not fight on if I did not hope for the birth of that France, so richly deserving that men should kill one another and die for her sake."[242] A notable exception, however, to this rising tide of patriotism among Protestants are the wartime meditations of Liberal Protestant theologian, Raoul Allier.

Raoul Allier: Abraham "Hesitates" for Individuals

In every great mass movement such as a war, we always find those with second thoughts, those who pause to contest, however subtly, the prevailing view. In the midst of the intransigent Catholic domination of the sacrificial ideology of warfare, the figure of Raoul Allier stands out, opposing, however prudently, the dominant Catholic view of sacrifice in warfare. This Protestant thinker considered matters closer to hand than the "high-diction" of war rhetoric would permit. What happens when we get down to the level of public sermons for a mass audience as preachers attempt to explain the meaning of the death of soldiers? Here, we can see how differences in Protestant and Catholic religious histories over the meaning of sacrifice begin to tell. Allier's sermons show, I believe, that the absence of the sacrificial Eucharistic ideology of expiation from at least liberal Protestant religiosity shapes a different understanding of the meaning of civic duty to serve, perhaps unto death, in war. Less in thrall to the divine right of kings, less enamored of royal absolutism by their tragic history in France, more informed by Protestant religious individualism, French Protestants saw Frenchness in the Enlightenment's celebration of the individual as sacred being. Here in the case of French liberal Protestants, then, is another example of how thinkers talked *about* the (civic) sacrifice of wartime duty while talking *with* the language of (ritual) sacrifice. In this case, however, liberal Protestants rejected expiation in their Eucharistic theology. In order to focus, let us consider, for example, what prominent Protestants thought about the extent of an individual's duty to the nation. For us, how is civic duty to be conceived, *once* it had already been conceptualized according to the rhetoric of sacrifice—as indeed it was during our period? Let us turn to the words of Raoul Allier.[243]

Raoul Allier was a philosopher in the tradition of Renouvier, a liberal theologian, historian of religion, and author of numerous books on La Compagnie du Saint Sacrement, a Catholic institution active in the French Counter-Reformation.[244] Despite his notorious biases, indeed because of them, Allier's reading of this part of the history of the Counter-Reformation gives us access to the mind of a politically and religiously committed republican and liberal Protestant. Allier, the liberal doyen of the Paris

Protestant faculty of theology was clearly hostile to the efforts of the Catholics to block the efforts of religious reform in France. Still in all, his Protestant colleagues, such as Jean Réville, felt he had been "rigorous and impartial."[245]

Throughout the dark year of 1915, Allier preached a series of eighty-one midweek sermons at various Protestant temples in Paris.[246] In what we must presume to be the full light of their historical religious significance, Allier returned again and again to the theme of political sacrifice in the course of war's seemingly unending slaughter. More than this, Allier's task bore an almost unbearable emotional weight for him. His son, Roger, had been killed in the very first weeks of the war. At first, it had been difficult to find the body of Allier's son and then almost impossible to identify it. Finally, the body was discovered in a common grave. But Roger Allier's face had, for some reason, suffered deliberate mutilation in order to thwart attempts at identification.[247] After a long period of mourning, the grieving father regained his energy, a result, Allier claimed, of "communion" with his dead son. Thus he was set upon a course of wartime preaching for which he became widely known.

In the course of these *conférences*, Allier sought to console the suffering, to encourage them to find in their own grief an "occasion for renewal, for religious experience."[248] He also pushed to the brink of theological crisis, and perhaps beyond. Doubtless a result of his own great loss, Allier broached issues perilous for a man of even his liberal theological cast. Against the grain of his own pacifism, he asked openly whether we can really pray for our enemies under the present circumstances? In the face of his own theological nurture, he challenged the Calvinist belief forbidding prayer for the dead. God is a god of life. If we pray for the safety of someone bound for a long journey, asks Allier, why not for those who have passed beyond life to death? Allier even paused over the subject of spiritism and the idea of how long a soul remains in a body once dead.[249] But most of all Allier meditated on what the faithful should believe, think, and do during those trying times. We will now see how his Protestant theological formation directed his politics of civic sacrifice.

In two sermons, *Le Sacrifice vivant* and *Sacrifice et récompense* (both of 1915), we see that the good patriot Allier accepts that national duty demands that citizens contribute themselves to the nation.[250] "'There is no surer foundation for civic heroism than Christian courage,'" Allier relates.[251] But how far does courage go? In what sense should losses of life in the pursuit of this ideal of courage be read? Not, apparently, as Catholic reactionaries did. In full awareness of the historical significance of Catholic political theologies of sacrifice, Allier tellingly denied "war as a divine institution, such as de Maistre and Moltke have said." Attacking the same Maistrean theological politics, Allier inverted justifications for war based upon expiation for collective sin, or of victimizing the innocent: it is rather "'the most valuable who die for the least.'" War is thus neither "divine law nor a providential expedient" but "election in reverse." Thus, while Allier makes room for thinking about the death of soldiers as an instance of civic sacrifice, he does so within a still discernibly Protestant worldview.

These themes flow together in Allier's meditation on the sacrifice of Isaac. One night, Allier tells us he was visited with a blessed hour's "luminous experience." There, he tells us, "I saw . . . what sacrifice ought and ought not to be." Allier's vision drew him away first to the ruins of ancient Carthage. There he saw the burnt offerings of infants to Baal-Moloch, "in despair" parents wept "as their children were sacrificed." At that moment, he "saw what humanity too often sees in sacrifice and why it revolts us." It means killing something, and then giving it to God—to "return it to *le néant.*" In this sense, "sacrifice is to make death, to surround the self with death, to make death itself. Our conscience protests!"[252]

Pursued by this gruesome "nightmare," Allier's vision-gaze then shifted magically to the patriarch Abraham trudging off dutifully to sacrifice Isaac on Mount Morija. "This was a pious and fervent man, who had understood God to have ordered him to offer his only son." And so it seems at first as if Abraham would repeat the ritual horrors of the devotees of Baal-Moloch. At this point, however, Allier asks more than simply why God so tested Abraham. Embellishing the narrative beyond the text's face value for his own hermeneutic purposes,[253] Allier asks why Abraham "hesitates" [*sic*].[254] Allier believes that in the moment of hesitation, which he reads into the biblical narrative, we can perhaps find a paradigm for a proper Christian attitude to sacrifice. What matters here, Allier assures us, is not the face-value divine command to Abraham. What matters is Abraham's inner *"résistance,"* his slight reluctance at God's grim demand—not his outward actions, which for all the world seemed bent on ritually slaughtering his own son. In short, God is merely testing Abraham, merely waiting for Abraham to "hesitate." What moral then is there to this well-known story? God wanted Abraham's inner *spiritual* submission to divinity, to offer Isaac as a living person, not his outward, *bodily* conformity in ritually killing Isaac. God wanted Abraham to "sacrifice" Isaac in the spiritual sense of *"sacrum facere"*—making him holy, making him "dead to sin," dead in spirit to iniquity, not literally dead in body.[255]

As if answering Roman Catholic wartime pastoral letters, Allier then explicitly links the story of Abraham and Isaac to the moral anguish of the French trying to comprehend the meaning of great loss of life during the War, remembering here the loss of Allier's own son. In the process, Allier implicitly rejects the intransigent Roman Catholic fixation upon bloody expiatory sacrifice for the nation. Like Abraham, "We are not (in reality) asked to sacrifice our sons and husbands. The truth is that our loved ones sacrifice themselves." This was how Allier dealt with the highly charged issue of the sacrifice of innocent "victims," posed in a "poignant fashion"[256] by the War. He drew back from the severe views we have seen dominating Catholic thought since the Joseph de Maistre.

Rather, he said, we should focus attention on the internal personal sacrifices all civilians need to make to the war effort. We need to shore up the bravery, steadfastness, and courage of our soldiers by putting their needs before our own: we need to sacrifice our own comfort and concerns for them! Drawing back from the horror of death mounting daily before the French public, Allier adds (with doubtless small comfort for the troops in battle), "As for us, fathers, mothers, spouses—it is ourselves and not them that we sacrifice." Allier concludes by trying in effect to do his best (lamely?) to deny the bloody logic of the author of the *Eclaircissement sur les sacrifices*. He rejects the severe vision of saving immolation effected by the sacrificial death of the innocent: "Our God is not a God of death. He doesn't want death. He is the living one; He is life; He wants life. He asks His worshipers to be likewise the living and to be of the living who make life. The Living One wants to create life."[257]

Whether persuasively or not, Allier argues that we are not required to be obedient to the authority of a divine command to sacrifice "Isaac." Allier's god respects the *individual* human conscience—both Abraham's, in not requiring such obedience of him, and Isaac's, in not demanding consummation. Then, Allier went further and read the story to undercut annihilationist readings: Abraham, of course, neither kills Isaac, nor does he really intend so to do (contrary to the literal sense of the story). The sacredness of the human individual beloved of French Protestants is maintained. Allier thus produced a view of the death of innocent soldiers during battle that contrasts to what we have seen in the rhetoric of expiation for national sins promoted by the reactionary Catholics. Rather than seeing the death of innocent young Frenchmen in war as victims in a sacrifice, expiating for sinful excesses of willful French individualism, Allier tried to save the individual and internalize sacrifice.

In this chapter, I have tried then to show how potent the classic Catholic ideology of sacrifice was in shaping cultural and social attitudes about sacrifice in the realm of nationalist discourse among a broad range of the French population, at least as late as World War One. I conclude by showing how these attitudes are contested notably by a figure working within the theological tradition of the Reformation. Allier's sermons on the war show us the beginnings of a process of how religiously informed sacrificial public policies are contested—from an equally religious perspective. I have in fact argued that Allier's subtle attack on theologies of extreme sacrifice in warfare derives from his own religious history of loyalty to an anti-sacrificial doctrine of the Eucharist made by the Reformation fathers. In the next chapter, I want to see how the same classic Catholic religious ideology of sacrifice made itself present in the case of Dreyfus and the "affair" that attended it, and then explore how this too was contested by one of Allier's coreligionists and close associates.

4

THE DREYFUS "MYSTIQUE" AND THE CONSERVATION OF THE SACRED

> La politique se moque de la mystique, mais c'est encore la
> mystique qui nourrit la politique même.
> —Charles Péguy[1]

From "Case" to "Affair" to "Mystique"

Although much is mundane and "merely" political about the Dreyfus
case, there is just as much that is not. An historian of our own day, Miche
line Tison-Braun, finds aspects of the case particularly "astonishing" and
"out of the ordinary" (*insolite*).[2] After the case had matured a while, Dreyfus became a living "symbol"—a development that in the process saw the
anti-Dreyfusard "nationalist movement . . . definitively transformed into
a militant religion."[3] Perhaps borrowing broadly from a usage made notable by Charles Péguy, Tison-Braun seems to pick up Péguy's idea of a
"mystique," which the great Catholic author felt surrounded Dreyfus in
his own day. Péguy observed, and I concur, that "the Dreyfus Affair was a
beautiful example of religion, of a religious movement, of the beginning
of or origin of a religion—a rare case, perhaps a unique case thereof."[4]
According to the "religion" of the nation, which came into being from at
least the French Revolution, Dreyfusards tended accordingly to see in
Dreyfus an embodiment of the Revolution's transcendent political ideals
of justice and the sacredness of the individual. In the mystical imagination
of the revolutionary tradition, the Dreyfusards saw arrayed against them

Dreyfusardism a conspiracism !?

and "the condemned" a cabal of scheming Jesuits linked with a pious Catholic military, ever-ready to overthrow the republic.[5] So profound indeed were these commitments for Dreyfusards like himself that Charles Péguy said that the "question was never whether Dreyfus was innocent or not—but whether or not we had the courage to assert it."[6] From the anti-Dreyfusard side, a similar process of demonic mythological and religious conceptualization of the accused took shape.[7] Dreyfus was the Jesuit and Catholic inverted, a Judas and the archetypal Jew, menacing the good Christian people of France.[8]

What is interesting as far as the subject of sacrifice is concerned is that from both sides of the debate over Dreyfus, he is assimilated into various discourses of sacrifice. Dreyfus is either an innocent victim, sacrificed to the powers of evil, or Judas, the traitorous agent of sacrifice, equally ready to betray France as to betray Jesus to the enemy. The bulk of this chapter will attempt to bring out the ways Dreyfus is linked to these symbol-laden sacrificial discourses. To begin this exploration into the religious and symbolic aspects of Dreyfus within such a symbolic sacrificial discourse, we need first to distinguish such a level of meaning from others attending the Dreyfus matter. Here, I separate out at least three aspects of the matter of the trial, conviction, and pardon of Dreyfus. I refer to these aspects as the "case," "affair," and "mystique" of Dreyfus.[9] In the same vein, Richard Griffiths argues that when the Dreyfus matter

> seems specifically concerned with justice and truth, . . . the issues appear simple. . . . [Yet] around the simple case of a miscarriage of justice there developed a battleground of conflicting political forces. In the process, the actual case became lost to view. Dreyfus himself often became forgotten; or else he became merely a "symbol," to the extent that many of his supporters were less concerned about his individual fate than about the fate of their cause.[10]

What then are these levels which one would like to distinguish in the matter of Dreyfus?

First, the judicial "case" involved the conviction by court-martial of a Jewish army captain, Alfred Dreyfus, in 1894. He had been charged with exposing details of France's military secrets to Germany. The army's charges appeared to have substance. Dreyfus was indeed well positioned in the upper echelons of the French security apparatus, with ample access to the military secrets that had been disclosed to the age-old enemy. The chief piece of evidence of the crime was the notorious *bordereau*, a handwritten letter detailing incriminating evidence of espionage and matching well enough, it was thought, the hand of Dreyfus. The "case"—or at least the first stage of the judicial section of Dreyfus's involvement with the military tribunal—concluded with Dreyfus's imprisonment on Devil's Island.

Second, we may speak of the Dreyfus "affair" as the controversy that arose from either contesting or supporting the "case." The first reactions against this conviction came from the Jewish journalist Bernard Lazare and dwelt on the so-called *erreur judiciaire* committed in the trial.[11] Composed as early as the summer of 1895, Bernard Lazare, published the first meticulous book-length study detailing judicial irregularities and failings, *Une erreur judiciaire: la verité sur l'Affaire Dreyfus,* appeared in November 1896. A measure of its fine-grained analysis of the case are pages of remarkable character-by-character examinations of discrepancies in the handwriting used in evidence to convict Dreyfus. At this point, Bernard Lazare's efforts ended in a denunciation of the condemnation on grounds of a scrupulous examination of the facts of the case. Yet this book had been preceded by several articles, published as early as November 1894,[12] denouncing the anti-Semitism stirred up around the condemned. So important were Bernard Lazare's writings that even the anti-Dreyfusard Charles Maurras admitted that without the "'publication of the first pamphlet of Bernard Lazare, bit by bit, the Affair would have simply been forgotten.'"[13] Of course, the intervention of Émile Zola's "J'Accuse" would make sure Bernard Lazare's impact was lasting.

In 1898, after months of Zola's intense strategic planning and the publication of a series of articles denouncing anti-Semitism among the French,[14] his "J'Accuse" struck like the proverbial thunderbolt.[15] "J'Acccuse" was written expressly as an open letter to the president of the Third Republic and published in the newspaper *L'Aurore,* where it would have maximum public impact. It charged that Dreyfus had been wrongly convicted, that various members of the army high command bore responsibility for the deed and worst of all, that the army sought to conceal the fact of Dreyfus's innocence. Years later in reflecting on his great achievement, Zola affected a perhaps ironic modesty and said of his provocation, "'My method was only to expose the Affair in full light.'"[16] The results of Zola's piece are well known. Together with Bernard Lazare's campaign to exonerate Dreyfus, Zola's classic letter split the nation into camps on either side of the issue of reopening the "case." Thus the "Affair" was born, with the "Dreyfusards" calling for "revision" of Dreyfus's conviction. On the opposite side of the "affair" were those upholding the original guilty verdict of the "case" against Dreyfus and trying in one way or another to discredit the arguments Zola first had made and which his successors would make thereafter.

A third venue for launching the "Affaire" was the avant-garde literary magazine, *La Revue Blanche.* The *Revue blanche* complained of a certain "'military bureaucracy,'" which prevented critical consideration of the possibility of Dreyfus's innocence, and also struck deeper chords by attacking the place of *raison d'état* and military authority in the proceedings against Dreyfus.[17] Among its notable contributors were the passionate Dreyfusards, Charles Péguy and Léon Blum.

But, third, there is, indeed was, much more in this skepticism about the "case" than quarrels with the efficient operation of the machinery of justice. Suspicions soon led to the view that nefarious activities were in play behind the scenes. Therefore, thinking about the fate of Dreyfus, according to some, broke utterly with the commonsense talk of "case" or "affair" and took off onto a discontinuous level of discourse entirely.[18] This is to some extent what Charles Maurras meant when he noted slyly that, at a certain point the "Dreyfus Affair became "The Affair" simply and nothing else." [19] To wit, hidden, underlying, and often conflicting mythologies seemed to take over the explanation of things to hand. To wit, among other motifs, talk of Dreyfus in terms of the logic of sacrifice appeared. Something big and cosmological lay behind the condemnation of Dreyfus. With the eruption of the Dreyfus Affair upon the national consciousness, the confidence of a generation—practiced in the "disenchanting skepticism" and relativizing distance of an Ernest Renan, for example— was badly shaken.[20] This transformation of the Dreyfus affair into a matter governed in part by a discourse and mythology of sacrifice is what I shall call its "mystique." Inquiring of the "mystique" of Dreyfus leads us then beyond both law and politics into the realm of religion.[21] There, Dreyfus comes to be seen by his supporters as the innocent Christ, abused and victimized in the name of faceless political power (figs. 2, 3, 5). Dreyfus was like the pure and gentle "lamb," unjustly and unwillingly led to sacrificial slaughter in the name of the angry god, *raison d'état* (fig. 13).[22] Even Maurice Barrès cast Dreyfus at first as what a recent critic has called an example of the "fine noble figure of the victim."[23] Opposed to the apotheosis of Dreyfus, Dreyfus's detractors cast him in the role of "Judas"—not simply a traitor,[24] but also the man who delivers Jesus to sacrifice. There is more then to the Dreyfus matter than mere political renderings would indicate. There is Dreyfus as part of the world of religious or symbolic discourse.

Dreyfus and His Six Mystiques

The "mystique" or religious dimension of Dreyfus, especially as it involved the logic of sacrificial discourse, can be seen in the development of the ways in which Dreyfus was represented. Partly because the Affair coincided with the rise of the popular illustrated newspapers and magazines, much of this representation will be graphic (fig. 1).[25] Yet the mystiques of Dreyfus are found in all modes of representation of the "case" and "affair." Thus, for a good portion of his defenders, Dreyfus was (typically unwitting) simply an innocent or "the condemned," as he is called. References to classic features of religious imagery such as sacrifice do not necessarily stand out. Yet others tended in the direction of applying religious metaphors to the condemned. Dreyfus took on something of a special sacrificial quality, and we can then begin to speak of the first mystique. He was a "victim." This role of Dreyfus at the center of a victimization narrative— an involuntary sacrifice for unknown or unstipulated purposes—put him into a powerful interpretative framework. Dreyfus might be the "victim," for example of anti-Semitic prejudice, and thus someone whose fate required one to posit models of explanation that went beyond the liberal assimilationist common sense of the day. This is the Dreyfus we can call simply Victim-Dreyfus. Later notions, involving elements of sacrificial exchange, such as Dreyfus's assimilation to Judas-like betrayal of the nation, which is seen as Christ, for monetary gain or as a heroic, even Christ-like figure, are not yet present. As the rightist Catholic paper, *Le Pèlerin* reported only weeks after Dreyfus's trial before the Council of War:

> The traitor is condemned for having dishonored the uniform of a French officer, for having sold the very France he was charged with defending. Like Judas, who betrayed his Master with a kiss, the Jewish officer betrayed France while pretending to server her in a position of honor.[26]

More in the same vein is yet to come.

But this early and minimal conception of Victim-Dreyfus would not last. Building on his meticulous examination of the evidence supporting the "case," the great Jewish journalist, Bernard Lazare, for example, was one of the first to cast Dreyfus as someone caught up in a larger cosmological religious drama as a "victim" in an anti-Semitic campaign. He was the first to take Dreyfus's part prominently and to declare that the "case" and "affair" were, as we will see, more mysterious than either mere judicial error or political brouhaha.[27] Evoking powerful religious imagery, Bernard Lazare says that in Dreyfus we have a "martyrdom" at the hands of hateful anti-Semites.[28] Indeed, as Bernard Lazare analyzed the attacks of the anti-Dreyfusards, it became clear that they had gone beyond common sense and cast him in the role of Judas, the traitor who delivered Jesus into the hands of those who would sacrifice him.[29] Beneath the conviction of Dreyfus was something more than judicial error, oversight, or even garden variety injustice. We have an anti-Semitism redolent with the centuries-old stench of Christian prejudice against the Jewish people everywhere. From Bernard Lazare, we thus get the universalized concept of "the Jew" in general being persecuted. Dreyfus is not merely one Jewish man being tried and convicted. Dreyfus represents all persecuted Jews throughout history.[30] This Dreyfus can then be called the Jew-Dreyfus (fig. 9). Under this conception, although it can be said that Dreyfus was a victim of anti-Semitism, it is unclear that, say, for Bernard Lazare Dreyfus's condemnation represents anything we might call "sacrifice." For example, there does not seem to be any sort of assuaging of divine anger or any *reciprocity* from God in exchange for Dreyfus's being victimized. In the anti-Semitic depictions of graphic and literary media, the Jew-Dreyfus is not yet seen as being offered for any good purpose. That will come. For now, there is just crime as seen by the anti-Dreyfusards and loss from the viewpoint of his supporters.

Fuller development of the sacrificial features of Dreyfus came in the form of his representation by the anti-Dreyfusards in several, sometimes conflicted, forms. Second was Dreyfus as "Judas Iscariot"—what I call Judas-Dreyfus, agent of sacrifice.[31] This Dreyfus fits sacrificial conceptions because Judas delivered Jesus to sacrificial death on Calvary and is even seen as an inverted Jesus—himself of course a classic sacrificial victim. Here, we find Dreyfus depicted as someone deserving his "degradation"—both literal and figurative—worthy to be cast out, as refuse, a "dirty" thing (figs. 4, 5, 6, 10, 11, 12).

Third and fourth are two versions of Dreyfus as Jesus. In one, Dreyfus is depicted by his supporters as suffering unjustly like Jesus (figs. 2, 3). This Dreyfus I call True Jesus-Dreyfus. Zola, for one, made a practice of referring to Dreyfus in Christ-like terms. In his letter to Madame Dreyfus printed in *L'Aurore* in 1899, the anticlerical Zola refers to the condemned as a "'the martyr,' 'the crucified,' 'the resurrected, emerging alive and free from the grave' . . . 'the man chosen by suffering by which universal communion comes into being.'"[32] Richard Griffiths also observes how Zola even casts Dreyfus as an expiating suffering servant. Griffith reports how Zola speaks of Dreyfus in classic, albeit spectacular, Catholic sacrificial terms. Although Griffith notes that Zola's produces "some of the most ineffective and inappropriate examples of religious imagery to appear in the course of the Affair," it is nonetheless there—and one might add that this discourse is nonetheless shot through with the classic Catholic rhetoric of expiatory sacrifice.[33] The condemned, says Griffith, is for Zola "the man of sorrows who had suffered on behalf of the world." As Zola himself put it:

> Whether he be honored, whether he be venerated, this man, chosen by his suffering, brings about universal communion by it. . . . It

is tomorrow's verdict which looms [over us]. That verdict will be a triumphal acquittal, a radiant reparation, [with] all generations on their knees and begging for the pardon of the crimes of their fathers in memory of the glorious condemned.[34]

Even the unchurched Clémenceau referred to Dreyfus as submitting to a "living crucifixion," as a "Jew . . . nailed to the cross as did the Romans 2000 years ago."[35]

Fifth, another representation of Dreyfus created by his enemies casts him sarcastically as Jesus (fig. 5). I call this the False Jesus-Dreyfus, since this image is propagated by those profoundly cynical about the matter of his innocence. Here, the enemies of the condemned vent their bitter hatred of Dreyfus and the Dreyfusards by insincerely casting Dreyfus as if he were innocent and indeed holy—just as the Dreyfusards believed him to be.

Sixth, Dreyfus is seen as a special sort of victim, closer to classic sacrificial motifs made popular by scholars like René Girard, a victim whose death or punishment wins certain returns for a given community (figs. 2, 13).[36] This is what I call Scapegoat-Dreyfus—partly at least in line with Girard's usage. In regard to this motif, Girard would have us believe that societies often protect themselves by substituting a victim in their place. This contrasts with the classic position of Hubert and Mauss, who approach sacrifice from the viewpoint of the person who *escapes* victimization and destruction. Speaking of sacrifice "from the ground up," so to say, Girard fixes on the hapless victim, substituted for the benefit of the sacrificer.

Now, in the case of Dreyfus in the late nineteenth century, the identity of the community (or communities) protected is ambiguous. It could at least be either French Jewry or the nation at large, in particular the army. For French Jews, Scapegoat-Dreyfus is a special sort of victim because the life of Dreyfus is surrendered in order to be given in exchange for the lives of French Jewry at large. Scapegoat-Dreyfus protects the Jewish community by deflecting the ire, otherwise concentrated directly at the Jews of France. Instead, Dreyfus absorbs the hatred of the mob, and carries it off with his perceived pollution to Devil's Island. In this role, Scapegoat-Dreyfus approaches Judas-Dreyfus in his being assimilated to something, at least on the surface, repellant and even dirty or polluting, even though for French Jews Scapegoat-Dreyfus was not necessarily presumed innocent. At the very least, except for Mathieu Dreyfus and Bernard-Lazare, the possible guilt or innocence of Scapegoat-Dreyfus was not very deeply investigated by French Jews. The point was first and foremost to put Dreyfus between a potentially vengeful France and the Jewish community.

Not very different in its uses of Dreyfus as scapegoat was the Scapegoat-Dreyfus of the radical right-wing Catholics of which we will see more shortly. Even while some Catholics may have suspected or even been convinced that Dreyfus was an innocent victim of judicial error, the overwhelming number did not. And even some of those who felt that he might be innocent affirmed nonetheless that he should be sacrificed for *raison d'état*—to protect the prestige of the nation and its army high command, with its predominantly Catholic officer corps.

Thus, what then began as a judicial "case" became an "affair" and then a "mystique"—a phenomenon with puzzling elements. All these cases of mystique link to the sacrificial discourse that we have seen thrive and renew itself with such vitality in France.[37] What began as a military court martial became first a political *cause célèbre* and then was seen as a public ritual, a religious action, indeed a sacrifice. It leads to a Dreyfus no longer a mere citizen, but Dreyfus either as much more or far less than a man—as a hero, a living symbol of justice and the sacredness of the individual for the Dreyfusard community (fig. 7). It is time to explore these cases in detail.

Judas-Dreyfus: Agent of Sacrifice[38]

Perhaps the most popular way in which Dreyfus was absorbed into a sacrificial mystique was through his identification with the apostle who betrayed Jesus—Judas Iscariot.[39] The first identification of Dreyfus with Judas to be published seems to have been by Catholic nationalist author Maurice Barrès the very day after Dreyfus's degradation. Entitled "The Parade of Judas,"[40] the piece was puzzling because it "mixed hatred and compassion."[41] Although Dreyfus is identified as a possible Judas, nonetheless he is also the object of sympathy. We do not know the exact circumstances and motivation for this remarkable piece—the peculiarities of which we will need to tease out as we untangle the complex rhetorics of the remarkable public talk about Dreyfus. Suffice it to say for the moment that in it one encounters a strange complex of contradictory views and feelings about Dreyfus—even an inexplicable sympathy for him from so unlikely a figure as the right-wing Maurice Barrès. But just why this should be so remains a mystery. In the present state of our knowledge of both the "Affair" and the human psyche, we are reduced to speculations about the perversities of latent anti-Semitism or the enthusiasms of a rabid nationalism.

More typical, of course, of Judas-Dreyfus is his role as object of hatred, generally informed by anti-Semitism. It would be well then to recall that the link between Judas and Jewry had already become stock-in-trade anti-Semitic libel long before the Dreyfus affair. Thus, a widely published

Catholic author, Father Vincent de Paul Bailly, wrote in the anti-Semitic *La Croix* of 18 April 1889:

> The savior was duty-bound to suffer all sorts of trials, and he suc-
> ceeded in getting through them. For example, he was sold like a
> slave in order to ransom us. But ever since this day, Judas, who re-
> ceived his blood money, has wandered the earth like Cain, marked
> by the sign of his curse. This sign is a sack of *ecus*. He carries it on his
> back, and it weighs down on him like a mountain. He will never get
> out from under it until his death. . . . The race of Judas inherits his
> chain of gold, his millstone of gold. The Jew, that eternal pilgrim,
> drags it around until he reaches hell. Judas! Worship your millstone:
> care for it, make it even bigger. But, die rich and scorned![42]

It only took the appearance of a Jewish officer accused of treason to
unleash the myth-making mind to produce to potent image of Judas-
Dreyfus. This image focuses on the analogy of Judas as traitor to Jesus being reprised in Dreyfus the betrayer of France. As Judas proper threatened the very existence of the nascent Christian community from within
its own ranks by removing Jesus from their midst to be made ready for execution, so too did Judas-Dreyfus put French security in danger from destruction from within by offering the security of the state to its enemy
(figs. 4, 5, 6, 10, 11, 12). As Judas delivered Jesus up to sacrifice with all
the cosmic consequences this entailed, so too, as several illustrations de-
pict, did Dreyfus deliver up France to her eternal enemy with the same
traitorous kiss. (figs. 4, 12). Other stock-in-trade anti-Semitic libels of Jewish avarice stand out as well. Both Jews—Judas and Dreyfus—performed
their treacherous acts for money. To the mythological mind of the time,
the wealthy, traitorous Dreyfus then was an inverted Christ, no doubt de-
lighting all those who saw something providential in his being exiled to
Devil's Island—literally to the domain ruled by Satan himself! (fig. 15).
Judas-Dreyfus was the image of impurity, who must be cast out of the body
politic, as indeed Dreyfus proper was cast out to Devil's Island, lest he in-
fect his countrymen, just as Judas proper leaves the company of Jesus and
his companions and dies alone and abandoned even by those to whom he
delivered Jesus for sacrifice (fig. 6, 10). For his crime, Judas-Dreyfus was
fit, literally and officially, to be degraded before his peers, and to have that
equally literal image of the triumph of his enemies published across the
land in countless "illustrated" magazines of the period.[43] In the same way,
Judas proper ends his days in equally ignominious style, either as a suicide
or as victim of a horrid accidental death (fig. 11).[44]

A further transformation of the Judas-Dreyfus myth finds him in a political cartoon of 1894, appearing in Edouard Drumont's anti-Semitic *La*

Libre Parole. It shows Dreyfus, doubtless representing Jewry in general in the minds of anti-Semites like Drumont, trying futilely to wash away his supposed transgression with money. Echoing Judas, who sold Jesus into sacrifice for money, but then comes to regret his decision, the cartoon's caption scolds Dreyfus in words that portend the violent death of the traitorous apostle, even as he may regret his act. Thus, as Dreyfus tries to scrub away his sin with the symbolic thirty pieces of silver resting before him, Drumont's caption admonishes him (and French Jewry): "Jews, for us in France, blood alone can get out a stain like that!!!" For Drumont, only the sacrificial death of the guilty Dreyfus can expiate the sin of his treason and the imagined "crimes" of the Jews of France against the nation (fig. 9).

While all these rather straightforward analogies between Dreyfus and Judas reigned in the mythological imaginations of Dreyfus's accusers, it would be a mistake to overlook how the symbol of Judas functioned in some profound sense to strengthen not only the forces of the coming leftist Dreyfus revolution, but also the rise of radical groups like Action Française. As such, Judas functions to make the sacrifice of Jesus possible. In the Gospel of John, Jesus announces to his disciples at the Last Supper, "I know those I have chosen. But the scripture must come true that says, 'The man who shared my food turned against me.' I tell you this now before it happens, so that when it does happen you will believe that 'I Am Who I Am.'" (John 13:18–19). After the disciples protested that none of them would betray Jesus, he answered that he would dip his bread into to the sauce served at the meal and give it to his betrayer. As the story goes, Jesus gave the bread to Judas, and tellingly says to him: "'Hurry and do what you must!' . . . Judas accepted the bread, and went out at once, it was night" (John 13:27–30). Without his betrayal by Judas, ironically, Jesus could not have fulfilled the prophecies of the scripture that he mentions and could not have realized his sacrificial destiny.[45] Judas's betrayal is not all that unusual, since it plays the same role as the original "sin of Adam," otherwise known as the *"felix culpa"*—the sin without which Christ would not even have been necessary. Thus, despite Judas's willful perfidy, there is something again of the notion of cosmic inevitability about sacrificial thinking that haunts the figure of Judas and unsettles attempts to grasp Judas in his role.

Is something of same true of Dreyfus? Did anyone see it this way? The case is hardly clear. To wit, would the Action Française, and the new darker regime of politics to which it led, have come into being without the belief among his accusers that Dreyfus betrayed his country? We know, for example, that Maurras certainly exploited the Affair for the purpose of creating his new politics.[46] While the Dreyfusards sought more often to decry the injustice done to Dreyfus than to prove the innocence of the Affair, the forces of the right wholeheartedly concentrated on casting him in mystical sacrificial roles such as Judas. Such identification roused the emotions and inspired a contempt which the anti-Dreyfusards used for their wider anti-Semitic ambitions.[47] Is this behind the representations of Jesus crucified, which are identified with Judas at the same time—albeit in a deeply cynical way (fig. 5)! Thus, in the French army captain's identification with the one who delivers Jesus for fulfillment of his divine expiatory destiny, Dreyfus is recognized to be more than a felon: he is a major player in great cosmological dramas, of perhaps confused narrative lines. Ironically, although one cannot necessarily credit the right-wing accusers of Dreyfus with such foresight, without Dreyfus their movement might never have come into being.

True Jesus-Dreyfus, False Jesus-Dreyfus

Yet, as his enemies typically viewed him, Dreyfus was the very inverse of Jesus. As he was guilty, unfaithful and treacherous, the savior was innocent, pure and faithful; while Judas delivered Jesus for sacrifice, Jesus was the sacrifice himself. But while the imagery of Judas as traitor is clear, the "mystique" of the Judas-Dreyfus thrived amid sometimes mind-boggling "confusion" typical of the symbolic imagination in France. We will recall that on 6 January 1895, the day after Dreyfus's degradation on the parade grounds of the École Militaire before a baying mob calling for his death, Maurice Barrès published his account of the ceremony called "The Parade of Judas."[48] In this extraordinarily ambiguous piece, Barrès tried to prevent a rush to judgment about Dreyfus's guilt. While Dreyfus is identified as a possible Judas, he is also seen as stoically suffering through the abuse hurled at him. Indeed, surprisingly, Barrès sees Dreyfus at first as a potential "heroic victim . . . symbol of dignity and courage in the face of collective hysteria." Dreyfus is in fact seen as a potential sacrificial *"bouc émissaire"*—the scapegoat of Jewish lore about which we will see more shortly. Was there not a chance that all this humiliation of Dreyfus was an elaborate scheme to deceive the Germans, since suspicions circulated that Dreyfus was a double-agent, whose *bordereau* was meant to lead the enemy astray.[49] In this piece, Barrès even tempered his anti-Semitism with a remarkable degree of "admiration and pity," says a recent critic, as Barrès merged the figure of Judas-Dreyfus with that of Job. Both men are models of suffering in loneliness, rejection, and abandonment; they deserve our sympathy.[50]

From an earlier period of French history, we will also recall how Edith

Flamarion showed that some of the success of the Brutus myth resulted from a similar kind of "confusion" during the French Revolution, although in that case a confusion of different historical Brutuses with each other. The result of this logic-defying confusion was really to achieve the desired ideological end of symbolically identifying the republican patriotism of all the "Brutuses."[51] The same kind of symbolic play takes place, but this time even more refractory to reason, in Dreyfus's being confused with both Jesus or Job, the victim of sacrifice and undeserved punishment and with his opposite, Judas, the perfidious agent delivering Jesus to sacrifice. This accounts in part for the black irony by which Dreyfus's enemies could both acknowledge his innocence all the while "blaming" him for it, and insisting upon his sacrifice all the more!

On occasion, for example, the anti-Dreyfusards played a deeply cynical mythological game by running together Dreyfusard imagery of the pure and innocent Jesus with the anti-Dreyfusard image of the wretched impure Judas. This yielded another turn of the religio-political imagination, which one may call the Judas/Jesus-Dreyfus. The same running together of notions of Dreyfus's possible innocence with his judicial guilt also emerge in the cynical language of the affair. Thus, while mocking devotion to Dreyfus's innocence, the accused opponents draw him as Judas assuming the place of Jesus crucified! In order to make this bitter sarcasm plain, Judas is also depicted as soft and paunchy, the very image of the "rich and avaricious Jew" propagated in anti-Semitic literature of the period (figs. 5, 9, 10, 11). Even in depictions of Dreyfus on Devil's Island, where he suffered great privations in leg irons and shackles, solitary confinement, and miserable conditions in tropical miasma, his haters chose to cast him as living a life of ease under the swaying palms, puffing away on a large cigar (fig. 11).

The deliberately confused theme of Dreyfus mythologized as Judas/Jesus-Dreyfus likewise seems reflected in the "cynical" anti-Dreyfusard language employed by Charles Maurras, founder of the Action Française.[52] Likening Dreyfus to Jesus again, Maurras said at one point that "as in the priestly circles of Jerusalem of Jesus, it was not unthinkable that an innocent man be punished for the greater objective of the general welfare."[53] Now, of course, Maurras never felt Dreyfus innocent, even less that he should represent Jesus. Yet he adopted this bitterly cynical attitude all the same, ostensibly to gall the supporters of Dreyfus by throwing their image of the unjustly condemned Jesus-Dreyfus back in their faces, creating the image of False Jesus-Dreyfus (figs. 3, 5). While this theme of Dreyfus as a false Jesus-like figure performing expiating sacrifice cannot be said to be prominent, it does turn up in unexpected places. Thus, Maurras even acknowledges that Dreyfus's suffering does achieve some sort of "expiation," as he mocks Dreyfus's family for their attempts to identify the real culprit. "The family of the condemned man decided to identify the one who according to them committed the treason that Dreyfus had expiated."[54] We will see how even this cynical perspective takes on unexpected character later in this chapter, as we meet other anti-Dreyfusards, such as the novelist Paul Bourget and the journalist Paul de Cassagnac, both of whom believed that even in the (admittedly for them unlikely) event of Dreyfus's innocence, the condemned should be sacrificed anyway![55] In this bitter, twisted logic of the right's confusion of Dreyfus, Judas, and Jesus, Dreyfus can also then be seen to recapitulate a nonetheless powerful politico-religious logic. Like Jesus in his impure state—the criminal humiliated outside the city walls on Calvary—at a safe distance on Devil's Island Dreyfus discharged the pollutants poisoning the nation.

Scapegoat-Dreyfus: Gentile and Jew

Beyond the Judas-Dreyfus myth, there are occasions when the Judas-Dreyfus not only merges "confusedly" with the ironic myth of Jesus-Dreyfus as we have seen, but also points to an often paradoxical sacrificial image of Dreyfus as the classic scapegoat of Jewish lore. In this guise, Dreyfus serves the function of unwilling victim, who bears the brunt of sacrificial immolation, which saves the people and the nation. The scapegoat" carries off the evil threatening a group and in doing so relieves the group of threats to its safety. For the anti-Dreyfusards, the "other" to be saved is the honor of the Army, and whether or not Dreyfus was guilty, he must be sacrificed to ward off even greater dangers to the nation. Here, René Girard's conceptions of the scapegoat (*bouc émissaire*) as related to the death of Jesus seem pertinent: "The scapegoat that takes shape under our eyes is the same as the origin of Judaic sacrifices. Caiaphas is the perfect sacrificer who puts victims to death to save those who live."[56] As if he has Dreyfus in mind, René Girard adds that Caiaphas is the "incarnation of politics at its best"—he saves the nation by sacrificing Jesus. "Scapegoating" therefore is what Girard calls a society's deflection "upon a relatively indifferent victim, a 'sacrificeable' victim, the violence that would otherwise be vented on its own members, the people it most desires to protect."[57] The scapegoat "takes it in the neck," as we say, for the sake of others who escape unscathed. In this way, sacrifice insures social order and social peace for those who escape the ordeal that falls upon the immolated victim. This then most perplexing feature of the sacrificial mystique of Dreyfus, the monstrous view that even though he may be innocent, Dreyfus should be sacrificed anyway, will occupy us here.

From this complex of mystical sacrificial perspectives of the anti-Dreyfusards, we can see both how Dreyfus is implicated in sacrificial discourse and why further it was thought that he ought to be sacrificed. The anti-Dreyfusards had many "reasons" for persecuting their victim—most of them mystical or mythological. (In this respect, of course, the Dreyfusards had just as many reasons to "heroize" the condemned, and for equally—though opposite—mystical or mythological reasons as well.) If he is guilty of betraying the nation, then as Judas-Dreyfus, he deserves to die for delivering the savior to his death (fig. 14). He further ought, like the "scapegoat," be carried far away with his impurities, to Devil's Island. Let us explore further some of these possibilities, and the confused, yet for all that, potent sacrificial imagery that englobed Dreyfus. Both pro-Dreyfus and anti-Dreyfus forces engaged in mythologizations that were largely, but not exclusively, formed by the traditions of Catholic France reinforced by the revolutionary tradition's appropriation and reconfiguration of them. When we reach the *fin-de-siècle*, we meet intransigent Catholics exploiting their reconciliation with the Third Republic and its *raison d'état*, along lines we have already spelled out in connection with the newly recovered Catholic patriotism for the Third Republic. Dreyfus fell into the hands of a party well socialized in both the Catholic theology and mythology of sacrifice as well as the French Revolution's transformations of it.

Memory, Scapegoat-Dreyfus, and Zionism

Now, what is puzzling in our story is that elements of this essentially intransigent Catholic ritual "mystique" of Dreyfus seem also to have been shared by the Jewish community of Dreyfus's day. This, in a way, is no surprise, since Jews taught Christians much of what they know about sacrifice. So, it would be as natural for Jews, as for Catholics, to trade on the theological lessons of their centuries-long experience with sacrifice, both as a rite and symbol to help make sense of their world. Yet the sacrificial conception of Dreyfus produced surprising results among French and foreign Jews alike, results that could not have been foreseen at the time—namely the birth of Zionism.

When we start sifting Jewish views about Dreyfus contemporary to the events in question, we discover a stunning range of opinion. Some French Jews, like Daniel Halevy, supported the accusations of the army and anti-Semites, even denouncing Dreyfusards, like Bernard Lazare, for being in the service of "'Jewish money.'"[58] Bernard Lazare himself at first wanted nothing to do with the whole matter. Even Durkheim, who played a prominent role in the defense of Dreyfus, at first excused his conviction by appeals to the dynamics of the crowd:

When society is in pain, it feels the need to find someone to blame for its troubles, [someone] upon whom it can avenge itself of for its disappointments. Naturally, singled out to play this role are those already held in bad opinion. These are the pariahs, and they serve as expiatory victims. Confirming my interpretation was the way the judgment against Dreyfus was greeted on the streets in 1894. The boulevards erupted in joy. People celebrated what was really an occasion for public mourning as if it were some kind of victory. "We finally know whom to blame for the economic troubles and moral wretchedness of our times. Our problems are the fault of the Jews. Now, this has even been officially established as a fact. And, because of that alone, everything seems already to be getting better, and we feel cheered up."[59]

But overall, French Jews early on tried to avoid the entire subject and thus said little or nothing about Dreyfus—at least in public. Later, when the "Affair" hit with full force, French Jews were still not active, much less conspicuous, in resisting a sacrificial reading of Dreyfus's condition. Nor were they conspicuous among those defending the accused.[60] The only exceptions were Mathieu Dreyfus, the captain's brother and the accused's immediate family, soon to be supported by Bernard Lazare. Thus, at least during the period of the Dreyfus "case," most French Jews, like their Gentile peers, neither saw the accusation nor the conviction of Dreyfus as anti-Semitic. Nor in the period of the "case," was Dreyfus in general seen as scapegoated victim or impure being, much less as an immolated pure and innocent "lamb led to slaughter."[61] These conceptions would come later as the "case" became the "affair" and ultimately a "mystique." Speaking of those early years, even before the "case" had become an "affair," Léon Blum sums up Jewish opinion of those times:

In general, the Jews accepted the condemnation of Dreyfus as legitimate and fair. They did not speak of "The Affair" among themselves. They evaded the subject, rather than stirring it up. A great misfortune has befallen Israel. But, they submitted to it without uttering a word, waiting for the passage of time and inattention to dissolve its effects.[62]

French Jews simply wanted to forget about Dreyfus.

Some prominent Jews, however, did suspect that the "case" against Dreyfus involved something more than things best left to the authorities. However slowly, they came to believe that Dreyfus's fate had been directed from far behind the scenes of public events. Some began to conceive of the "affair" along the lines of a "mystique"—that Dreyfus had been scapegoated. Typically, however, such thoughts were quickly suppressed. René Schwob, editor of the literary supplement of the anti-Dreyfus *L'Echo de Paris,* was typical in keeping his personal feelings about Dreyfus's innocence scrupulously private in such a hostile professional environment. He only revealed his suspicions in private correspondence with his mother and then as late as 1898.[63] Leon Blum himself also tells us that it was the gentile head librarian of the École Normale Supérieure, Lucien Herr, who granted him what he called "'Dreyfusard grace,'" but then not until 1897—four years after the condemnation! Thus, enlightened by Herr, Blum mercilessly criticized his own French Jewish community for thinking that they could sacrifice Dreyfus at no cost to themselves. Such sacrificial prophylaxis would not work in the end, concluded Blum:

> The rich Jews, the Jews of the middle bourgeoisie, Jewish civil servants feared the struggle undertaken on behalf of Dreyfus. . . . They thought only of lying low and hiding. They imagined that anti-Semitic passion would be deflected by their cowardly neutrality. . . . They did not understand . . . that no precaution . . . would delude the enemy and that *they remained the victims offered to triumphant anti-Dreyfusism.*[64]

It was only because of the efforts of Jewish intellectual and cultural notables, such as Bernard Lazare that progressives began seeing Dreyfus as a scapegoat—albeit to preserve others than themselves—in the sacrificial drama staged by intransigent Catholics. They then began campaigning for the revision of Dreyfus's conviction.[65] Therefore, so-called Jewish solidarity simply did not exist in the early years of the case. It was more a myth propagated, typically by anti-Semites seeking to support the idea of a "Jewish conspiracy."

Such dynamics in the French Jewish community then fit René Girard's shrewd general observations on the "scapegoat," and may even explain something of the silence of French Jewry. Girard tells us that the "scapegoat" marks the "the strange propensity to seize upon surrogate victims, to actually conspire with the enemy and at the right moment toss him a morsel that will serve to satisfy his raging hunger." [66] If Charles Péguy, Bernard Lazare, and Léon Blum can be believed, this approximates what the French Jews did to one of their own.[67] But given this, can one imagine the French Jewish community volunteering such a description of themselves?[68] By comparison, early Christians had an advantage in declaring the "scapegoated" nature of Jesus' death, as they saw it, since the altogether more appealing symbol of the "lamb of God" was available to them. For early Christians, says Girard,

The expression scapegoat is not actually used, but the Gospels have a perfect substitute in the lamb of God. Like "scapegoat" it implies the substitution of one victim for all the others but replaces all the distasteful and loathsome connotations of the goat with the positive associations of the lamb. It indicates more clearly the innocence of this victim, the injustice of the condemnation, and the causelessness of the hatred of which it is the object.[69]

Thus, even had French Jews mustered the courage to speak out for Dreyfus, one could argue that in terms of available religious imagery they were reduced to silence. It would have been shameful to admit that Dreyfus was a "scapegoat" and far too Christian to refer to him as a "lamb of God." At the very least, French Jewry seemed silenced by the impossibility of representing Dreyfus in a favorable way.

Compounding Jewish difficulties in representing Dreyfus, not to mention their ambivalence in the Dreyfus case, was the attitude of Dreyfus himself. Always insisting he was merely an "artillery officer," he shunned any religious or "mystical" construction of his situation.[70] Dreyfus never believed that anti-Semitic victimization or scapegoating had determined his accusation or condemnation.[71] Indeed, after his rehabilitation, he resumed his career in the army, serving in two of the bloodiest battles of the First World War—Verdun and Chemin de Dames—as commander of a supply column! For his service to the nation, he was made an officer of the Legion of Honor in September 1918.[72] Naively or not, he refused to play the "victim" in the several sacrificial narratives that sought to capture him for their own purposes (fig. 7). If Dreyfus cast himself in a narrative role at all, it was as eventual victor. As the perfect loyalist, Dreyfus resisted to ritualize his condition as victim or scapegoat. Dreyfus always remained firm in his belief that some bizarre error had been made, catching him up in a nasty drama under someone else's direction. When the mystique finally cracked, when the mistake was recognized, he was convinced that the army and the nation would put it right. There was in this sense an "affair without Dreyfus."[73]

While to us, this childlike faith in impartial justice may even seem pathetic, at least in the period of the Dreyfus "case," it is nonetheless plausible for Dreyfus to have assumed that his Jewishness had not influenced the judgment of the army. Although the Paris populace and the Catholic popular press did indeed play at explicit and vociferous anti-Semitic politics, the army revealed no overt signs of anti-Semitism in their official deliberations.[74] Private communications, however, may tell a different story. Although Dreyfus's Jewishness was never mentioned in the judicial processes, one need not forget that most of the officer corps of the army were inclined toward anti-Semitism.[75] But on the other side of the debate, one could point out that some of the key players in the "case," while anti-Semites themselves, do not seem to have acted on their prejudices. Georges Picquart, the Catholic army officer who began the investigation eventually exonerating Dreyfus, provides a case in point. Although he disliked Jews in general and found Dreyfus himself unsympathetic, Picquart nonetheless did not act upon these prejudices and exposed Esterhazy as the real author of the *bordereau* that had originally incriminated Dreyfus. Indeed, Picquart's action in pressing ahead with the investigation, which ultimately exculpated Dreyfus, cost him greatly.[76]

For their part, of course, the French Jewish community never would admit that they believed that Dreyfus's conviction protected them from attack. Yet Jewish commentators like Léon Blum, as we have seen, confirm that this belief was a widely held among French Jews.[77] It was simply suppressed. According to this scenario, French Jews were enthusiastic in their patriotic feelings toward the republic;[78] their confidence in the French judicial system was great; they cherished a profound respect for the Army, especially for the high command.[79] As good patriots, like other members of their economic and social class, they were concerned that an attack on the prestige of the army would weaken its ability to quell serious internal social unrest, such as that caused by the anarchists, syndicalists, and other proponents of "social revolution" threatening the middle classes in the waning years of the nineteenth century.[80] Jews did not, in short, see themselves as candidates for sacrifice, as special targets for victimization—and certainly not as characters in a drama of annihilation for the sake of expiation of national sinfulness. Most of all, French Jews feared standing out and providing easy targets for their enemies. One might say that a significant number of French Jews wanted not only to forget about Dreyfus, but also themselves.

But, if philosemitic commentators of the time are to be believed, French Jews eventually cast Dreyfus in the role of scapegoat preserving the Jewish community. A philosemitic Catholic, Charles Péguy, claimed that French Jews "would only ask to sacrifice Dreyfus in order to ward off the storm."[81] Fearing that identification with Dreyfus would target them to the fiercely anti-Semitic crowds demonstrating and brawling in the Paris streets at the height of the "Affair," French Jews acceded at least to the structure of the scapegoating sacrificial logic. With a significant portion of the Jewish community, Dreyfus's life substitutes for that of the community and not in this case for the sake of the army or the French state's *raison d'état*.

For Reasons Unstated

The sacrificial motif of the scapegoat may have been original to the history of the religion of the Jews. But neither it nor the creation of Scapegoat-Dreyfus would be either a solely, or perhaps even mostly, Jewish venture. Far more influential than any Scapegoat-Dreyfus narrative "told" by the Jews of France—if only by virtue of demographic realities—was the use of the Scapegoat-Dreyfus motif by the anti-Dreyfusard intransigent Catholics. Indeed, although some French Jews did justify their own inaction in behalf of Dreyfus by thinking about the punishment of Dreyfus as a renewal of the venerable rite of sacrifice, it was highly doubtful that Jewish ideas about sacrifice dominated thinking about Dreyfus as a sacrifice. Certainly, it was Catholic conceptions, like Judas-Dreyfus, that held sway in the popular mind, not the narratives that the tiny Jewish community of France might tell. After all, French Jewry numbered only a few tens of thousands at the time, a mere .05 percent of the French population. This means that we must look to those rightist Catholic notions of sacrifice, which in various degrees appeared so prominently across the broad range of opinion in French civic thought in the late nineteenth and early twentieth century. In doing so, they provided an efficient and pervasive rationale for the active conversion of Dreyfus into a number of sacrificial subjects, whether Judas-Dreyfus, Scapegoat-Dreyfus, or even True Jesus-Dreyfus. The anti-Dreyfusard intransigent Catholics had available to them several convenient narratives for locating Dreyfus. He was the guilty traitor delivering Jesus to sacrifice, the possibly innocent victim nevertheless required to fulfill the scapegoating narrative of sacrifice for the good of the nation, or the guilty one again masquerading as the good and innocent suffering Lord. The intransigent Catholics had overdetermined Dreyfus for victimization.

If the scenarios entangling Dreyfus in a sacrificial narrative are many, one above all challenges our sense of logic and justice more than others. Indeed, if Dreyfus had betrayed France as his accusers claimed, he would have deserved being cast in the role of Judas-Dreyfus. Neither do we need to linger over the unedifying, if understandable sacrificial logic of Scapegoat-Dreyfus imputed to French Jews by Léon Blum, Charles Péguy, and others. Not only does demography matter, but rational fears based in Jewish historical experience cannot be discounted.[82] Nor do I have in mind the heroic Dreyfus cast in the role of the Jew-Dreyfus, the pure, Jesus-like "lamb" innocently accused and punished, nor of course much less the False Jesus-Dreyfus of cynical anti-Dreyfusard thought (figs. 3, 5). Rather, this is the sacrifice of Scapegoat-Dreyfus, Dreyfus victimized for *raison d'état* by his enemies. What gives this logic its Maistrean character is that there were some cynical participants and observers of the day who held that even if Dreyfus were innocent, he should be sacrificed anyway—in this case in order to maintain the honor of the nation and army (fig. 13).

Nationalist leader, Maurice Barrès, for example, discerned a certain cunning social utility in the condemnation of Dreyfus—even if he were innocent. "'Let us content ourselves with speaking of social preservation,'" says Barrès. As Barrès expands his thought, it is clear that he stands for a drastic and mystical absolutizing of the interests of the state over the individual. Confounding common sense, Barrès went so far as to deny that any injustice had been done to Dreyfus at all—even if his innocence were declared! In Maurice Barrès's perverse redefinition of morality, one only speaks of injustice when the interests of the nation-state are not in play. "'Speak of injustice,'" says Barrès, only "'when one man condemns another.'" Since the trial of Dreyfus pitted the state against an individual, and since by implication, the state must be protected at all costs, Dreyfus cannot in principle suffer injustice! For Barrès, the only logic operative in the matter of Dreyfus was the logic of *raison d'état*. In this light, not only are apologies unnecessary, but with a sadism perhaps unparalleled in modern politics, Barrès urged that the scapegoat should be persecuted all the more! "'As for the deplorable victim of such a judicial error, one thing must be refused all the same: pardon for his defenders. . . . For the rest, if he is not a traitor, he should perforce be ashamed at having aroused such sympathies.'"[83] Pressing the same point, those enemies of Dreyfus loyal to the principle of *raison d'état,* felt that even if Dreyfus were innocent, he should be sacrificed nonetheless.[84] What effrontery for the scapegoat to stumble upon the altar of the knife-wielding priest! Notable in this number was the founder of the Action Française, Charles Maurras.

Maurras's transcendent loyalty to the principle of *raison d'état* led him to further perverse interpretations of the acts of a key figure in the Dreyfus "Affair," Colonel Hubert Henry. An officer in the intelligence corps, the Deuxième Bureau, Henry found evidence showing that the handwriting on the *bordereau,* which had originally seemed to incriminate Dreyfus, matched even better that of a fellow officer in his own section, Major Ferdinand Esterhazy. Furthermore, unlike the monied and prudish Dreyfus, Esterhazy was amply motivated to enrich himself through espionage. Both plagued by debts and a notorious "bounder," Esterhazy enjoyed equal access to the secret materials available to the condemned.[85] However, once Henry took stock of the politics of his discovery, he began a shameless effort to conceal what he had learned. He feared that discoveries exculpating Dreyfus would become widely known and cause a revision of the case against Dreyfus. He thereupon forged a letter addressed to the German mission in Paris falsely implicating Dreyfus in espionage. In the end, Henry was caught and promptly took his own life; Dreyfus was eventually pardoned. Along with Maurras at the height of the revelations about Colonel Henry, the most cynical anti-Dreyfusards affirmed all the more that individuals meant nothing when compared to the interests of the state. Partly in irony, but deeply revealing at the same time, anti-Dreyfusard Paul Léautaud declared in a slogan "'All for order! Down with justice and truth.'"[86]

But how did Maurras react to Henry's exposure? He confounded all morality and normal logic by celebrating Henry for inventing facts and perpetuating the myth of Dreyfus's guilt! Apparently marching to the beat of a perverse drummer indeed, Maurras addressed the memory of Henry in the following words: "'You have misled your fellow-citizens, but, it is for the good and honor of all. Your slogan, "Allons-y!" which had become proverbial, is now invested [by your sacrifice] with a profound and mysterious significance.'"[87] Moving even further into "mystical" realms, even in contemplating the possibility of Dreyfus's innocence, Maurras cannot restrain his lust for sacrifice for the sake of *raison d'état.* "If by some accident," says Maurras, "Dreyfus was innocent, he should be nominated for Marshal of France. But then we should go out and shoot a dozen of his chief defenders for the triple offense they have done to France, to Peace, and to Reason."[88] What Maurras tells us, in effect, is that anti-Dreyfusard myth is better than the reality of Dreyfus's innocence; the mystical trumps the logical. What I believe we should see here is that the "mystical" can well trump the "logical" when that mystique is imbued with the magic of a symbol like sacrifice, which has been so embedded in the nation-state and history of France.

Although Maurras's call to serve *raison d'état* was picked up in the anti-Dreyfusard Roman Catholic press,[89] it was also given a brilliantly wicked turn as well by the occasional liberal Catholic, such as Captain Pierre Félix, commander of the 6th Company of the 22d Infantry. As a military man, Félix tells us that he can accept the death of individuals for the common good. Surely, in the present situation of potential civil war between contestants in the Affair, he would consider

the sacrifice of an innocent man and some of his most notable fellow-travelers. But, taken in all, it would seem to be fairly easy and perhaps even more just and more moral—and therefore preferable—to sacrifice some of Dreyfus's accusers or persecutors in sufficient numbers "to insure peace." To start, it would not at all seem that the death of Drumont—or that of Georges Berry as well—(for

Drumont launched the famous formula "innocent or guilty") would be considered a greater public calamity.

But as for the "voluntary sacrifice of Dreyfus," which his tormenters seek, tongue firmly in cheek, Félix throws back into the face of the likes of a Maurras and his ilk the contradictions of their Maistrean logic—the guilty don't make good and acceptable sacrifices.

> As for the voluntary sacrifice of Dreyfus, I must confess that it would not be lacking in a certain loftiness—as long as it were necessary. But in reality, it is not the *patrie* that needs this sacrifice. The salvation of the country, by definition, can never consist in the consecration of an iniquity. This is the glory of Drumont and his anti-Semitic party. Oh, I well understand how precious to France and the civilized world the reputation of the infallible prophet Drumont is—a reputation that the uncontested success of the anti-Dreyfusard conspiracy would have consecrated forever. But one is also permitted to admit that Dreyfus and his partisans had preferred the triumph of truth to the care of that reputation.[90]

But given the French Revolution's transfer of sacrality to the nation, begun a generation earlier by Rousseau, Charles Maurras's statist interpretation of events should not surprise us. In asserting the infallibility of the General Will, all citizens are required to submit unconditionally to it. In effect, the revolutionary tradition reprised the authoritarianism of the *ancien regime*'s Divine Right of kings in nationalist form, along with its guiding principle, *raison d'état*.[91] As the great historian of French religious history, Adrien Dansette, noted of the revolutionary tradition:

> real deity was still composed of the principles that the Revolution claimed to incarnate. The constitutional cult had strictly subordinated the spiritual to the temporal. It made no distinction between what was God's and what was Caesar's because, as in the world of antiquity, Caesar or the State was God. That was what Robespierre meant when he demanded that the revolutionary tribunal should punish "those who have blasphemed against the Republic."[92]

In the fusion of Catholic and revolutionary traditions following the debacle at Sedan, these deeper affinities could then burst forth in explicit form. When the nation was perceived to be in danger, Catholic royalist arguments in favor of the national sacrificial imperative were virtually indistinguishable from their Jacobin counterparts. We have noted how both Catholic royalist and Jacobin *étatiste* read Rousseau to support the subordination of the individual to crown or state, respectively. Matching Robespierre, we will recall, was the influential royalist journalist, Abbé Thomas Marie Royou, who argued, for example, that "individuals in a state of nature, realizing the inadequacy of their abilities, had surrendered all their rights to society as a whole. This surrender was "absolute, unlimited, irrevocable, and perpetual." Thenceforth, individual interests had to suffer if necessary for the welfare of all.[93] A "Catholic" thinker like Maurras could easily claim that the state should subordinate the fate of Dreyfus to the interests of *raison d'état*. The arguments had been prepared many years earlier.[94]

As a result of the succession of sacral kingship by sacral nationhood, we should rather expect Dreyfus's situation to be ritualized. Instrumental considerations—who really passed information to the Germans?—are put aside, and ritual ones—how do we maintain a national image?—come to the fore. *Raison d'état* is not in this way primarily a principle of political statecraft as much as it is an assertion of the divinity or sacrality of the state, with all this implies for the ritualization of Dreyfus's fate. Thus, in the right's insistence on saving the reputation of the army and nation, we meet yet another example of the religion of nationalism having its way. That Dreyfus can be sacrificed for *raison d'état* already tells us that the state has been well sacralized. Why would the state be worthy of sacrifice unless it were not already sacred, unless it already embodied ultimate value?

My focus on the extremes of French nationalism should not, of course, imply that the *raison d'état* is a French matter alone. Nothing could be farther from the truth. It is a commonplace that the nation-state system operates precisely upon the basis of *raison d'état*. In this sense, a Jewish state is no exception to the rule of nations that will require "sacrifice" of its citizens for *raison d'état*. Thus, Herzl's perception that Jews without a nation are vulnerable to such scapegoating or simple victimization by the *raisons d'état* of their host nations is central to our discussion of sacrifice, but the dynamic of the nation-state does not exclude a Jewish state. Thus, in 1890s when the likes of Charles Maurras appealed to the *raison d'état* of France in persisting in the punishment of Dreyfus, Jews lacked an equal right to appeal to a Jewish *raison d'état*, since there was not yet a Jewish "state" in the required sense.[95] Only by becoming a nation themselves could Jews begin to call for their own sacrifices of purity instead of being victims of the sacrificial strategies of others.[96] Therefore, once a nation, the same celebration of sacrifice of totality, purity, and innocence emerges in Israel as we have witnessed in France—without, as far as I know, the extremity of a Charles Maurras. In the famous Israeli nationalistic poem, "The Silver Platter," we meet a young couple—significantly pure and innocent—confronting the nation with the sacrificial price which must—inevitably again—be paid for the continued existence of nationhood itself. The poem concludes with their final words:

> We are the silver platter
> On which the Jewish state has been given you.
> . . . Then enveloped in shadow at the people's feet they fell.
> The rest will be told in the annals of Israel.[97]

Thus, except for Zionism, which in effect propels us *out* of French history and into a new phase of Jewish history, French Jewish anxieties about Dreyfus as a sacrificial victim tell only part of the story of Dreyfus's many roles in the narratives of sacrifice.[98]

A religious logic is at work here in the anti-Dreyfusard roots of this extreme form of nationalism, which, when applied to the political scene, may be called political theology or religious ideology, according to one's tastes. As theological as it was political, the logic of the belief in the overarching value of the punishment of Dreyfus cannot be understood without resort to an analysis of theologies and theories of sacrifice current at the time. Again, among the varieties of thinkers about sacrifice known and respected at the time, we must number Joseph de Maistre and his meditations on the desirability of political sacrifice.[99]

Catholic Sources of the Habits of Obedience

What influences fed the thought of those like Charles Maurras, who held the belief in the efficacy of sacrifice in behalf of the nation, even the sacrifice of the innocent? And, what would these influences tell us about the ideologies informing conceptions of sacrifice in the late nineteenth and early twentieth centuries?

To the extent Maurras thought about Dreyfus—even cynically—as a scapegoating sacrifice of the innocent, one would certainly want to look to Joseph de Maistre. There is in any event much of de Maistre behind Charles Maurras, given de Maistre's high popularity among "Catholic" rightist thinkers and readers of the day.[100] Early in his life, Maurras declared explicit allegiance to "'our Catholic traditions,'"[101] perhaps obliquely referring to Maistre, widely regarded as a champion of Catholic thought at the time. And despite Maurras's own later agnosticism and the Church's condemnation of the Action Française, Maurras remained loyal throughout his life to the proposition that the essence of France was "the language, the Church, the Roman administration and its law."[102] What did this mean? Especially in light of the fact that Catholics flocked to the Action Française in overwhelming numbers, the ideological unity among rightist Catholics and the Action Française is manifest. Eugen Weber has argued, for example, that the Action Française and the Church sought the same ends: "authority, hierarchy and discipline."[103] Not accidentally, both Charles Maurras and Joseph de Maistre saw the essence of life as the craving for "suffering, sacrifice and surrender."[104]

But do these Maistrean affinities with Maurras help us understand the Dreyfus Case? One reason to believe that Maurras's Maistrean thinking may inform his attitude to Dreyfus is that the assertion of "authority, hierarchy, and discipline" conforms to the principle of *raison d'état,* beloved of the Catholic right wing in the late nineteenth and early twentieth centuries.[105] Anticipating Maurras, de Maistre's submission of the individual to the will of the monarch or state is equivalent and in some cases identical to—in religious terms—the submission to the magisterial will of the church reaffirmed so unambiguously in the Syllabus of Errors and at the First Vatican Council. As a political parallel to the Oratorian celebration of annihilating "consummation" of the individual in their Eucharistic spirituality, Joseph de Maistre's theology of sacrifice rehearsed the convictions that defined the intransigent Catholic party from its inception and that were renewed in the *fin-de-siècle*.[106] Further notable in Maistre's view of sacrifice, and at the same time aligning him with the political theology of the Oratorians, is the severity of his views.[107] Sacrifice for both is annihilation in pursuit of expiation, a total giving up of the victim in sacrifice. As Isaiah Berlin notes regarding de Maistre's bracing convictions: "Men must give, not merely lend, themselves. Society is not a bank, a limited liability company formed by individuals who look on one another with suspicious eyes—fearful of being taken in, dumped, exploited."[108] This is so for Maistre because society is not an "artificial association based on calculation of self-interest . . . but rests at least as much on . . . the impulse to immolate oneself on the sacred altar without hope of return."[109]

De Maistre's vision of sacrifice was given explicit political life in those who followed him in the late nineteenth and early twentieth century. Their role was to initiate a struggle to command and control the symbolism of sacrifice. Consider first the coercive force of the code of behavior of the members of the military tribunal that condemned Dreyfus. Albert S. Lindemann has argued that having declared for Dreyfus's guilt, the minister of war, General Auguste Mercier, succumbed to habits of obedience and respect for authority, thereby rendering him (and others) incapable of dissent. In like manner, the Dreyfusard press produced analyses of the so-called military mentality and its responsibility for abuses leading to the condemnation of Dreyfus—often contrary to the testimony of facts. One remarkable document, published under the pseudonym "L. Vérax," is devoted entirely to the subject of the relation of the military mentality to the mistreatment of Dreyfus by the army and its courts.[110] Unrelenting in his condemnation of the military mind set, Vérax calls it "ghastly," since it is replete with "entrenched prejudices, excessive credulity, and an obstinate partisanship against reconsidering anything" (fig. 16).[111] Assuming all the sense of superiority of a haughty Church hierarchy, the military "believe themselves charged with a mission which is far above that of other citizens. It has something of the sacred character of a priest to it."[112]

But where, one must ask, did these habits originate? Out of what sort of ground did they take their nourishment? Although a "garden variety" authoritarian military culture cannot be gainsaid,[113] especially as it was reinforced in times of perceived national peril, in a "Catholic" country like France, and especially among a predominantly intransigent Catholic corps of military leaders, we need go no further. Thus, one should not be surprised to read how Charles Maurras's conceptions of Dreyfus as scapegoat for *raison d'état* are found among the military—at least if we are to believe Dreyfusards like the mysterious "L. Vérax." If he can be believed, the conclusions one must draw point directly to the power of intransigent Catholic among the military. Vérax reports:

> I have heard directly from the mouth of a military man that revolting saying. To wit, if Dreyfus should be innocent, it is better that he be let to perish on Devil's Island than to overturn his condemnation. The interests of the *patrie, raison d'état,* require that he just go away and that justice never be granted him.[114]

Worse yet, Vérax adds, this serviceman feels the family of Dreyfus should join in sacrificing their own and in effect embrace the sacrificial image of Scapegoat-Dreyfus for a *raison d'état* as their own! "I well understand," the soldier goes on,

> other fathers, wives and sisters upholding that monstrous theory. They indeed would add that in the higher interests of the state, the family of the condemned should desist in their efforts at rehabilitation. Instead, they should immolate the innocent on the altar of the *Patrie.*[115]

What was the *"raison"* within their *raison d'état*? What could have justified for them an appeal to the overriding interests of the state against the equally compelling French imperative of the *droits de l'homme*? Vérax offers that this *raison d'état* is actually a fake. It is really only the "pride of the military bound tightly to their own interests."[116] And those interests have their home, for Vérax at least, in the deeply entrenched Catholicism mixed with political absolutism of the golden age. The military, like most

French people, are "steeped in antiquated ideas," such as ideas of "absolute monarchy. Such blind confidence in the government is a prejudice dating from another age."[117] It is the duty of modern French citizens to throw off this mentality. Otherwise, the "interests of the individual will be obliterated by the congregation in which the soldier finds himself as surely as it is among those in religious orders."[118] Despite Vérax's partisan stance, is it so implausible that the "intransigence" of the mind-set of this overwhelmingly Catholic officer corps was the same "intransigence" characterizing the dominant wing of Catholic theology and spirituality of the late nineteenth and early twentieth centuries? The "absolutism" of the military mind-set is here a local variant of the absolutism and "spirit of domination" characteristic of the Catholicism of this period.[119] What other sort of political culture might more plausibly emerge from the culture of intransigent and integral Catholicism (fig. 8)?

Raison d'Etat *and the Conservation of the Sacred*

Mercier and the other Catholic officers judging Dreyfus were informed by at least two major tenets of French political and, as we will see, "religious," culture. The first was the principle of statecraft, *raison d'état;* the second was the related notion of the sacredness of the nation. Both militated against the exoneration of Dreyfus and thus conditioned the Catholic officers of the tribunal to resist revision.

The first deliberate application of Machiavelli's theories of statecraft to the affairs of a great state seems to have been in France. *Raison d'état* had effectively been employed in statecraft by the French crown from at least Catherine de Medici's regency. Catherine was in this way a worthy member of her family, for Lorenzo di Piero de' Medici was the prince to whom Machiavelli's great work had been dedicated. Even though he was reported to have ignored Machiavelli's unsolicited advice, Catherine seems to have followed the lessons of her family's would-be counselor. To secure the Catholic cause, while at the same time shrewdly conciliating the Huguenots, she contrived the wedding of Protestant Henri of Navarre (later King Henri IV) to her own daughter, Margaret of Valois. But Catherine followed up this show of tolerance by allegedly ordering the St. Bartholomew's massacre. The Huguenots never really recovered from this decapitation of their leadership. In later years, the Medici connection proved good insurance for the Catholic cause, when Henri married Catherine's distant relative, Marie. After his assassination, Marie de Medici ruled France as regent largely in the interests of Bérulle's *"parti dévot,"* right up until the maturity of their son, Louis XIII. Marie later arranged the marriage of Louis to Ann of Austria, thus cementing an alliance with one of the major Catholic powers in Western Europe during the time of religious warfare. Ann, in turn, kept the lineage of Italian masters of Machiavellian statecraft alive in France by appointing Cardinal Mazarin as Richelieu's successor as first minister to the king. Mazarin (Giulio Mazarini) himself hailed from the Abruzzi and was a confirmed disciple of Machiavelli. In this way, chiefly through the Medicis and then the Bourbons, the lineage of chief ministers schooled in Machiavellian statecraft was planted early in France and maintained an unbroken line into the eighteenth century.

Raison d'état served Catherine and her successors well in freeing the French crown's political ambitions from religious or moral restraints. Thus, as wise Machiavellians, the French monarchs did not confuse those virtues necessary for maintaining the state with those one might like to see prevail among individuals ruled by "Christian charity." In order for the prince to act "virtuously," he acts according to *raisons d'état* and not, Machiavelli argues, as one might behave among loved ones. Where honesty is a virtue at home, so to speak, it is dissimulation and deception that are "virtues" at court.[120]

Now despite this deliberate attempt by politics to cut itself free from religion, I am arguing that in France a politics governed by *raison d'état* came to take on a sacred character nevertheless. What began as a crass principle of statecraft ended up defining a new realm of sacrality. Indeed, the very assertion of an absolute principle like *raison d'état* was *ipso facto* to assert that the interests of the state are ultimate and thus, in this way, sacred. *Raison d'état* thus demands a fidelity as intransigent as anything coming from the mouth of the Catholic intransigent theologians of our acquaintance.[121]

Making the mixture of politics and religion in France especially potent was the fact that *raison d'état* was paired with the medieval French belief in the sacrality of the body of the king and, in the period of our study, with the assertion by Louis XIV of the divine right of kings.[122] By the seventeenth century, the cult of the French monarchy had reached a "critical mass." The *"majesté"* heretofore reserved for God alone, now englobed the monarch, replacing the traditional attribute of "dignity."[123] While it is true that medieval French kings were seen as priests, now they were likened to Christ, the man-God Himself.[124] The state thus became divinized, and further "the State as personified by the king" took on divine character.[125] The absolutism inherent in these formulae reveals itself as nothing more than a "kind of religion."[126] What then began as a formula for a secularized politics, expressing Machiavelli's declaration of the independence of politics from the restraints of religion, in France, certainly by the time of Louis XIV, ironically was married solemnly to a divinized politics in the form of the sacred monarchy of the later Bourbons.[127]

What is critical for us in dealing with events of the late nineteenth and early twentieth centuries is how the nation-state ever since the French Revolution and into Dreyfus's day sought to retain the divinity of the French kings, even while disavowing the sacred character of their new politics. With the French Revolution, the nation may have replaced the monarch, but the Machiavellian principles of statecraft imported by the French kings stayed in place. Thus, the ascent of the modern nation-state in the wake of the French Revolution only changed the idioms of this divinized politics. When the monarchy fell, the sacrality of the king merely passed on to the nation-state, which deployed its sacrality where it would, now under a re-sacralized reincarnation of the old secular principle of *raison d'état*.[128] Thanks in part to the intellectual work done a generation earlier by Rousseau, "reason of state," as embodied in the General Will, was sufficient unto itself, and as unanswerable and absolute as the whims of the Sun King. By virtue of this logic, sacrifice became the natural disposition of the true patriot. In Liah Greenfeld's sharp words, "patriotism implied complete renunciation of self, the effacement of the private in front of the public. Civil liberty lost much of its meaning."[129] Dale van Kley dubs this process as governed by the "law of the conservation of the sacred"—a process not without its costs to those seeking to disenchant the world of traditional religious values, but one, at any rate, that restores sacrifice. Thus, the revolutionaries ended with a resacralized politics—the

> price paid for the desacralization of the remaining symbols of transcendence was an ideological resacralization of a "regenerated" body politic—the nation, the *patrie*—along with anathematizing or eliminating those deemed impolitic by the new secular order.[130]

As Dreyfus was sadly to discover, his fate was to be sealed in part by the "law of the conservation of the sacred," as it was now embodied in the politics of the *fin-de-siècle*. Dreyfus had the misfortune of falling into the clutches of a French polity and its rituals of political sacrifice, which had in fact been formed out of the remnants of the forces of reconfigured absolutism and freshly reinterpreted theologies of the sacrificial Eucharist. One, but not the only, thinker forming this tradition, which was still potent in the time of Dreyfus, was none other than that genius of rightist thought and sacrifice for the sake of the collectivity, Joseph de Maistre.[131]

Albert Réville and Protestant Resistance to Sacrificing Dreyfus

I have been arguing that intransigent Catholic notions of sacrifice and state, rooted in the sacrificial Eucharistic theology of the École Française de Spiritualité as further developed in the political theology of the absolutist thought of Joseph de Maistre, shaped attitudes to the fate of Dreyfus. A final test of this thesis might be made along the following lines. If the ideological heirs of Joseph de Maistre in the *fin-de-siècle* were renewing the culture wars of the seventeenth century over the meaning and significance of the Eucharist, then we might expect to find Protestants of the turn of the century joining the fray against all that de Maistre and the sacrificial reading of Dreyfus entailed.

Indeed, this is what we do find. Given the central place of the symbol of sacrifice in the ideology or political theology of the Catholic right wing, we might expect as well that the Protestant combatants in the *fin-de-siècle* culture wars raging round Dreyfus, should likewise be engaged in a struggle for hegemony over the meaning, application, and propriety of sacrifice in the modern nation-state. Their repugnance for the Catholic ideal of sacrifice, used now to excuse the condemnation of Dreyfus, stemmed in part from centuries-long Protestant resistance to the dominant spirit of Catholic intransigence, a resistance that was renewed in the present day. The Protestants of the Third Republic, even those fallen from observant practice, had not "forgotten the persecutions of the seventeenth and eighteenth centuries."[132] Indeed, Protestant "memories of old feuds kept returning."[133] Or, as Eugen Weber has dryly observed, "in France, the dead live longer than in other places."[134]

The Maistrean logic of sacrifice, so strange to us today, was recognized for what it was by leading French intellectuals of the *fin-de-siècle,* especially politically minded liberal Protestants loyal to the cause of vindicating Dreyfus. Likewise, these Protestants were keenly aware of how deeply de Maistre's ideas of sacrifice informed the political ideologies of their enemies among the anti-Dreyfusard intransigent Catholics. They knew well how the mystical Maistrean logic of sacrifice demanded the civic sacrifice of Dreyfus and how that logic needed to be defeated in order to pursue the struggle for Dreyfus. Years before the crisis of national conscience provoked by the Dreyfus Affair, Protestant scholars, like Edgar Quinet, posited an inner relation between reactionary political culture and the sacrificial religious mentality made prominent by the integral Catholics.[135] In 1880, the *Encyclopédie des sciences religieuses,* edited by the dean of the Protestant faculty of theology, Fréderic Lichtenberger, published the article, "Maistre (Marie-Joseph, Comte de)." There, the author notes that despite de Maistre's remove from the religious events of the day, his "role is quite important in contemporary religious history": he was nothing less than the "theoretician of theocracy in this century."[136] De Maistre preaches a "God who is pleased by sacrifice,"[137] a God who "loves it that the innocent pay for the guilty."[138] Ending this article in an ominous tone, the author warns that de Maistre's thought represents "an apologia for the executioner, admiration for war and the warrior—all those paradoxical theses which have not been easily maintained before the nineteenth century in France."

In terms of the place of religious factors in the Dreyfus "Affair," perhaps the most interesting figure vocal in opposing the sacrificial condemnation of Dreyfus was Albert Réville (1826–1906), liberal Protestant theologian, religious historian, and public intellectual.[139] In this opposition to the sacrifice of Dreyfus, Albert Réville was then working out the implications of a political theology developed by liberal Protestants for some time. The way of resistance to the sacrifice of Dreyfus had then already been prepared for a Protestant like Albert Réville by those dead in France of whom Eugen Weber speaks as living "longer than in other places."[140]

Born in 1826 during the antiliberal reign of restored Bourbon, Charles X, Réville was descended from a pious Huguenot Norman family of Dieppe. He followed his father into the liberal Calvinist ministry, after studying biblical history and theology at the Protestant faculties in the universities of Geneva and Strasbourg. As an avid scholar of the New Testament, he was deeply influenced by the "echoes" of the critical teachings of Ferdinand Christian Baur while abroad in Tübingen. Witness to the failure of the revolution of 1848, Réville left France and, from 1851 to 1873, he was pastor of the Walloonian church of Rotterdam. But in 1873, after the evangelicals seemed about to enforce doctrinal discipline at the Synod of 1872, Réville resigned his ministry. In the same year, following the fall of Napoleon III, he returned to France, and began to exploit the newly available political opportunities of the day. Réville rallied to the support to the new republic, and established his reputation among the newly invigorated political and religious liberals of the Third Republic. He spent the years 1873–1880 in his home city of Dieppe, writing in behalf of various republican causes. He intimately knew the leading liberal figures of the birth and early years of the Third Republic; he wrote for progressive newspapers and journals in France, even while abroad in Holland.[141]

With his "call" to the chair in history of religions at the Collège de France (1880), where Gambetta referred to Réville as "*his*" personal candidate,[142] he soon entered Parisian intellectual life at the highest levels. But Réville was also very much a man of the world academic scene. He was well known in England, delivering the prestigious Hibbert lectures in 1884. He attended the 1893 World Parliament of Religions in Chicago[143] and organized the first international congress of the history of religions 1900 in Paris. Albert Réville dominated the study of religion (and thus sacrifice) in France for the last two decades of the nineteenth century up until his death in 1906. As head of the École Pratique des Hautes Études,

Fifth Section, he was the principal authority and voice for the study of religion in France. With national and international prestige to give his views credence, he began to exert the wide influence on the study of religion, which we will consider at length in the next chapter. In 1886, he became the first president of the École Pratique des Hautes Études, Fifth Section, where he taught extensively under the rubric of history of (Christian) doctrine. No Protestant was more important in terms of the scholarly issues concerning ritual sacrifice than Albert Réville. His son Jean, a close co-worker and colleague at the Fifth Section, was a keen observer of the intellectual scene and among the leading Protestant critics of the work of Hubert and Mauss.

In the course of his busy life he was acquainted with some of the most illustrious politicians and academics of his day: British prime minister William Gladstone, Edouard Schérer, Charles Renouvier, Friedrich Max-Müller, and others. Réville was likewise in personal contact with the leaders of theological liberalism in France—with Auguste Sabatier, Alfred Loisy, Ernest Renan, and others. He had even advised Charles Renouvier on theological matters and was, as will see, an early Dreyfusard.[144] As a deeply political man, he was especially suspicious of Roman Catholic intentions toward religious tolerance and democracy; he was also an active philosemite.[145] Opposed to anti-Semitism on universalist and humanist, rather than particularist, grounds, Albert Réville saw anti-Semitism as an attack upon anyone who was *not* a Roman Catholic.[146] Albert Réville never lost his suspicions about the Catholic threat to individual liberties, doubtless heightened by the reinvigoration of religious authoritarianism with the First Vatican council.[147]

Although Réville grew up in the humanist environment of French Protestantism, his embrace of the Arminian or Remonstrant wing of Calvinism in Holland decisively reinforced Réville's liberal theological as well as political and economic thought.

Best known perhaps for their denial of predestination, the Remonstrants held economic positions well suited to the individualist and "opportunist" liberal bourgeois Third Republic. The Remonstrants stood for principles of economic individualism over against the statist views of their Calvinist peers. In the same theological breath, so to speak, they supported religious tolerance, freedom of conscience, *and* individualist capitalist commerce.[148] One of Albert Réville's biographers tells us that the Dutch devotion to the *"libre ésprit,"*[149] reminiscent of Hugo Grotius,[150] apparently marked Réville for life. In the spirit of the worldly Grotius, Réville's liberal political passions show how well integrated were his religious and political beliefs.[151] He advocated what he called political prophetism. For him, "the old trunk" of reformation liberationist theology now "spread out into branches" of liberal political (and religious) reform. For Albert Réville, "religious reform, religious spirituality, emancipation from oppressive authority, war against corrupt institutions . . . are various titles of its representatives in the modern world."[152]

In fact, Albert Réville's politics were thoroughly informed by his Protestant religious valuation of the sacredness of the individual over against that of the state. We are a long way from an absolutizing *raison d'état*. Réville was one of the first prominent French intellectuals to go on public record in defense of Dreyfus. His defense was not based so much on his abhorrence of anti-Semitism, as upon his deeply felt Protestant belief in the transcendent value of the human *individual*.[153] Not confining his defense of the sacredness of the individual to France, Réville supported the abolitionist cause in the United States, always couching his arguments in terms of the dignity of the individual. His 1860 biography of Theodore Parker (1810–1860), the American Unitarian abolitionist and "prophet" of human liberation, stands as a testimony of his belief in the universal and thus transcendent sacredness of the individual.[154]

By 1872, Réville had reached a point of crisis in his religious life, as many of the positions developed in Holland began to emerge in his public quarrels with more orthodox French Protestants. Along with the prominent young "extreme" liberal theologians whom we have already met, Réville took part in a spectacular defection from the main body of conservative Protestant orthodoxy.[155] The rebels denied the inerrancy of scriptures, original sin, as well as the divinity, incarnation, and resurrection of Jesus. In place of this supernaturalist view of Jesus, Réville saw Christ in classically individualist terms—as incarnate in humanity at large. For him, the spiritual history of humanity was a uniform story of evolution culminating in the individualist value of equality:[156]

> spiritually speaking, humanity in any case is one. It is one same spirit that animates it and is developed in it; and this, the incontestable unity of our race, is likewise the only unity we need care to insist on.[157]

In arriving at the conclusion of the equality of all people, Réville believed we were swept once more into the divine presence. The absolute value of the individual was, after all, basically as religious a matter as the absolutism of a state informed by the principles of *raison d'état*.

> In setting forth the intellectual and moral unity of mankind, everywhere directed at the same successive evolutions and the same spiritual laws, it brings into light the great principle of *human brotherhood*.

This common "evolution," in turn, forms a "basis of reason" for the "August sentiment of *divine fatherhood*. Brother-men and Father-God!—what more does the thinker need to raise the dignity of our nature?"[158]

Albert Réville Meditates on Sacrificing the Humanity of Dreyfus

Now, the upshot of the lessons that Albert Réville learned in his life was to affirm the sacredness of the individual, not only in political life but also, as we will see, in what I am arguing is the internally related theoretical work on sacrifice that Albert Réville produced. Despite the efforts of some of his coreligionists later in the century to accommodate altruism to the principle of self-interest, liberal Protestants like Albert Réville always gave individualist self-interest top priority. The accumulated weight of Réville's political alignment with the Radical Party, his nurture in the individualist theological culture of French Protestantism and, more recently, his experience of the Arminians in Holland, tipped the balance against alternatives to individualism. This also explains why Réville remained a steadfast opponent of the sacrifice of (the individual rights of) Dreyfus and at the same time a scholarly critic of sacrificial religions in *"science religieuse."*

Albert Réville gave his own Protestant humanist reply to the Maistrean mythology of sacrifice of Dreyfus in a poignant, anonymously authored little book called *Les étapes d'un intellectuel* (1898).[159] Indeed as a personal diary, it even conforms to a certain paradigm of Protestant individualist literature. An intimate record of an honest individual's attempt to examine his conscience in the light of changing information about the Affair, Réville carefully records how his own inner states, his doubts, his suspicions, his convictions shifted over the span of years 1894–1897. In its striving for purity of intention, closed within the ambit of a personal diary of inner reflections upon the daily course of the Dreyfus case, Réville displays some of the most characteristic features of French liberal Protestant sensibility. In effect, he religiously confesses his inner feelings. From the viewpoint of sacrifice, it is thus instructive to heed both what and how Réville speaks to us.

The first conviction of Dreyfus was redolent with the stench of the sacrificial symbolism of victimization in behalf of *raison d'état*. To wit, even if Dreyfus was innocent, it mattered little to the court whether his life should be spared sacrifice on Devil's Island. This is so in Maistrean terms because the judicial immolation of an innocent Dreyfus, far from offending our sense of human dignity, would strengthen social bonds all the more. Like several of his peers, Raoul Allier for instance, Albert Réville was persuaded that Catholic theological teachings merely repeated at a religious level what at the same time were political positions.

Réville records the day-to-day events reported in the newspapers, and we become privy to an inner dialogue of his meditations about why Dreyfus was accused and whether he could be guilty. Although disposed to give some benefit of the doubt to the results of the court martial, Réville early on doubted Dreyfus's guilt and immediately suspected nefarious plots. After all the arch-anti-Semite Drumont had eagerly published the news of Dreyfus's arrest in his *La libre Parole*.[160] Suspicion of anti-Semitic motives grew in Réville's mind as considered the case,[161] and indeed all soon became obvious.[162] Did not Dreyfus himself say at his "Dégradation," reports Albert Réville, that his "'misfortune was to have been born a Jew'"?[163]

But, without denying the reality of anti-Semitism, Réville shifts ground to the violation of the sacredness of the individual, which he feels is at the root of the problem. Against the racist slanders of a visiting German academic, Réville replies that French Jews are not really a "race."[164] They are "*French by law* and by their hearts," because they subscribe to the principles of 1789—in effect, the *individualism* enshrined in the Declaration of the Rights of Man.[165] Furthermore, French Jews have thrown their support to religious tolerance and have thus "signed" the social contract that made of religion a matter of *individual* conscience.

Sealing this judgment, Réville asks rhetorically about the source of human strength. His reply is that it is not "social and religious collectivism," but "individuality which makes the man, which makes the man strong." Thus, what we most frequently read is not an elaborate analysis of the plight of the French Jewish *community*, but Réville's feeling for the plight of an *individual*, the all-important loss of dignity. He records again and again the offenses committed against elemental human dignity, one of the root values of the creed of individualism.[166] Albert Réville's pain at the "degradation" of the victim and his sympathy for the "*misérable*" both speak to the anguish of loss of human dignity. Heightening this mood, Réville plays on the formal ceremony of cashiering an officer and stripping him of his insignia—literally his "de-grading"—but also unmistakably of an individual's loss of value. Such powerful links between a military rite and the reduction of one's individual integrity come out graphically in the powerful images circulating in the illustrated media of the day, an image so powerful that it is repeated again and again: Dreyfus, stooped, round shouldered and humiliated, stripped of his honors before his triumphant and splendidly uniformed executioner who, with a sharp blow, snaps Dreyfus's sword in two over his knee.

In his own way then, Albert Réville issues a judgment against the Maistrean, and thus intransigent and integral Catholic, visions of national expiation by means of judicial sacrifice of the innocent. When Réville considers transcendent Protestant values such as individual human dignity, Réville must refuse the civic sacrifice of a Dreyfus he feels to be innocent. In this little meditation of Albert Réville's, we have then seen emerge a pattern of individualist Protestant religious and political thinking, leavened, as we might expect, by a universal humanism, the result of liberal Protestant affiliations with Enlightenment religion of humanity.

"For Reasons of State"—An Old Story Retold

Part of what makes Albert Réville's opposition to the Maistrean theology of victimization and civic sacrifice so powerful is the way it reapplies deep historical structures and reinstalls ancient historical templates that we have unearthed in discussing the links between political absolutism and the theology of the Eucharist articulated by the "École Française de Spiritualité." There, we will recall that on the theological plane, a sacrificial and annihilationist conception of the Eucharist conformed, on the political plane, to an absolutist theory of monarchic government. In France, it is as if the same fundamental battles are periodically refought along the identical lines as they had been drawn hundreds of years before. Only the labels identifying the participants change. In Albert Réville's liberal Protestantism we therefore replay his own Calvinist[167] incipient republican skepticism of, if not downright opposition to, absolute monarchy—even though he was not opposed to constitutional monarchy. Along with resistance to the hierarchic ideal of absolute monarchy, as I have argued, was Calvinist opposition to the sacrificial theology of the Eucharist. Theories of Eucharist and government replicate one another, van Kley argues, because French monarchy from the late sixteenth century was "implicated in sacramental conceptions." The monarchy associated itself symbolically with the "consecrated host" and thus with a particular theology of the Eucharist as sacrifice.[168] The upshot of this identification is that the modern notion of "reasons of state" directly succeeds and continues the rule of divine right of kings or absolute monarchy. Both represent the "divinization" of politics.[169] Thus, although much changed with the Revolution, such as the transfer of sacrality from the monarchy and the body of the monarch to the people and the nation, the religious quality of these orders of sacrality did not.[170] The appeal to *raison d'état* to justify the sacrifice of the individual victim, Dreyfus, differs only in its mode of expression, not in its fundamental logic. By raising the people and nation to a level of sacrality above, in function and kind, that enjoyed by the absolute French monarchs,[171] the leaders of the Revolution gave new life to absolutism just when they thought they were eliminating it.

The Dreyfus Affair continues to fascinate us because it so well exemplifies the perennial crisis for the new liberal order created by the Revolution, or indeed for any liberal order. In the Dreyfus Affair, as Durkheim notably and brilliantly argued,[172] it is fundamentally contradictory for the Third Republic to compromise the dignity of the individual for *raisons d'état,* because the Revolution and the republic stand upon the value of the absolute dignity of the individual—or so Durkheim argued. As Durkheim put it in the heat of his polemics in the Dreyfus Affair,

> the liberalism of the eighteenth century which is, after all, what is basically at issue, is not simply an armchair theory, a philosophical construction. It has entered into the facts, it has penetrated our institutions and our customs, it has become part of our whole life, and if we really must rid ourselves of it, it is our entire moral organization that must be rebuilt at the same time.[173]

Albert Réville is doing no more than exposing this painful—and perhaps irresolvable—contradiction to the benefit of the accused. It remains a dilemma that liberals have had to face ever since.

FIGURE 1
Félix Vallotton,
"The Age of Paper"
(L'Age du Papier),
Cri de Paris, 23
January 1898.

FIGURE 2   Anonymous, "Republican Delights" (Délices républicaines), in John Grand-Carteret, *L'Affaire Dreyfus et l'image* (Paris: Flammarion, 1898), 265.

FIGURE 3
Henri-Gabriel Ibels, "A Lick of the Sponge"
(Le coup de l'éponge), *Légendes du siècle*
(Paris: Le Siècle, 1899).

FIGURE 4
Anonymous, "Dreyfus,
France and Christ"
(*Dreyfus, La France et
Le Christ*), *La Croix*,
7 November 1894.

FIGURE 5
Alfred Le Petit,
"The Golgotha
of a Traitor and
the Holy Women
Constantly Waiting
for the Resurrec-
tion of Judas" (*Le
Golgotha d'un traître
et les saintes femmes
attendent toujours
la résurrection de
Judas*), *Mon Droit*, 3
June 1899, in John
Grand-Carteret,
L'Affaire et l'image
(Paris: Le Siècle,
1899).

FIGURE 6
Lionel Royer, "The Degradation"
(La Dégradation), *Le Journal
Illustré*, 6 January 1895.

— Pere, une histoire!

FIGURE 7
Félix Vallotton, "Father, A Story!" (Pere, une histoire!) "Oh no, no. *I* was merely an artillery officer who had his career derailed by a tragic mistake. *That* Dreyfus, the symbol of Justice, *that* wasn't me. He was what the rest of you invented." (*Mais non, mais non. Je n'étais qu'un officier d'artillerie qu'une tragique erreur a empêché de suivre son chemin. Le Dreyfus symbole de la Justice, ce n'est pas moi, c'est vous autres qui avez créé ce Dreyfus-là.*), *Cri de Paris,* 1 October 1899.

FIGURE 8
F. G. Keronan, "The New Siamese Twins" (Les Nouveaux Fréres Siamois), *Le Père Peinard,* 30 October 1898.

FIGURE 9

J. Chanteclair, "Fruitless Soaping" (Savonnage infructueux), *La Libre parole illustrée*, 17 November 1894 (the caption reads: "Jews, for us French, only blood can take out a stain like that!!!" [*Juifs., chez nous, en France, le sang, seul lave une tache comme celle-la!!!*]).

FIGURE 10

Alfred Le Petit, "Rendition of a Tableau by Prud'hon: Justice and Vengeance Pursuing the Crime" (*Traduction du tableau de Prud'hon: La Justice et la Vengeance poursuivant le Crime*), *Mon Droit*, 13 May 1899, in John Grand-Carteret, *L'Affaire et l'image* (Paris: Le Siècle, 1899), 16.

FIGURE 11
Alfred Le Petit, "The Expiation??? by Bobb" (*L'Expiation??? par Bobb*), *La Silhouette*, 13 January 1895, in John Grand-Carteret, *L'Affaire et l'image* (Paris: Le Siècle, 1899), 3.

FIGURE 12
Montèqut, "He Usurped the Uniform of France" (*Il a usurpé l'uniforme français*), *Le Pèlerin*, 4 November 1894.

FIGURE 13
Pépin, "The New
Religion" (*La Nouvelle
Religion*), *Le Grelot*,
27 February 1898, in
John Grand-Carteret,
*L'Affaire Dreyfus et
l'image* (Paris: Flam-
marion, 1898), 113.

FIGURE 14
Montèqut, "He Has Dis-
honored the Uniform of
France" (Il a déshonoré
l'uniforme français),
Supplément au Pélerin,
18 November 1898.

FIGURE 15
Anonymous, "Dreyfus
Taking Leave of the Devil:
'Farewell Mr. Alfred, and
Pleasant Memories to My
Compadres, the Jesuits of
France'" (*Dreyfus Prenant
Congé du Diable: "Adieu,
Monsieur Alfred, bons
souvenirs à Compères les
jésuites de France"*), *El Hijo
del Ahuizote* (Mexico), in
John Grand-Carteret,
L'Affaire et l'image (Paris:
Le Siècle, 1898), 46.

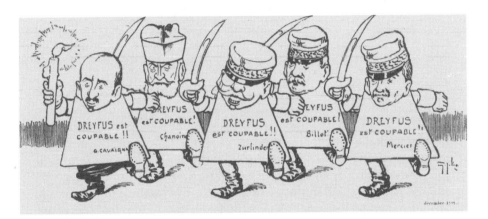

FIGURE 16   Julio, "And for Every Argument, the Sabre. Dedicated to the Five War Ministers" (*Et Pour Tout Argument Le Sabre. Dédié Aux Cinq Ministres De La Guerre*), *La Réforme* (Brussels), December 1895, in John Grand-Carteret, *L'Affaire et l'image* (Paris: Le Siècle, 1898), 31.

5

TARTUFFE, THE PROTESTANTS, AND REPUBLICAN SACRIFICE

The children have the feeling that I am giving them something of myself, and I am glad of it.

—Letter from an anonymous *instituteur* to Ferdinand Buisson[1]

Plus ça Change

I have argued that a distinct ideology of sacrifice developed in France in modern times primarily under the successive, not always continuous, efforts of Catholic thought. Key moments in the history of this sacrificial discourse can be found, for example, in the writings of such figures as Joseph de Maistre or among devotees of the Sacred Heart, the *École française de spiritualité*, and in the patriotic rhetoric of sacrifice for the nation articulated in the Enlightenment and French Revolution. Further, I have argued that this ideology or theology, as one would have it, set the terms of debates about sacrifice. In this sense, I am also saying that Roman Catholic thought (at least in its rightist forms) and its revolutionary transformations could be said to "own" or control the symbol of sacrifice during the late nineteenth and early twentieth centuries. It was from their formulations of the conception and meaning of sacrifice that the bulk of French people—whether folk or elite—took their point of departure in speaking and thinking of sacrifice thereafter.

This is not to say, however, that Catholic hegemony was never contested. As we have seen, Protestants took issue with Catholics in the late

132

Isn't Strenski now trying to do this?

nineteenth and early twentieth centuries in several venues. They exploited their prestige in the educational sectors of the Third Republic by trying to dominate academic teaching and writing about sacrifice, a notion at that time thought central to understanding religion. Comtean and Protestant, linguist and polymath, Raoul de la Grasserie, for example, was just such a one who challenged the prevailing theories of sacrifice of the time.

In 1900 at the prestigious first International Congress of the History of Religions in Paris, de la Grasserie delivered a major address, entitled "Du rôle social du sacrifice religieux."[2] In it, he addressed the question of why peoples in the past had sacrificed. Three reasons occurred to de la Grasserie. His investigations, not surprising for a man of his ideological persuasions, revealed to him a gradually progressive development in human cultural evolution toward this troublesome rite. At the first and lowest levels of civilization, the most rudimentary of peoples think that sacrifice nourishes the gods. In feeding the gods, people gain union with them and assuage divine anger. Second, advancing higher on the scale of civilization, people perform sacrifices in order to strengthen their own social cohesion or to restore the cosmos to proper running order. Third, and higher still, people sacrifice—in effect like Grasserie's Roman Catholic contemporaries—to expiate sin. Even though this sort of sacrifice remains "sacred butchery," it promotes a selfless attitude, which de la Grasserie concedes has some noble qualities to it. Fourth, at the loftiest level of human development, and once humanity has definitively forsaken these baser motives for doing sacrifice, de la Grasserie believed sacrifice expressed pure altruism of intention and purpose.[3] At best, sacrifice remained, for de la Grasserie, only "the kernel of social religion," and social religion would always stand below the "religion of the individual."[4] There, the proper forms of the religious life are prayer, asceticism, and ecstasy—the very stuff of the religiosity developed over the centuries by French Protestants, which stood in stark contrast to the sacramental ritualism of Catholics.

Although theoretical discussions of sacrifice like de la Grasserie's are not to be confused with orders to leap out of a trench in an "attaque à l'outrance," Catholic theology has had consequences for the formation of nationalist ideology, as I have argued in Chapters 2 and 3. In France surely, and in general arguably, religious ideas can inspire or (even retrospectively) legitimize social policies as readily as, if not more than, any other set of ideas. At the very least, they help us make sense of the practical courses of action people pursue by linking social policies with broader aspects of their worldviews, such as religious affiliation and belief. In the previous chapter's discussion of Albert Réville's literary intervention into

KEY

the Dreyfus Affair and Raoul Allier's meditations on sacrificial death in World War One, we saw how Protestants opposed political expressions of intransigent Catholic celebrations of sacrifice, no matter how nationalist they otherwise were. It is no accident, I argue, that the same men should also belong to a religious tradition that had been theologically set against the sacrificial Eucharist and the suffering Christ since the sixteenth century.

In this chapter, I wish to show that even in their attempts to *depart* from the Roman Catholic tradition of discourse about sacrifice, avowed Protestants, Free Thinkers, and anticlericals of the Third Republic reverted to most, if not all, Catholic structures. I shall argue that while Third Republic Protestants, Free Thinkers, and anticlericals strove to distance themselves from the intransigent Catholic position on sacrifice, they nonetheless were obliged by the logic of nationhood, to articulate their own conception of sacrifice, one that was more palatable to their religious commitments than that offered by the dominant Roman Catholic discourse. Ironically, this attempt to articulate and conceive sacrifice in behalf of an avowedly secular civic duty to the republic presented contradictions for the liberal Protestants. Thus, although, the Third Republic was itself called by its critics, "the revenge of the Reformation," its Protestant adherents installed—at another level and with new vigor—analogous conceptions of sacrifice to those devised by Catholic theologians and theorists of state. Thus, ironically, the Protestants repeated in their own way some of the sacrificial discourse which typified Catholic discourse on sacrifice, reaching all the way back to the language of sacred kingship and absolutism distinctive of Catholic apologists of the divine right of kings in the seventeenth century and carrying further to the anti-individualism of the Catholic integralists and intransigents of the late nineteenth and early twentieth centuries.[5] But compromise as they did with the more dominant discourses of sacrifice dominated by Catholic though, the French Protestants resisted to the very end the Catholic notion of sacrifice as annihilation of the individual. They totally rejected sacrifice as expiation or substitution, and emphatically rejected the desirability of the sacrifice of the innocent. But even in doing so, they were not always able to avoid—especially in the extreme conditions of warfare—embracing the symbols of sacrifice itself and echoing much of what the Catholics had insisted on centuries earlier.

The application of this old template might be used in part to explain, as I have argued in chapter 2, why the French fought World War One as they did. Despite great differences between clerical and anticlerical, monarchist and republican parties during the nationalist revival before World War One, virtually all parties (with the exception of Jean Jaurès)

They reached the point where they recognized submission as the only
means of survival. Their logic was right. The Brits never met these
circumstances

agreed about the need for unconditional sacrifice for the nation. It was
only after it became clear what sacrifice without limit meant—in terms of
its bleak, tragic, and futile results—that attitudes changed and the old
template fell apart.[6] The "defeatism" of France in World War Two and the
surrender, however delayed and disguised, of French national sovereignty
under Vichy showed dramatically how little the French could respond to
the once potent "high diction"[7] of sacrificial discourse, typical of the
rhetoric of World War One for all parties.

*Its about
reproduction
success, silly.*

Reformation, Eucharist, and Sacrifice

Readers may recall the judgment of an American observer of the French
religious scene in the early years of the twentieth century. The historian of
philosophy J. A. Gunn exaggerated a fact of religious life in France bearing on the arguments of this book. "We may note," Gunn reported, "and
this is important, that in France the only form of Christianity which holds
any sway is the Roman Catholic faith. Outside the Roman Church there is
no religious organization which is of much account."[8] Although commentators like Gunn implicitly discount French Protestants in the France
of the *fin-de-siècle*, the role of the French Protestants cannot be so cava-
lierly dismissed. This is especially so for the late nineteenth and early
twentieth century, particularly in fields like government and education,
which were influential in the formation of a national *morale*. There, the
influence of the meager Protestant minority was many times greater than
demography would lead one to expect. In fact, Protestant participation in
the political and academic debates about sacrifice, Eucharist, and the rest
were important in the cultural struggle being fought over the meaning of
sacrifice in the *fin-de-siècle*, especially as it impinged on the political sphere.

From my survey of the French royalist Catholicism of the *réaction* and
its successors, I have tried to demonstrate how in the late nineteenth and
early twentieth centuries, the sacrificial Eucharistic theology of French
Catholicism supported the anti-individualist, integrist political culture
created by it. In this chapter, we will see how leading Protestant scholars of
the study of religion, lodged primarily in the École Pratique des Hautes
Études, Fifth Section, well understood the political meaning of Catholic
theories or theologies of sacrifice. In response, the Protestants contested
these Catholics views of sacrifice. They sought both to delegitimate the
Catholic views of sacrifice as well as to set up alternatives of their own. As
we will see, Protestant thinking about sacrifice tried to associate the *denial*
of a Catholic sacrificial reading of the Eucharist with modes of political
culture *opposed* to the authoritarianism of integral Catholicism.[9] This sort
of thinking retraces familiar ground, but, as it were, treads in different

places. Consider first the classic and formative period of the Reformation of the sixteenth and seventeenth centuries.

Unlike the Catholics (even the "protestantizing" Jansenists),[10] French Protestants rejected a sacrificial theology of the Eucharist and its assertion of priestly ritualistic powers of consecration. Both aspects of the Catholic position on the Eucharist flew in the face of the Protestant view that *majesté* belonged to God alone. Christ's sacrifice on Calvary was sufficient unto human salvation, and no ritual Eucharistic celebration could hope to re-create it, any more than the human ritual performance of the Mass could hope to make holy what only God could sanctify. The power and authority attributed by the Catholics to the Church and its priests had natural political implications, which were amplified by the theology of sacrifice put forth by the "École Française de Spiritualité" with its emphasis on virtues like domination, submission, annihilation, and expiation. By contrast, although French Protestants were ready to reap the benefits of royal power and protection, we do not find in their policies any preference for royal absolutism, which later became so important for Catholic thinkers. Instead, the Protestants seem to have sought to nurture a bourgeois republicanism and varieties of individualisms.[11]

Naturally enough, Calvin's positions against both the Eucharist as sacrifice and transubstantiation, as Dale Van Kley notes, were correlated with congruent political positions. Notably, Calvin criticized Catholic image worship, relics, and miracles not only from a theological perspective but notably as "politically subversive."[12] Thus, Calvin's anti-hierarchical views of the organization of Christianity were part and parcel of his rejection of the classic Catholic theology of Eucharistic sacrifice that we have examined.[13] Since its religious value was so identified with its political one, sacrifice was charged both positively and negatively with political and social value. For French Protestants thereafter, affirming an individualist political culture and bourgeois republicanism required the rejection of the importance of sacrificial interpretations of the Eucharist in their religious thought, and vice versa. For them, sacrifice diminished as a religious value not only because the Protestant communion rite was deliberately not conceived as such, but also because it was in terms of sacrifice that Catholic royalists conceived *both* the nature of Eucharist and the king. "The French monarchy," says Dale Van Kley, was "implicated in sacramental conceptions," indeed associated with the "consecrated host." This was played out symbolically insofar as the king's body was likened to Christ's and the physical, mortal person of the king symbolically identified with the Eucharist.[14]

In this regard, the Jansenists present us with an interesting comparative test case. At first, their example seems to contradict the associations between theologies of the Eucharist and political values that I have tried to maintain. Thus, the Jansenists enthusiastically affirmed the sacrificial nature of the Eucharist, along with the royalists, but at the same time tended toward both a political and religious "republicanism" or laicism like the Calvinists.[15] But, contrary to appearances, the Jansenists seem the proverbial exception that proves the rule. While it is assumed that a major issue dividing them from other Catholics of the time, especially the Jesuits, was the question of the *frequency* of communion, their Eucharistic spirituality altogether differed from those royalist advocates of the sacrificial annihilationism, the "École Française de Spiritualité." Instead of putting self-effacing sacrificial immolation at the center of the mortal person's relation to God, and despite their affirmation of the exclusive majesty of God, Jansenist spirituality of the Eucharist was governed by the ideal of charity and love: "Love God with your whole heart!" and "Everything in Christianity leads to love!" proclaims Arnaud, one of Port Royal's leading spiritual teachers.[16] Additional records of his views about appropriate attitudes toward the Eucharist further contrast with the negating theology of the "École Française de Spiritualité." Thus, Arnaud tells us in his discussion of the nature of Eucharistic spirituality that "the state of grace [is] conceived as the effective and enduring rule of charity in us."[17] Further, he tells us that "To be converted . . . is to live for God—that is to say—to live by charity."[18]

What the Jansenist case tells us is that *mere* acceptance of a sacrificial notion of the Eucharist does not in itself mechanically necessitate annihilationist spirituality or favor the affirmation of political absolutism. The Jansenists were religiously offended by royal absolutism's claims to rule by divine right because it assigned to the king the *"majesté"* proper to God alone or at least to God and his Church taken as a whole.[19] Divine right of kings in effect gave the monarch a direct line to God, minimizing in this way the mediating role of the Church and mystical body of Christ. This Jansenist spiritual "republicanism,"[20] so to speak, insisted on granting local parish clergy greater dignity within the church, thus tending toward what would become political and religious individualism—the doctrine that the human person was in itself sacred. Louis XIV' s view that the Jansenists constituted a "new form of Calvinism" may not therefore have been far from the mark.[21]

Tartuffe and the Return of the Huguenots in the Fin-de-Siècle

Recounting this history serves several purposes. Foremost among these for the present volume is showing how the theological positions and clusterings of religious and political ideas lived on into modern times. Neither Catholics nor Protestants would allow matters to die that were so formative of their identities. Events of the sixteenth and seventeenth centuries became paradigms or templates for interpreting the events of political and religious life well into the Third Republic. One of the leading liberal Protestant theologians and scholars of religion in the Third Republic, Jean Réville, explicitly reasserted the classic Calvinist position on the nature of the Eucharist, thus undercutting the Catholic assertions of the *École Française*. In a book on the historical origins of the Eucharist,[22] Jean Réville surveyed sacred literature of the first century and a half of Christian history. That normative literature, Réville discovered, flatly contradicted the sacrificial reading of the Eucharist given voice by leading theologians of the Catholic Golden Age, such as the Oratorian Charles de Condren,[23] to name only one of the leaders of the "École Française de Spiritualité." Jean Réville concluded in triumph that the "Eucharist is not presented in any document as a redemptive sacrifice—or indeed of any other kind of sacrifice—in which Christ would be the sacrificer or victim."[24] While in some documents, Réville concedes, the "Eucharistic act of sacrifice" tends to be likened to "the sacrificial meals of the pagans . . . or with the sacrifices of the covenant,"[25] these are not what God desires. Appropriating the authority of Justin Martyr, Réville notes that, in the eyes of this second-century Christian Church Father, only pagans and Jews offer these so-called material sacrifices.[26] By contrast, "the only sacrifices that Christians might offer to God are of the spiritual order."[27]

It is not at all clear that the political implications of Jean Réville's scholarship reached very far or that they were avidly appropriated for political use. But given the tense, intertwined political and religious situation of the *fin-de-siècle*, such attempts to discredit political positions by debunking theological positions were not often made explicitly. In fact, one of the most potent attacks on the integral Roman Catholic politico-religious position of the *fin-de-siècle* was made under the guise of ideologically neutral historical writing. Here, I refer to the Protestant Raoul Allier's series of books on the history of various chapters of the Compagnie du Saint Sacrement, one of the main agents of sacrificial Eucharistic thought and devotion in the seventeenth century.

Before considering Allier's project, we must enter a caveat. In Allier's conception, the Compagnie du Saint Sacrement was a precursor to the kind of sacralized politics of "immanent" Catholicism, which the late nineteenth- and early twentieth-century Catholic right wing sought to establish in France. But recent scholarship has raised objections to this long-held view.[28] Yes, the Compagnie wished to transform France along the lines of their conception of Christian moral reform. But according to the French historian Alain Tallon the Compagnie did so unofficially, that is to say neither as an arm of the Church nor of the Crown. As an independent lay organization, the Compagnie sought to transform individuals according to Christian ideals, one by one. Only by changing individual hearts, could the Compagnie feel that they could effect large-scale Christianization of French society.[29] Thus, unlike the integral Catholics of the late nineteenth and early twentieth centuries, the Compagnie of the seventeenth century had no plan for changing the gross *structure* of French society and political culture. Nor, what is more to the point, did the Compagnie have a conception of what such a Christianized social structure would be. By contrast, those who went by the name of an "integral" Catholicism were well equipped with mythical models adapted from the middle ages ready to implement their desired structural transformations. Chief among these was the overthrow of republican government.[30] In light then of Tallon's work, Allier's histories of the Compagnie are thus best understood as weapons in a war of words, moves in a struggle between Catholics and Protestants over the meaning of institutions like the Compagnie. Allier's histories are not evenhanded treatments. Against this background, what propaganda points was Allier trying to make, and what is their significance for the arguments of this book?

Allier's point of departure is clever. To most French Catholics of his day devotion to the blessed sacrament, the reserved Eucharist, would seem the purest of private religious affairs. Indeed, much of its spirit derives from the great movement to withdrawn religious devotion typical of the Counter-Reformation. Surely nothing political could be linked with a religious practice carried out typically in the meditative silence of a side chapel before the reserved sacrament? Yet we also know that in a time of intense religious and political struggle that we should hardly expect that the Compagnie, as one of the chief agents of the *réaction* to the Reformation, was innocent of religious politics even if acting as independent agents. In late nineteenth and early twentieth-century France, a period as charged with religious politics as the seventeenth century, the enthusiastic republican, liberal Protestant Raoul Allier was unapologetically partisan in his attacks on the Compagnie du Saint Sacrement. He referred to the Compagnie as the *"Cabale des Dévots"* to expose what he felt was its grotesque attitudes of militant anti-Protestantism, broad religious repression, violence and cruelty, typical of a "cabal" of pious religious partisans hiding behind a public image of innocent piety. To Protestants and other religious dissenters, the rigorism of the Compagnie no doubt seemed to threaten the wholesale regulation of religious and moral life. Although the Compagnie never officially or publicly sought the revocation of the Edict of Nantes, partly because, as Tallon has argued, it operated outside both official state and ecclesiastical structures, Allier claims that it worked secretly to undermine the Edict or erode its protections. Allier claims that the Compagnie influenced judges to interpret the Edict to limit concessions to Protestants and among the Parlements to oppose any possible Protestant infringements.[31] In this and other things, Allier may well have the balance of truth on his side, since other scholars have argued that it was the constant pressure such as the Compagnie brought to bear over the years that finally provoked the crisis which eventuated in the revocation in 1685.[32] Whatever may actually be true of the role of the Compagnie in these affairs, the tragic history of Protestantism in France and the threats to the republic issuing from integral Catholic sources made it impossible for Allier to speak kindly of the Compagnie. Just how much this is so can be seen in his indictment of the activities of the Compagnie in the provinces—notably contested by Tallon.[33] Allier says:

> One thing is certain. The Compagnie du Saint-Sacrement had developed its sacred espionage in tandem with its organization of charitable works. The distribution of alms served to make the souls of the wretched more receptive to Catholic preaching; suffering would have tended to put them off. But the Compagnie did not only afford a way of indoctrinating the poor with catechism using the lure of a piece of bread, they made it possible to invade the lives of the needy—to ferret out all their secrets, to learn about the skeletons in their closets, to track all their bad thoughts. Thus, the Cabal developed spiritual police operations. . . . The official administration organized professionals who merely sought to make a living in this occupation. The Compagnie du Saint-Sacrement had fanatical agents, among whom, doubtless, were some who gave birth to and enhanced the love of art, but who, above all, loved souls ferociously, and in their zeal to save them were utterly unscrupulous about the methods they employed. Sanctified by the purity of their intentions, [they committed] what their simple consciences would have otherwise called dirty tricks.[34]

Worse even than this is the willing part Allier claims the Compagnie played in the violent repression of religious dissent. Allier thus records the enthusiastic role of the Compagnie du Saint-Sacrement in punishing various categories of religious offenders, even though Tallon has argued that these cases occurred rarely.[35] In one of its pamphlets from 1655 against blasphemy, the Compagnie noted that

> "This [offense] merits nothing less than temporal fire, pending the eternal fire which they cannot avoid so long as they persist in this miserable condition." The Compagnie took seriously its duty to re-

store the peace of souls. It had a particular horror of "public blasphemers," and craved their punishment by any means "so that they
would serve as an example." The joy of the Compagnie was great
when it had avenged the honor of God.[36]

The critical point to be appreciated in Allier's charges, is how they reflect his conviction of perceived kinship of spirituality existing between
the Compagnie itself, a Eucharistic society, and the type of theology of the
sacrificial Eucharist exemplified by the Oratorian theologians and Joseph
de Maistre. It is not hard to understand why Allier should associate the
two. We know, for example, that for some years it was "incontestable" that
this sacrificial Eucharistic theology and certain social formations were
closely related to each other.[37] Père Charles de Condren, the second "general" of the Oratory was, for example, one of the Compagnie's founders
along with the Duc du Ventadour. Jean-Jacques Olier, his successor, followed Condren's example and worked diligently to introduce the Compagnie to the members of the Oratory.[38] From our survey of Roman
Catholic theories of sacrifice, as articulated in theologies of the Eucharist,
I have argued that these annihilationist theologies of Eucharistic sacrifice
ought to be seen as theological counterparts to theories of political absolutism reigning in the France of the later (perhaps *dévot*[39]) Louis XIV.[40] I
say this despite the fact that Louis XIV suppressed the Compagnie in
1660 and indeed that the Compagnie as an independent lay movement
stood in considerable tension with both the desire of the Church and
State to control everything.[41]

Allier's treatment of the Compagnie du Saint Sacrement then brings
out two points. First, the social character of the Compagnie conforms well
with its theological pedigree. The Compagnie gladly embraced the annihilationist ideal of holiness learned from the "École Française de Spiritualité."[42] I would suggest that this willingness to make the annihilation of
the self, even if done in the interest of mystical union with God, weakens
any potential sense of the integrity of individual. Thus, we ought not be
surprised that the Compagnie was authoritarian in social matters, if not
absolutist, because the devaluing of individual choices and rights fit well
with the spirit of a sacrificial Eucharistic theology of annihilation.[43] As
profound devotees to the monarchy, for example, the Compagnie had a
horror of republican inclinations of the day, such as they were.[44] The
Compagnie ranked the king and the pope at the highest levels of dignity
and authority,[45] never contesting ecclesiastical authority or for that matter the authority of the Crown.[46] The individual conscience seemed to
have little integrity in such a scheme.

On the other side, Tallon cautions us to recognize that the Compagnie conditioned its understanding of both ecclesiastical and royal authority by expecting that representatives of both powers would adhere to their sacred duties. The Compagnie, despite its unreserved loyalty to the Crown, also believed that kings could go bad too—although this would not sanction regicide in their view.[47] King Louis XIII, the Compagnie thought, showed by example what their model good king could be. He would rule by the principle that the eternal salvation of his people is the first law of the realm. To Louis XIII, this meant purging the realm of prostitutes, mountebanks, and blasphemers, but also Jews, actors and feminine vanity![48] The end result of these attempts by the Compagnie, in effect, to preserve its independence and to stress its primary loyalty to God himself was, Tallon claims, to have resisted the absolutism typical of the age. From Allier's point of view, such distinctions failed to produce significant differences; either way the world desired by the Compagnie was authoritarian, if not absolutist in the strict sense of the term. The individual still stands submissive to authoritarian superior powers of a hybrid religious and political kind, and in effect accepts annihilation, albeit in God, as its highest goal.

Second, Allier's treatment of the Compagnie made it an object of study at exactly the same time as the Third Republic (and therefore its Protestant adherents) came under attack by the integral Catholics we met earlier.[49] In the minds of liberal Protestant republicans, the Compagnie, the Eucharistic theology it represented, and the attendant anti-individualist ideology of the Catholic *réaction* came to form a set of symbolic equivalences bearing the same meaning. They thus gave voice to their bourgeois social ideology of individualism by attacking either (or both) the Compagnie and/or the Eucharistic theology related to it. In doing so, the Protestants felt that they could reaffirm the wisdom of their antisacrificial theology of the Eucharist by pointing out its political consequences in such social formations as the Compagnie. In the *fin-de-siècle*, Allier's histories of the "Compagnie du Saint Sacrement" were then, in effect, liberal Protestant republican counterparts to Catholic attempts to rally its forces around devotion to the Sacred Heart and all this cult represented in terms of the authoritarian, nationalist politics of the Catholic integralism.[50]

One will recall that in 1873, the National Assembly voted to build the Basilique de Sacré Coeur as an offering of national humility and repentance after the defeat to Prussia of 1871. But in 1874, Albert Réville took pains explicitly to attack the revival of the cult of the Sacred Heart—what he called "this great *humbug*." He indicted ritual devotion to the Sacred Heart wholesale. This could be traced back to its inception in the ecstatic devotions of Marguerite Marie Alacocque, who herself had been in league with the Compagnie.[51] To Albert Réville, devotion to the sacred heart was nothing more than another example of the way in which Catholics "need to make use of religious forms, as if they were indispensable receptacles of the divine reality."[52] To Albert Réville and those like him favoring the separation of State and Church, this charge not only indicted ritual religious practice. It made a political statement against the kind of identification of the French nation with Roman Catholicism, which the Catholic integrists of Albert Réville's time labored to achieve. Thus, in their theological talk about sacrifice and in the institutions that fostered its elaboration and practice, both French Catholics and Protestants knew quite well that they were also engaging in a kind of politics of the sacred by contesting various key symbols.

Albert Réville, Aztec Sacrifice, and Labor Unions

For Réville, the illiberal political formations that the Catholic right wing promised could not be separated from a species of sacrificial religiosity, which in fact gave those political practices and institutions their legitimacy. Both the practice of ritual sacrifice and the illiberal politics that Albert Réville hated were, for him, aspects of the same integral Roman Catholic religious politics that he fought throughout his life.[53] Thus, public policy in an enlightened republic must reject both the political and religious expressions of what is in effect the same reality. It must reject sacrificial thinking emanating from the writings of someone like Joseph de Maistre and his latter-day followers as well as Roman Catholic doctrines of Eucharist as sacrifice, since both held sacrifice up as an ideal worthy of pursuit and emulation. For a son of the Reformation like Albert Réville, Catholic attitudes to sacrifice as, say, expiation should be rejected out of hand as ritualistic superstitions—as magic. Rituals had no power to remove sin or the effects of sin. So building churches like the Basilique de Sacré Coeur had no effect at all on the collective state of sin of the French people. Part of being a Protestant meant rejecting the divine or cosmic efficacy of (necessarily human) ritual action. Believing so was the worse sort of offense against the majesty of God, since He alone could remove sin or the effects of sin.

For Albert Réville, this condemnation of the Catholic belief in the power of ritual to expiate human sinfulness was necessarily part of a global attack on the prestige of ritual in human culture across the board. Not only Catholicism deserved censure for promoting the prestige of sacrifice. All ritualistic religions shared the blame for fostering superstitions. As an historian of religions, Albert Réville noted that, far from being an exclusive property of Roman Catholicism, sacrificial practice was very widespread among the religions of humanity. What might this historical depth and ethnological breadth mean? As an evolutionist Albert Réville was equipped to answer this puzzle: sacrificial religions were seriously defective in some deep way because they offended what all right thinking people knew to be essential human values. Albert Réville, as an evolutionist, felt that religions that practiced bloody sacrifice—especially human sacrifice—had not yet risen to the level at which they could grasp the, for him, highest principle of true religion—the belief in the sacredness and inviolability of the human person. All societies governed by such retrograde values must surely in the long run show themselves fatally inferior and thus vulnerable to conquest and extinction. But how to prove this to those who did not share his values?

In 1882, Albert Réville, seized an unusual occasion to deepen his sweeping indictment of ritual sacrifice and those societies that built upon it as a social value. He engaged in a little exercise in comparative study of religion to make a religious point that was just as certainly political in its implications. At the time professor of the Collège de France, Réville addressed the general assembly of the Société Protestant du Travail on the reasons for the victory of Cortez over the Aztecs. His speech was later published as "Fernand Cortez and the Real Causes of the Conquest of Mexico." Here Réville tried to show how a society centered around ritual sacrifice would inevitably produce a weak and vulnerable political system.[54] At first glance, this seems indeed an odd subject for an address to an audience of trade unionists! But Réville was no academic prig; he knew how odd this topic would at first sound to his audience of red-blooded workers. He prepared them for what he had to say[55] by appealing to memories of France's defeat by Prussia in 1871, which was still fresh in mind. For Réville, the Aztec defeat by Cortez mirrored France's defeat by Prussia. The Aztecs fell to the Spaniards because sacrifice had weakened the national fibre of the Aztecs. By the same token, if sacrifice became as central to French religious consciousness as it had been to the Aztecs, it too would weaken the French body politic in equal measure.

Réville saw in the Aztec nation a historical example of autocracy, with its "first principle" being ritual sacrifice.[56] Thus, as if anticipating Joseph de Maistre from afar, Aztec sacrificial religion was in effect a politics of absolute submission to authority. Far from signaling the ferocious vigor some have seen in de Maistre's writings, the dominance of the sacrificial spirit revealed a weakness in the Aztec nation, which smoothed the way for Cortez's campaign. Aztec society operated on the principle of mindless submission of subjects to authority. By means of such a principle, subjects went cheerfully off to their sacrificial deaths. Further, when it came time to defend the realm, they fell for Cortez's claims of superiority, because they did not think critically. In a flurry of republican rhetoric, Réville ended by symbolically linking the authoritarian aristocracy of his own France to the top-heavy Aztec aristocracy, which had demanded ever more sacrifices. But if French workers refused to submit blindly to authority and instead asserted their independence, then France could win back what it had lost. The Germans should not imagine that just because they defeated a badly led French army that "the warrior power of France" had been extinguished.[57] Were the future of the nation entrusted to the hands of freedom-loving workers, France's fortunes would be assured.

Réville's abhorrence of ritual sacrifice seemed then to arise out of his collective historical memory of French political and religious history, from the formative Protestant opposition to the ideology of ritual sacrifice embedded in the annihilationist sacrificial Eucharistic Catholic ideology of the seventeenth century—and the fatal politics of the Revocation with which it was connected. So, it should not be surprising that Réville gave ritual sacrifice, even in distant Aztec society, a contemporary political application, which he damned in the process.

The New Protestant Ethic of Civic Sacrifice

I have been arguing all along that even though Catholic attitudes toward sacrifice were for all intents and purposes rejected by the secular or non-Catholic republicans, even opponents were, in many ways still held captive by these ways of thinking. Comte's positivist religion of humanity, for instance, promised that altruism would generally increase in proportion as his new religion of humanity grew.[58] The flow of events seemed to vindicate this prophecy. Especially after 1870, the Free Thinkers or laïcs turned increasingly nationalist and humanist. As they did, so also did their anticlerical allies among the Protestants. Partly under the sway of Michelet's writings, the humanists forged a vision of the French nation as a special embodiment of humanity. As such, the nation, standing as it did for humanity, became a worthy object of civic sacrifice. So fervent was this nationalist and humanist piety that adherents of this religion of humanity were the virtual equals of integral Catholics in their affirmation of the ideal of civic sacrifice, or altruism. They urged a spirit of collective solidarity based on "humanitarian ardour" and "mutual love."[59] The Free Thinkers or laïcs were also strengthened by movements derived from Henri de Saint-Simon and the early pantheists and socialists who succumbed to his influence.[60] All this aided the articulation of a republican political theory and a moral theology of civic sacrifice virtually indistinguishable—except for its Maistrean excesses—from what the Catholic rightists. This whole discourse on sacrifice was produced out of what

CHAPTER FIVE

Georges Goyau called the "subconscious Christianity [which] . . . still survives in the soul of France, and which incites it to sacrifice."[61]

I shall conclude by arguing that the weight of history inclined non-Catholics to assume an essentially Catholic theory of sacrifice and in addition the exigencies of life inside the nation-state called forth its own "religion." *Raison d'état* is simply the rule of modern nationalism, no matter how "secular that nation may believe itself to be. And, as I have argued, *raison d'état* is finally a religious principle, a baseline of the nation-state's belief in its own absolute right to exist and to do what needs to be done to further its own interests. Once Protestants in France found places for themselves within the Third Republic, once the nation became in a way "theirs," they were caught in a conflict pitting their native individualism against the exigencies of *raison d'état*. I shall devote the final part of this chapter to Protestant intellectual strategies for resolving this dilemma.

What (Protestant) Sacrifice Means: Hamelin's Death

An incident that captures the spirit of French "secular" feelings about sacrificial morality is the death of the Protestant rationalist philosopher, Octave Hamelin.[62] One illustrative reaction to that death comes from a close colleague of many years, none other than Émile Durkheim himself. As the story goes, Hamelin had drowned at the seaside in an attempt to save two young women, by some reports his nieces—even though reports also have it that Hamelin did not swim. Shortly thereafter, an obituary for Hamelin appeared in *Le Temps*. Durkheim was so unhappy with it that he protested directly to the editors. In effect, Durkheim said that Hamelin deserved far more than the "summary mention" he had received from *Le Temps*. Hamelin had been slighted, and much more was to be made of the death of the philosopher. Later in 1907, Durkheim volunteered his own tribute to Hamelin in the Paris daily to set the record straight.[63] In it, Durkheim, invokes the rhetoric of constructive sacrifice and heroism. Hamelin died nobly, said Durkheim, since he died a *sacrificial* "victim." Not only was the greatest living philosophical heir of Renouvier a "great mind," he "was at the same time a great soul: he died in sacrificing himself [en se dévouant] for others."[64] To Durkheim, this extraordinary act of heroism moreover exemplified the way Hamelin practiced and preached the conduct of everyday life—in selfless but meaningful, devotion to others.[65]

Significantly for someone devoted to pedagogy like Durkheim, the sociologist suggested that Hamelin's selfless death was consonant with the philosopher's selfless career in pedagogy. A moral point was to be made here. Durkheim recounted how Hamelin's scrupulous care for students prevented him from acquiring the professional peer recognition his academic achievements merited. Hamelin's masterpiece, *Essai sur les éléments principaux de la représentation,* lay unpublished for years while he attended to the teaching duties so favored by the spirit of the Third Republic's educational ideology. Durkheim noted finally that Hamelin's *"dévouement"* constituted a form of moral investment in creating an entire generation of philosophers—here perhaps thinking of his own efforts with the *L'Année sociologique.* Thus, mirroring his heroic attempts to save innocent lives, Hamelin also exemplified the new Republican civic morality of sacrifice in word and deed. As a devoted, self-sacrificing teacher of the young *and* a prophet of personalism, Hamelin also embodied the new republican civic morality informing the young teachers serving in *"instruction publique."*[66] Such a vocation afforded young French republicans a chance to combine their dedication to the development of the individual with the pursuit of collective goals requiring personal "sacrifice" for the welfare of the nation.

Schools for Republican Sacrifice: "Instruction Publique"

For us, Hamelin's death carries with it a surplus of meaning because he was first of all a teacher, imbued with the republican spirit of devoted service to secular public education, which informed the corps of *instituteurs.* He was secondly a successor to *the* philosopher of the Third Republic, Charles Renouvier, and thus a theoretician of civic morals in the highest academic circles. Let us then first consider how Hamelin's self-sacrificing and heroic death reflects the sacrificing spirit of the republic's corps of *instituteurs.*

Part of the Third Republic's commitment to education can be traced to the prominence of Protestants in the appropriate ministries of governments even before the inception of the republic. Official Protestant prominence in public mass education did not come into being until Louis Philippe's Protestant de facto prime minister, François Guizot, in effect, made it so in the universal free public schooling law of 1833.[67] Although limited, this law decreed "universal . . . free public elementary schools for those who could not afford to attend private institutions."[68] With the inception of the Third Republic, Protestant influence in educational reform quickened especially under the leadership of liberal Protestants like Jules Ferry, Félix Pécaut,[69] or Ferdinand Buisson, reinforcing among disgruntled Catholics the idea that the Third Republic was little more than "the revenge of the Reformation."[70] After 1870 and the beginnings of the nationalist revival, educational reform was given even further impetus by the perception that "Protestant" Prussia had beaten "Catholic" France. Renan, for example, spoke sternly of lessons the French needed to learn from the severe "Prussian schoolmaster."[71]

Competition with Germany stirred the French educational establishment to a new sense of dedication, resulting in the articulation of a concrete and practical ethic of sacrifice among the corps of *instituteurs*. Leaders in the field of education, such as Félix Pécaut and Ferdinand Buisson became models of a sensibility eagerly encouraging civic sacrifice for the Third Republic. For example, Pécaut administered the program of the women's École Normale Supérieure at Fontenay-aux-Roses, which he had conceived and created under Ferry's direction in 1880. Appealing to the historical memory of the Protestant-like Jansenist religious community crushed by Louis XIV, Fontenay was popularly known as the "'Port Royal of the Third Republic.'"[72] It was there that women were to be educated for a career of dedication to teaching. By contrast, Catholic education of women had been carried out in a system of convent schools and was still designed to maintain women in traditional domestic roles.

No one was more important, however, for articulating and inculcating notions of civic sacrifice in these prospective *instituteurs,* whether male or female, than Ferdinand Buisson.[73] From 1879 to 1896, Buisson directed primary education at the Ministry of Public Instruction, and was the "man most responsible for the practical implementation of the Ferry Laws."[74] He also articulated and conceived the rationale for a scheme of moral education from his chair at the Sorbonne, largely in terms of the ideal of civic sacrifice.[75] In 1902, Buisson was succeeded by Durkheim.[76] The language of sacrifice was entirely fitting with Buisson's conception of his role. Despite his republican free thinker convictions, he embraced a religious interpretation of the humanism that inspired his efforts in public education: "'it is by religion that it [religion] is irreligious'" said Buisson asserting his preferences for "'the interior God of the conscience'" over institutionalized religion.[77] In proposing a national morality for all school children, he saw the state as the "church of the multitude," which would replace traditional religions.[78] To him, traditional religion was only an infinitely extended form of this national lay morality, and thus only performed supplementary functions to it.[79] The lessons of religious propaganda were thus adapted by the secular Third Republic in pedagogy. The old pedagogical techniques of Roman Catholic catechism instruction were put to work by republican *instituteurs*. Students in secondary schools memorized appropriately patriotic answers to questions put to them in their *manuels scolaires:* "'For what reasons do those who died for France occupy so great and brilliant a place in the history and memory of men?'" asked one such stock query. "'Who are, in your opinion, the greatest martyrs for our *patrie*?'" asked another. In the army, officers were urged to develop "'in the heart of their men the great ideas of sacrifice and devotion to the *patrie*.'"[80] Ernest Lavisse, the influential Sorbonne historian and author of textbooks whose sales numbered in the millions, is credited by Pierre Nora as being the "director of the national *conscience*" during the last decade of the nineteenth century and the first of the twentieth. He had an "incomparable place" in the formation of the national morality, Nora tells us.[81] In recapitulating the lessons of his twenty-six volume history of France, Lavisse concluded on a note celebrating the sacrificial: "The history of France culminates in heroism."[82]

It was through a corps of *instituteurs*, devoted to such an ethic of altruism and functioning accordingly as a lay priesthood that Buisson spread the word. As graduates of the École Normale Supérieure, they saw themselves as secular missionaries commissioned with the great task of displacing traditional religious belief with a new republican creed: "standing across the path to progress were superstition and violence. Rationalism, the philosophical basis of their anticlericalism, was the secular faith which they sought to spread through the educational system."[83] Buisson also commissioned and wrote textbooks that selected civic virtues for special attention. Conspicuous among these virtues was devotion to the republic and its ideals, in a word devotion to a veritable cult of civic sacrifice. Among the more touching tokens of these sentiments were the many letters sent back to the ministry by teachers stationed in the provinces, many attesting to the trials and hardships, but still in all, displaying their devotion as lay missionaries of the Third Republic.

A common theme was the rather modest economic status enjoyed by these educators, although they were comfortable by contrast to the peasants they served. In the eyes of respectful provincials, the *instituteur* was something of an aristocratic. In reality, however, they lacked the requisites of prestigious living. Teachers routinely took outside employment to make ends meet;[84] they were subject to clerical as well as local governmental abuses of authority. An *instituteur* in the Haute Loire reports:

> Monsieur the Mayor comes into the school as if it were his own house, or rather as if it were a barn, to drag the teacher off to the town hall, while the pupils dance in the classroom. Another day he sends the teacher to the next hamlet for an entire afternoon in order to help the tax collector, who is allotting the firewood in the forest. . . . A small farmer said to me one day in speaking of his son, "I should like to make a teacher out of him but for the fact that he would have to be everybody's dog."[85]

Frequently they suffered sacrifices of privation in being far from familiar surroundings: "Lost in the country, I felt so alone and so inexperienced that a great sadness filled my heart,"[86] an anonymous writer related.

Yet along with their chronicle of suffering, the *instituteurs* seemed conscious of their role in combating narrow selfishness and of the sense that they were spreading a spirit of civic sacrifice. A teacher from the Saône-et-Loire wrote:

> Let us note, therefore, without pride but at the same time, without foolish modesty, the part which this unobtrusive government employee takes in the work of social renovation, which is going on under our eyes and which tends more and more to replace narrow individualism by the principle of unity and the spirit of cooperation.[87]

The sacrificial spirit is likewise reflected in the anonymous words of another: "The children have the feeling that I am giving them something of myself, and I am glad of it."[88]

Now as far as the practice of sacrifice goes, the stories of these devoted souls show how clearly the republic's *instituteurs* saw themselves acting in a sacrificial drama. Absent the extravagance of Catholicism's baroque spirituality and its severe ideals of expiation and annihilation, the *instituteurs* seem every bit as self-sacrificing as a Condren or Alacoque. Alongside their lives of everyday sacrifice, we find republican thinkers assembling theoretical frameworks to accommodate and further rationalize civic sacrifice—but without embracing what they felt were the deficiencies of the Catholic efforts in this domain. It was as if the moral philosophers of the Third Republic needed to counterbalance the intellectual output of centuries of Catholic theological articulations of the sacrificial ideal. Philosophers like Octave Hamelin and Charles Renouvier (also "philosophers" like Émile Durkheim, as we will see) sought nothing less than to construct "counter-Catholic" philosophies of sacrifice. It is to these efforts that I wish now to turn.

Seeking the Mean: Renouvier's Republican Civic Theology

Renouvier offered the most durable attempt by a pious and thoughtful republican to reconcile the ideals of both self-interest and altruism, and thus *both* the tradition of republican and Protestant individualisms *and* the rationalistic religion of humanity that took form in revolutionary times. His civic ethic of sacrifice was consciously developed in relation to his own incipient Protestant theological reflections and the realities of national life at risk. Charles Renouvier thus reflects an attempt to reconcile Reformation theological judgments against the sacrificial nature of the Eucharist and Catholic theological annihilationism, which we met earlier, over against the needs of the nation for civic sacrifice and national cohesion.[89] Renouvier sought, in short, a formula that would allow him and those like him to break the monopoly that right-wing Catholics had over the control of the meaning of sacrifice.

Although relatively much is known about Renouvier the rationalist republican philosopher, little is appreciated of how he sought to enthrone the principles of reformed Christianity as he understood them in the heart of the Third Republic. Thus, he was at one time, like many of his peers, in the forefront of liberal Protestant *and* republican thought. To many of Charles Renouvier's peers, no real difference existed between the two. Thus, while neither dismissing the possibility of any nonreligious origins of revolution and republic, nor forgetting the religious roots of much that the revolution and republic stood for, it is only by taking the liberal Protestantism of Renouvier's thought seriously that one can comprehend him. The fact is that Renouvier was *both* republican and Protestant and that he at any rate saw the two as standing for the same values.

Known as a neo-Kantian or "neo-critical" philosopher, Charles Renouvier was commonly regarded as the official philosopher of the Third Republic;[90] at the same time, he was one of the most self-consciously "Protestant" thinkers of his generation,[91] although he is reputed not to have been received into the Eglise Réformé until 1873.[92] He was also personally affiliated with leaders of the Liberal movement, such as Albert Réville.[93] His weekly journal, *La Critique philosophique,* numbered such prominent liberal Protestants as Auguste Sabatier and William James among its contributors. In its pages, Renouvier argued that France could better solve its social and economic problems if the French would convert *en masse* to Protestantism![94] Renouvier tells us that his philosophical doctrine, "Criticism," was "'in philosophy what Protestantism is in religion.'"[95] A companion periodical, *La Critique religieuse,* gave Renouvier a platform for his more straightforwardly theological ambitions. He sponsored articles on topics such as Luther, the relation of free thought to liberal Protestantism, Vatican authoritarianism, the origins and future of religion, and so on.[96] Like many a French liberal Protestant, Renouvier was a hostile critic of the Vatican. And even going further than the Constitutional Church of the Revolution, he held up the rebellious image of Jesus, loyal to his own conscience, against the authoritarian spirit of lamblike obedience promoted by the Roman church. As such, he opposed the Church's role in education, and campaigned early (1879) for lay schooling.[97]

Renouvier's theology came straight from his liberal Protestant heart, being both intensely personalist and democratic. This theology required a limited deity, neither omniscient nor omnipotent. Gone was the picture of divine power and human insignificance that the Oratorian theologians like Olier advanced: "The deprivation that [a] . . . master of the interior life [such as Olier] preached implies 'a pessimistic judgment about human nature' about which a Free Thinker or "laïc" may be alarmed."[98] De Maistre's "'theocracy'" too was far from the ideals of democratic social life.[99] Likewise this anti-rationalist thinker posed further problems for Renouvier with his strong ultramontanism. De Maistre actually anticipated by sixty years what seemed to Renouvier the authoritarian doctrine of papal infallibility pronounced at the first Vatican council.[100]

Renouvier, on the other hand, emphasized the morality, freedom, and intrinsic value of both God and humans. Renouvier's God does not desire the annihilating sacrifice or self-sacrifice (recall Allier) of human beings to God. As a person himself, God respects the personality of every other person as if it were his own.[101] Striking another dissonant chord with the spiritual fathers of the integral Catholics was Renouvier's exposure of the affinity between the structures of one's theology and political ideology. Like Montesquieu, Renouvier felt that certain religious formations fit naturally with parallel political regimes. While Montesquieu thought Christianity, unlike Islam, hindered "despotic power" (bk. 24, chap. 3),[102] Renouvier made no such distinctions. He held that monotheism in religion favored monarchism—and absolutism—in politics, and vice versa. He favored instead a "republican" theology, rather than the absolutist sort we saw develop continuously from the *réaction* through de Maistre and in both the secular and Catholic integrisms of Durkheim's day. A republican theology would conform directly to religious humanism. Instead of developing a notion of a single world deity, surveying the universe like a monarch in splendid absolute isolation, Renouvier's theology is an anthropology. Centered on a doctrine of human "immortality, it is based on the belief in the value of human personality . . . on an energetic affirmation of personal liberty, mutual respect and liberty of faith."[103] Thus in the Protestant thought of Charles Renouvier, we see both individualist and altruist dimensions represented, both the traditions of French Protestantism characteristic of the periods before and after the French Revolution.

Renouvier's balanced embrace of altruism was refined to become a kind formula for reconciling self-interest and self-sacrifice. Here, it is well to recall that Renouvier had first been a Saint-Simonian altruist. Yet he eventually overcame what he later called his Saint-Simonian "'madness,'" and in doing so eschewed its extreme altruistic or self-sacrificing morality. His earlier flirtations with the Saint-Simonianism thus mellowed into a moderate altruism, a prudent love for others.[104] Accordingly, Renouvier rejected the annihilating ideal of an Absolute "Being" into which individuals are duty bound to dissolve themselves.[105] Renouvier recognized both individualism and our need to avoid being trapped within ourselves. As his formula put it, our duty to others is our first duty to ourselves, says Renouvier.[106]

Much of what Hamelin offers is already contained in Renouvier.[107] Hamelin, for example, embraced service to others, while disapproving of personal recklessness and absolute altruism.[108] "Duty toward oneself," argued Hamelin, is always subject to an appeal by a "better informed conscience"—namely one's own.[109] Hamelin accordingly noted with approval Renouvier's individualist view that the obligation of altruism is only incumbent upon the saint. Ordinary people are only expected to adhere to their obligations.[110] In the spirit of Renouvier and Hamelin, Durkheim also tries to balance egoism and altruism.[111] In the context of his discussion of mutual obligations of society and individual citizen, Durkheim declared that "in holding to his fellows and his group, a man should not sacrifice his individuality. And the agency on which this special responsibility lies is the State."[112] Further, Durkheim argued that altruism and egoism are "two concurrent and intimately intertwining aspects of all conscious life."[113] In these negotiations about the limits of individualism and altruism, thinkers like Renouvier, Hamelin, and Durkheim conformed to the larger national preoccupations of the day, which overrode their own various particular religious formations. In the words of William Bruneau, "The French required of their moral theorists that they keep the self-interest/altruism distinction clear and that they live between the two outlooks and move with the times."[114]

Even the Protestants

What is remarkable in the articulation of this civic morality of self-sacrifice, however modified, is its attractiveness even to Protestants. How was this possible, given traditional Protestant resistance to the ideal of self-effacing sacrifice? I am arguing that Protestant identification with the Third Republic and nation, and thus Protestant "hallowing" of the nation, is responsible for such an unexpected development. In hallowing the nation came, ironically enough, unintended identification with values once solely the mark of hated Catholic religious culture—the values of self-effacing sacrifice, once reserved for the discourse of absolutism, sacral king, and Eucharist.

With the rise of the Third Republic, and increased opportunities for Protestants, ambitious men increasingly wanted to take their places in the leadership of the national community.[115] More than any other religious grouping, the liberal Protestants dominated the creation of the Third Republic, perhaps justifying the widely held view that it was a work of "secularized liberal Protestantism."[116] Feeling this loyalty to the republic, feeling that they belonged to it and had a stake in its future, French liberal Protestants adopted or, as need arose, designed their own ideology of civic sacrifice.[117]

Both the new civic morality of the Protestant politicians and the epistemological innovations of the academics seemed to represent a new sense of confidence and security of French Protestants in the wake of the vindication of Dreyfus as the nation united for the coming war with Germany. Traditionally individualistic liberal Protestants thus drew closer to the altruistic pole of moral sensibility.[118] As we have seen, many liberal Protestant spokespersons of the period, such as Raoul Allier, supported patriotic sacrificial death in wartime, even if they did so with great difficulty.

But even though Protestant behavior may have changed, French Protestants were required by their new situation to have an *account* of how the sacred individual of traditional Protestant morality would fit into the new collective life organized around the Third Republic and the coming war with Germany. Thus, as the First World War drew closer and nationalist trends grew stronger, the need for legitimation of collective national political sacrifice increased accordingly. To this end, two strategies had to be pursued simultaneously. French Protestants had first at least to lower ideological barriers to a belief in nationalism—the belief in the sacredness of the national community. The greatest barrier to the embrace of the sacredness of the nation was of course the Protestant belief in the sacredness of the human individual. But French Protestants needed more than a reluctant acceptance of the need for national collective sacrifice; they needed a positive theology or ideology of civic *sacrifice* in behalf of the collectivity.

Prominent figures at the very heart of the Protestant community were troubled by these dilemmas. They felt, for example, that Protestants needed to develop an ideology of national sacrifice because Protestant individualism tended too often merely to be "jealous."[119] To these internal critics of the Protestant community, Protestant individualism tended to be little more than a form of "opportunism" which the nation could ill afford.[120] Writing as late as World War One, the celebrated liberal Protestant intellectual Paul Sabatier[121] complained that "Protestants cannot unify because of 'spiritual pride.' A Protestant only seems able to give himself up to his individual task. He isolates himself from the past and the present, and 'searches the Scriptures.'"[122] But, despite this individualist tendency of French Protestants, no less prestigious a figure than Liberal Protestant Maurice Vernes called for a uniquely Protestant ideology of sacrifice at the height of the nationalist fervor.[123] Vernes argued that Protestants needed to search their own religious heritage and reclaim a basis for a sacrificial ethic from it. A religious source of sacrificial values was required, because Vernes believed that secular thinking—so-called free thought—"was incapable of deriving an ethic of sacrifice from egalitarian altruism."[124] Nicely recapitulating this two-phased strategy, that most Protestant of Roman Catholics, Ernest Renan, similarly moved from a position before 1870 in which he decried the "'terrible harshness of the proceedings by which the ancient monarchial States obtained sacrifice of the individual'"[125] to a later view in which he defines the essence of the nation as the "'outcome of a long past of efforts, and sacrifices, and devotion.'"[126]

In this chapter, I have tried to show what the civic morality of the Third Republic's "Protestants" looked like, whether they be self-identified free thinkers or Protestants proper. I have also tried to show how, at least from the beginnings of the Third Republic, despite their deeply entrenched, theologically-grounded individualism,[127] even Protestants began to articulate an, albeit novel, moral theology of civic sacrifice, and with it, a justification of altruism close to that developed by Roman Catholics. Here, the Protestants joined the nationalist preoccupations of the day. The struggle for control over sacrifice had at last been joined, even if preliminary results were inconclusive.

6

DURKHEIM AND SOCIAL THOUGHT
BETWEEN ROME AND REFORM

Other Struggles, Other Venues

agency?

During the course of this book, I have tried to show how religious myths, symbols, and ideas conspired together with politics to produce national discourses and practices of sacrifice. I have argued that a certain Roman Catholic religious discourse about sacrifice—articulated first in the Counter-Reformation and renewed periodically since then in its more or less independent variants—can be seen to have informed a range of political and social policies and practices in the France of modern times. We have also seen how this discourse did not go unchallenged. In the late nineteenth and early twentieth centuries, it was engaged and contested, primarily by liberal Protestant theologians and some Third Republic free thinkers, with varying degrees of success. In this concluding chapter, I want to show how the dominant Catholic discourse was both contested and, to a degree, embraced by an unexpected, but somewhat more familiar, source—the Durkheimian sociology of religion.

Many readers will be familiar with the work of the founder of sociology in France, Émile Durkheim, and the school he assembled around himself. They may even know of his famous periodical, *L'Année sociologique* and the wide range of interests sponsored by this lively group of scholars. What needs to be noted about the activity of the Durkheimians is that they not only practiced sociology, as say Durkheim did on matters like suicide and division of labor, but that they cared very much about matters of social policy and the reform of French society. I want to show in particular how the Durkheimians, especially Henri Hubert and Marcel Mauss, contested Roman Catholic theological models of sacrifice at the level of academic social theory with important implications for civic morals and public policy. The efforts of Hubert and Mauss in the domain of sociology of religion attempted to change the way *fin-de-siècle* French people thought about the moral qualities of sacrifice; it was also part of a program of social policy aimed at influencing the French to embrace a new, distinctly non-Catholic ethic of sacrifice in daily life and in the great debates about national social policies of the day. In what some might see as a neo-religious move, the Durkheimians wanted to challenge Catholic civic morality by providing their own answers to the question of liberal social life—what does the individual owe to society? Does citizenship in a liberal democratic society require the total "giving up" of individual life and treasure, assumed by the intransigent Catholic view, which the Durkheimians opposed? Or does it only demand a sincere but prudent "giving of" the goods and lives of its citizens, closer to the Protestant and free thinker views of a Renouvier? How much, if any, sacrifice is required? And if so, what norm, what understanding of it, ought to rule? I shall argue in this final chapter that much of the Durkheimian view of ritual and civic sacrifice is only understandable as having been shaped within this contest over the normative understanding of sacrifice. Their view of sacrifice is understandable as an intervention into a polemic against the views of the intransigent French Catholics, and to a lesser extent the French Protestants as well.

In order to argue my case, I need to address a few preliminaries. Is it first of all reasonable to believe that Durkheimian social theory was written within the context of any sort of polemic with the religious communities of France? Were not Durkheim and his group just social "scientists," and thus neutral to local and national politics and religious viewpoints? Let me address these issues head on, first by considering the matter of the formation of social theorizing.

The Polemics of Social Theorizing

Although I think that social theorizing can and does often happen in and for itself within a creative intellectual space, it is also true that even academic social theorizing often occurs as part of a polemic with other theories—even if this is sometimes hard to tell. A new theory sometimes responds explicitly to another it seeks to overturn, replace or supplement. Thus, Weber's hermeneutic and idealist sociology arose in part to counter Marxist and materialist accounts of the place of religious affiliation in the rise of capitalism. Often as well, the real opponents of a rising theory may not be explicitly acknowledged, and thus hard to identify. The new theory is sometimes silent about its targets, often for polemical reasons. If the Hollywood maxim is true that there is no such thing as bad publicity, then perhaps identifying the target theory simply publicizes it, thus granting it more importance than it would otherwise have.

But there are also cases when the polemic of social thought spills over the walls of academe into society itself. Sometimes, the politics of a theory are not just academic, but external to the academic setting and public.[1] A new social theory may challenge a political or social ideology embedded in society itself, however implicitly. Sometimes social theorists become social critics, however unintentionally, largely because social theories often embody social values. In this light, it is surely not controversial to note that Durkheimian social thought in part affirmed the value of a socially conceived individualism, to take just one example.[2] By affirming a certain social value in this way, the new social theory may threaten to subvert some or all of the principles upon which a state or political power structure may rely. When this is the case, prudent social critics may seek camouflage; they may disguise the nature and target of the attack and the nature of the change proposed.

This scenario of concealing polemic targets for political reasons was, I believe, rather common practice by the Durkheimians.[3] Thus, although Durkheim was known for his antipathy for the Roman Catholic church, calling it on one occasion a "monstrosity,"[4] it is remarkable how little explicit criticism of the Church we find in Durkheim's writings. Although, for example, the Durkheimians shared the values of freedom of intellectual inquiry and a scientific approach to sacred texts advocated by Roman Catholic Modernists like Alfred Loisy, they never spoke in defense of Loisy's condemnation by the Vatican in the way even the Jewish liberal Salomon Reinach did.[5] On the other hand, the Durkheimians seldom spared Jews[6] and Protestants from direct, sometimes severe, even *ad hominem* criticism. In a major review for *L'Année sociologique,* Henri Hubert was not above deriding Reinach's *Orpheus* as a "pamphlet" and a work written for "women and young girls."[7] As for the leading Protestant scholars of their day, such as Auguste Sabatier, Mauss noted that his progressivist story of religious evolution is "broad and facile."[8] Going further, Mauss says of Sabatier's work that "It is a matter less of analyzing facts than of demonstrating the superiority of the Christian religion."[9] Why did the Durkheimians behave with what might seem to be uncharacteristic deference to the Catholics?

Part of the answer of this reluctance to attack the Catholics lies in the Durkheimian desire for self-preservation. Given the political realities of life in "Catholic France," diplomacy was a prudent necessity. It inclined the Durkheimians carefully to weigh their temptations to attack the Church. Unlike the relatively well-entrenched social position of Catholic theory, which was, as we have seen, embedded in long-standing French attitudes and backed by the powerful institutional formation of the Church, Durkheimian sociology was new, only then in the *fin-de-siècle* on the verge of becoming institutionalized. It was thus a relatively frail and vulnerable thing, subject to social and political pressures. In "Catholic France," open attack on the Church entailed material risks and possibly fatal confrontation. Thus, while Durkheim's credentials with the anticlerical party were impeccable, a public record of anticlericalism would only have stiffened Catholic resolve against his policies. Diplomacy had to govern the public attitude of the Durkheimians to the Church, if he wanted to succeed in seeing his policies implemented. Better to lie low.

In dialectic with their will to replace the Catholic teaching, and to disguise these intentions as well, one caveat should be entered, which complicates our appreciation of the Durkheimians as insincere anticlericals camouflaging their true feelings toward the Catholics. To wit, the Durkheimians actually admired Catholicism in some respects, as their distinctive attitude to sacrifice will reveal. Beyond just trying to maintain a facade of fair-minded and "scientific" evenhandedness towards the Catholics dictated by Durkheimian diplomacy and self-interest, the Durkheimians realized that they and the Catholics shared some vital central values. In education, for example, Durkheim generously credits the contribution made by the Catholic teaching orders in France's past.[10] He recognized Catholic Christianity as having contributed to the ideal of the sacredness of the human individual.[11] As Louis Dumont did decades later, Durkheim showed how Christianity contributed to the development of the idea of the individual.[12] Furthermore, Catholicism had retained and continued some of the primitive sources of social life and vitality, which the Durkheimians felt the nation needed. Referring explicitly to the Roman Catholic Mass, Hubert and Mauss say in *Sacrifice*, "By the same ritual processes *our priests* seek almost the same effects as our primitive ancestors."[13] "Scientific" historian that he was,[14] Henri Hubert chastised Reinach's *Orpheus* for neglecting the splendor of medieval Catholic art and philosophy, while emphasizing only the squalid facts of the Inquisition.[15] The facts are the facts, so to speak. And the good facts about Catholic Christianity are nonetheless facts, for all their being about Catholicism. Finally,

Durkheimian attitudes toward sacrifice reveal that the Durkheimians believed, along with the Joseph de Maistre and the intransigent Catholics, that sacrifice was, in some, yet-to-be articulated sense, necessary to the very existence of society: no sacrifice, no society. Hubert and Mauss's *Sacrifice* was the treatise in which the Durkheimians worked out this conviction, while trying to modify the "theory" of sacrifice assumed by the French Catholics. To return to a theme enunciated from the beginning of this book, the Durkheimians simply attempted to co-opt and transform the symbols of Catholic thinking for their own purposes.

Whatever the ultimate reasons, Durkheimian policy initiatives required diplomacy. These initiatives had to be cloaked in neutral garb, while at the same time holding fast to the reforms the Durkheimians wanted to make. For the Durkheimians, the historical basis of the French nation was in part informed by its Catholic past was therefore a thing to be *reformed* rather than effaced. This is especially true in the case of sacrifice. The Durkheimian theory of sacrifice is an example of diplomatic social theorizing, made primarily at the expense of what I have discussed throughout this book as the intransigent or right-wing Catholic theory or theology of sacrifice, replete with its various updatings. At the same time, the Durkheimian theory of sacrifice also takes its cues from the Catholic example, reshaping and reforming it without totally rejecting it. In either case, of course, the Catholic doctrine remains the point of departure even for a *soi-disant* secular and scientific theory.

Reforming the Reform

Many of the same reasons for Durkheimian diplomacy and positioning regarding the Catholics shaped Durkheimian polemics with the Protestants about sacrifice.[16] On the whole, we can see Durkheimian views of sacrifice as somewhat more socialized versions of the positions laid out by the Protestant philosophers, Charles Renouvier and Octave Hamelin. Their spirit, as we have seen, informed the sacrificial morality of the Third Republic's educational ideology as seen in the attitudes of its corps of *instituteurs*. Durkheim, as is well known, had always been close to the republican, disproportionately Protestant, educational leadership of the Third Republic ever since his appointment in Bordeaux and study tour of Germany in the 1880s.

Yet, in the interests of science over theology, the Durkheimians also sought to reform the positions on sacrifice laid down by other leading Protestant theological contemporaries. Durkheimians had good political reasons for engaging Catholic views about sacrifice, the Protestants, although a tiny 1½ percent of the French population, could not be ignored because of their dominance in the university and government ministries of education so important to the Durkheimians and to the formation of young minds throughout the nation. We have noted in connection with Mauss's reviews of Sabatier, a certain Durkheimian deference to Protestant power in academe. The Durkheimians sometimes withheld their criticism of the scholarship of liberal Protestant members of the Fifth Section, because doing so might conceivably have prejudiced the candidacies of Hubert and Mauss for chairs in the Section, where their radical reputations had already jeopardized their chances of appointment.[17]

Despite their sympathy for the liberal Protestantizing philosophical synthesis engineered for the civic morality of the Third Republic by Renouvier, the Durkheimians found the liberal Protestant theologians lacking the social sense in a way overdeveloped by the Catholics. Liberal Protestants made of the individual an abstract and isolated entity, while the Durkheimians felt that individuals are who they are in effect because of their embodiment of social norms. Therefore, unlike the Catholic annihilationist theology of sacrifice, Protestant thought reflected enduring commitment to the sacred value of individualism. As a result, Protestant attempts to encourage civic sacrifice were always offset by considerations for the sanctity of the individual. Their approach to the issue of civic sacrifice always had the look of compromise. Rather than the seamless self-abnegation of the Catholics, Protestant appeals to civic sacrifice reflected sometimes tortured attempts to balance their theological preferences for self-interest against the new political need for a theology of altruism. We saw signs of this conflicted thinking with Allier's agonizing treatment of the sacrifice of Isaac at the height of the First World War. Allier's meditations on the meaning of civic sacrifice in the war showed that individualism and self-interest did not exclusively rule the thought of French Protestants. No matter how reluctant, Allier did entertain the civic sacrifice of the *individual*—even including his own son. More conspicuously than the Catholics, who at least since the seventeenth century had made a place for a theological doctrine of sacrifice, the liberal Protestants agonized over reconciling ancient antisacrificial doctrines with the new dominance of an officially secular nation-state in which they fully participated. Hubert and Mauss's *Sacrifice* reflected the same condition of compromise between individualism and annihilating statism, not primarily because they were "influenced" by Renouvier—although they surely were—but because they and Renouvier reflected the same reaction to an identical existential situation. This meant in brief that like their philosophical comrades—the socially-minded Protestant thinkers, Charles Renouvier and Octave Hamelin—the Durkheimians would affirm the necessity of sacrifice, without trying to reduce it either to a psychological attitude or to a form of communion. Even more perhaps than Renouvier or Hamelin, the Durkheimians accepted stoically that society leveled real "costs" upon individuals, even if the Durkheimians eschewed the Catholic logic of sacrifice as expiation and the annihilationist "giving up" of the self that characterized it. Nevertheless, the Durkheimians advocated the need for individuals to "give of" themselves for the health and security of the society.

But the intransigent or right-wing Catholic theology of sacrifice takes on an unrecognized importance—even beyond what I have argued it already has within French political and religious history.[18] It is the principal target of Durkheimian polemic in their theory of sacrifice. A theory of sacrifice written in France about so highly charged a religious notion as sacrifice could not possibly be understood by its audience or its interpreters without some reference to the prevailing sacrificial discourse of this dominant "intransigent" cultural milieu. I believe that we can better understand the Durkheimian theory of sacrifice by locating it with respect both to its semiotic opposition to the classic intransigent Roman Catholic view of sacrifice and to its place in advancing Durkheimian social policy in the Third Republic. It is an unidentified target of the Durkheimian theory of sacrifice; it is the silent partner in a contest for control over the symbolism of sacrifice in the France of the *fin-de-siècle*. I believe therefore that the Durkheimians not only sought to contest academic theories of sacrifice, but also wished to reshape social ideologies of sacrifice embedded in concrete French social arrangements and moral discourse. I am arguing that it was in part to address the cultural hegemony of the Catholic theory of sacrifice that Durkheimian social thought shaped its own theory of sacrifice as it did. The Durkheimian theory of sacrifice trafficked both in elite academic discourse and in practical social and political discourse.

Hubert and Mauss's "Sacrifice" at the Center

I have referred continually to "Durkheim's" theory of sacrifice and at other times to "Durkheimian" theory of sacrifice. It is time to remove this potential source of confusion by speaking directly to the issue. Is there a difference? And how does this affect how we proceed at this point?

Clearly, "Durkheim's" theory of sacrifice is that which we can attribute to the great founder of sociology in France, Émile Durkheim (1854–1917), as found in his 1912 classic, *Elementary Forms of the Religious Life*. When I speak of "Durkheimian" theory of sacrifice, I mean that theory of sacrifice developed by the consensus of the group of co-workers Durkheim gathered about him in Paris to edit and contribute to the *L'Année sociologique* from about 1897 until his death in 1917. In fact, when it comes to sacrifice, by "Durkheimian," I mean none other than Henri Hubert and Marcel Mauss. In 1898, they published a short monograph, *Sacrifice: Its Nature and Functions,* which in effect articulates what I believe to be "the" Durkheimian theory of sacrifice.[19]

But things are not all so simple when we come to the scholarship of the entire Durkheimian circle, the great man himself included. Thus, while we know that Durkheim, Hubert, and Mauss worked in the most extreme conditions of collaboration, and that it is quite impossible definitely to separate out the ownership of individual ideas in any exclusive manner, still a conventional demarcation can be made on the basis of the authorship of their works. Thus, although Hubert and Mauss contributed much to Durkheim's classic *Elementary Forms of the Religious Life,* I conventionally call it "Durkheim's" book; by the same token, although Hubert and Mauss most certainly learned their sociological approach to religion from Durkheim, and although their classic, *Sacrifice: Its Nature and Functions* conveys just the sort of sociological sensibility taught by Durkheim, for convention's sake, I refer to the book as "Durkheimian"—as authored by the Durkheimians, Henri Hubert and Marcel Mauss.

Now, this distinction bears directly upon how we understand what "the" Durkheimian consensus about the nature of sacrifice was. I have argued elsewhere that the classic statement of this Durkheimian consensus is not to be found in Durkheim's *Elementary Forms of the Religious Life* at all, but rather in the little monograph published by two of Durkheim's closest confederates, Henri Hubert and Marcel Mauss's *Sacrifice: Its Nature and Functions.*[20] In brief, my argument is that Durkheim's fullest statement of his theory of sacrifice is really what Hubert and Mauss concluded in *Sacrifice: Its Nature and Functions* more than a decade before the publication of *Elementary Forms of the Religious Life.* Durkheim, in fact, conceded points made by Hubert and Mauss—a case which was at odds with an earlier view of Durkheim's taken over from William Robertson Smith.[21] What then was this consensus Durkheimian view?

Hubert and Mauss's "Sacrifice: Its Nature and Functions"

In 1898, Henri Hubert and Marcel Mauss published their study of less than a hundred pages, "Essai sur la nature et la fonction du sacrifice" (hereafter *Sacrifice*). No museum piece, Hubert and Mauss's effort still remains fresh, says Louis Dumont, while, by contrast, Frazer's masterpiece, *The Golden Bough,* whose second edition appeared only two years before *Sacrifice,* is today thoroughly antiquated.[22] Even its critics concede that *Sacrifice* was a "major contribution and without doubt decisive on most points."[23] *Sacrifice* thus continues to be the single most influential book

- the arguments abt altruism boil down for religion ets to issues 1) self-sacrifice, which diverts attention away fr. ritual sacrifice (of anyone other than self)

CHAPTER SIX

ever written on sacrifice, if not the required point of departure for almost every subsequent theoretical effort in the field.[24]

Published at the head of the second volume of *L'Année sociologique* as the second of the two "Mémoires originaux," Hubert and Mauss's *Sacrifice* appeared in the distinguished company of Durkheim's own classic "Concerning the Definition of Religious Phenomena." Durkheim argued that religion is the "germ" from which all of social life grows,[25] while sacrifice mysteriously sustains society and makes it possible. Although the origins of literature, the arts, and morality are to be found in religion, the religious origins of morality were to be found in sacrifice.[26] Thus, "family relations," said Durkheim in 1898, "started by being an essentially religious bond; punishment, contract, gift, homage are derived from the expiatory, contractual, communal, noble *sacrifice.*"[27] Even more impressive, Durkheim maintained this view of the relation of morality to sacrifice right to the last years of his of his life. In 1914, he said that "There is no moral act that does not imply a sacrifice, for, as Kant has shown, the law of duty cannot be obeyed without humiliating our individual, or, as he calls it, our "empirical" sensitivity."[28] Few notions could therefore claim importance in the Durkheimian scheme of priorities comparable to that assigned to sacrifice and developed into a Durkheimian consensus statement about what sacrifice meant to them.

"Let's Go! I Love a Fight!"

Recently discovered evidence affirms that, like some other sensitive Durkheimian studies, Hubert and Mauss's *Sacrifice: Its Nature and Functions* was one of those camouflaged subversive pieces in the culture war of which I spoke at the outset of this chapter; it intended to upset both right-wing Catholic values as well as to challenge the individualism of the French Protestants. Here, we are privileged to have a "smoking gun," that reveals the subversive intentions of Hubert and Mauss in producing social theory that trafficked in matters of social policy and civic values.

In their private correspondence, Durkheim's closest confederates, Henri Hubert and Marcel Mauss, revealed an arrogant contempt for their opposites in the camps of the traditional religions. In a tone of determined, if cloaked, combat, Hubert wrote Mauss in 1898 that he relished the mischief their "polemics" on sacrifice would spread among the religious powers of the day:

> We shouldn't miss a chance to make trouble for these good, but badly informed, souls. Let's stress the direction of our work, let's be clear about our aims so that they are pointed, sharp like razors, and

so that they are treacherous. Let's go! I love a fight! That's what excites us![29]

Thus, Hubert spoke not only for himself but also for Marcel Mauss, his lifelong companion in scholarly collaboration. He gave voice to the vigor and flair of two twenty-six-year-old, intensely patriotic, Dreyfusard, humanist, philosemitic, socialist, rationalist, somewhat anticlerical, iconoclast, historicist, scientific, upstart intellectuals. Hubert and Mauss were fully conscious of the effect they wished to achieve, even though they camouflaged their intentions and never revealed their scheme publicly.

However diplomatic they tried to be, such zeal did not pass unnoticed among Hubert and Mauss's Catholic contemporaries. In its day, Hubert and Mauss's *Sacrifice* was recognized for its radical departures from the conventions of scholarship. The otherwise friendly liberals in the Catholic scholarly community chided Hubert and Mauss for their brash dogmatism, for imagining that they could gather the entire phenomenon of sacrifice under their theoretical cloaks. These "good, but badly informed, souls," in Hubert's memorable words, saw *Sacrifice* as little more than a Durkheimian theology of sacrifice—"a kind of *philosophy* of sacrificial ritual."[30] It pretended to be "*the* theory of sacrifice, but is [only] *one* of the theories which explain certain aspects of sacrifices in certain circumstances of time and place."[31] They were right.

Being Excused from Annihilation and Expiation

Let me therefore consider certain salient points in the Catholic theological ideology of sacrifice and see how the Durkheimian polemic matches up. We will recall from our earlier discussion that the intransigent Catholic position could be reduced to two major points and as we will see, a series of complementary points. The major points were first that sacrifice was assumed by the Catholics to be total *self*-sacrificial annihilation and that this annihilation was believed to effect the cosmic consequences of an expiation for human sin.

Take first of all the matter of the status of the individual. In wholeheartedly rallying to civic sacrifice such as we saw in Catholic attitudes to death in warfare, the intransigent Catholics took up the annihilationist position. Where were the Durkheimians? While approving of civic sacrifice, and thus in some part taking the side of the Catholic right wing, Hubert and Mauss were clear about qualifying the limits of sacrifice. In *Sacrifice: Its Nature and Functions,* they conceived a relationship of the individual to the group that in serious measure opposed the legacy of the Oratory and de Maistre. As if proposing a theory of sacrifice tailor-made for members of the liberal individualist bourgeoisie to which they belonged, Hubert and Mauss argued for the norm of prudence when it came to sacrifice. "Giving *of*" the self, rather than "giving *up*" the self was their rule.

This is a theory of substitutionary sacrifice.

> In any sacrifice there is an act of abnegation since the sacrificer deprives himself and gives. . . . But this abnegation and submission are not without their selfish aspect. The sacrificer gives up something of himself but does not give up himself. Prudently, he sets himself aside. This is because if he gives, it is partly to receive. Thus sacrifice shows itself in a dual light; it is a useful act and it is an obligation. Disinterestedness is mingled with self-interest.[32]

Unlike Roman Catholic theorists, Hubert and Mauss excuse human beings from the *duty* of self-immolation to any social body, whether church or, in principle, even the state. This relief from the demands of sacrifice as articulated by the intransigent Catholics shows how well, for example, the Durkheimians continue the line of thought developed by their like-minded "Protestant" mentors and colleagues, Renouvier and Hamelin.[33] The civic sacrifice expected of the ordinary citizen was a "giving *of*" oneself, not a total "giving *up*" of oneself.

Hubert and Mauss felt that this conclusion was justified because it rested on excellent ethnographic and historical religious grounds. For them, the source of the intransigent Catholic annihilationist argument is the death of Jesus. As Jesus lived and died, so also should Christians. But Hubert and Mauss rejected making the example of Jesus' self-annihilating sacrifice a fit model for the sacrifice expected of citizens. The main reason Hubert and Mauss held this view was that they believed that the evidence of history indicated that Jesus' death was modeled on the so-called sacrifice of the god from Frazer. In all such sacrifices, Jesus included, the god is sacrificed—rather than a lesser victim—because only the god can provide a necessarily perfect sacrifice. Only a god can give up himself without self-interest corrupting the act. Only a god can give up himself in perfect purity of intention and execution. That is the secret buried deep within Christianity accounting for the reason so innocent and lovely a being as Jesus (to Christians at any rate) not only *was* sacrificed, but also *necessarily must* be the only perfect victim acceptable to a transcendent almighty god.

Kantian

Now this logic notwithstanding, Hubert and Mauss noted that the empirical historical record shows that these sacrifices were altogether rare and exceptional, indeed perhaps totally imaginary. Perfect sacrifices in religious documents the world over, the sacrifice of the god for instance, first of all, occur very infrequently. Hubert and Mauss argue this because these supposed epitomes of sacrifice, as exemplified by the sacrifice of

The thing to bear in mind is that the "sacrifice" of Jesus is anti-sacrificial, the death to end sacrifice, the ritual to end ritual.

the god like Jesus, never actually happen. Although the death of Jesus, for example, is held up as an ideal of self-sacrifice, in reality Jesus was literally the subject of judicial execution, not a ritual sacrifice. His death on Calvary was *interpreted* by Christians *as* a sacrifice, even if in fact it was not a literal sacrifice such as, for example, the temple sacrifices in Jerusalem of Jesus' day. The sacrificial death of Jesus is, in Durkheimian terms, a *représentation* of an ideal. Rather, the sacrifice of the god is a mythologicly projected ideal of what perfect sacrifice might be—sacrifice completely free of self-interest or calculation typical of human efforts.[34] The sacrifice of the god—even if that god be Jesus—cannot therefore be an "elementary form" of the institution of sacrifice in either ritual or civic senses. Sacrifices of the god therefore cannot be typical or normative sacrifices and thus cannot be the model humans would *normally* be expected to follow in their own behavior in real life. More typical of human religious history—and thus better candidates for being an "elementary form" of sacrifice—were the vast number of sacrifices requiring a mediating victim to intervene to *protect* the sacrificer, to save the bourgeois individuality of the persons giving "*of* themselves." Proper bourgeois individuals do not "give *up* themselves."[35]

In a second part of their implicit attack on the intransigent Catholic view of sacrifice, Hubert and Mauss challenge the would-be prestige of expiatory sacrifice. Taking down de Maistre and (Bonald as well) with a single blow, Hubert and Mauss note that simply on empirical grounds alone "expiation" does not mark "a real type of sacrifice."[36] It is not clearly separable from other forms of sacrifice, and as such "cannot thus form the basis for a general and rigorous classification of sacrifices."[37] To be sure expiation may be a factor in sacrifice, but it is not for Hubert and Mauss its center. Thus, the intransigent Catholic view of sacrifice as total self-sacrificing annihilation and expiation does not find support as typical of the data of sacrifice available in ethnographic and historical literature. The Catholic view, then, needs to be decentered and placed into the wider context of sacrifice the world over, where it can be seen as exceptional, rather than normative.

Sacrifice, a Machine for Making Jesus Holy

An indication of how thoroughly the Durkheimians sought to displace Catholic notions of sacrifice may be seen in how they rooted out even the implications or complementary points that flow from their central arguments against the Catholics. For instance, beyond opposing the antihumanist implications of the intransigent Catholic theology of self-annihilating sacrifice, Hubert and Mauss also tackled Catholic Christological claims directly. In the judgment of Hubert and Mauss, Catholics are mistaken about the status of sanctity in sacrifice. The pre-existent, already sacred, divine *logos* does not, as it were, "parachute" into history trailing holiness behind him. The *rite* of sacrifice—itself a social act—begins the process of consecration—as the name *"sacri-ficium"* (literally, "to make holy") itself implies. Thus, in classic Durkheimian sociological style, society, as embodied here in a ritual, itself manufactures the holiness of beings. The social act of ritual makes "gods" of them and/or sustains the gods in their divinity. Far from conceiving of sacrifice as some "saving event" intruding from afar into history, Hubert and Mauss propose that they have discovered an elementary mechanism of sacrificial ritual and that this mechanism converts what was profane into something now sacred.[38] The intention of Hubert and Mauss was to assert that this social consecrational structure underlay not only sacrifice among the primitives, but also the Roman Eucharist itself. The heart of Catholic ritual piety, like the religious rites of all our contemporaries, has built upon ancient pagan "models,"[39] they state. It arises from social causes, because ritual is itself social. Jesus becomes holy as a result of being assimilated to the social act of ritual in which the holiness of a victim is achieved through the power of the group gathered in ritual action.

The Durkheimians observed, for example, that Jesus' judicial execution becomes a sacrifice by being assimilated to the sacrifice of the Paschal Lamb. But it is the sacrifice of the Paschal Lamb in the Passover rituals conducted by the collectivity of the Jewish temple priesthood that makes the lamb holy and thus Jesus into the "lamb of God."[40] As Hubert and Mauss see it, the lamb becomes sacred in the first place as victim in an actual "objective," self-interested and practical agrarian sacrifice of the kind so well described in the ethnographic and historical literature. In Israel prior to Jesus, "not only was the life of the firstborn among men redeemed by the blood of the paschal lamb, but every Hebrew was also freed from danger."[41] Now, this sacrifice rendered the lamb indeed literally godly, precisely because as a victim in an institutional sacrificial act, it had been "consecrated." But in the period of the rise of Christianity, the mythological imagination of Christian theologians took up the old Jewish image of the sacrificed lamb and "represented" Jesus' execution and death in the metaphors and images of the Paschal Lamb. "Sacrifice has furnished the elements of divine symbolism."[42]

But there is a twist. Implicitly taking aim at the Roman Catholics, Hubert and Mauss say that Jesus' death becomes a "sacrifice," and indeed "a sacrifice of the god," because as a victim in a ritual sacrifice—the Paschal Lamb—he had already been *made sacred* by the social act of a ritual sacrifice. While not holy by *nature,* Jesus is a god when he ascends the mythological altar of sacrifice on Calvary, because in being associated with the "lamb of god" he has been identified with a fully *consecrated* being, that is to say, one *made sacred* because *sacri-ficed* in a ritual. The mythological and religious imagination in effect recognizes this by dealing with Jesus' death as a sacrifice of the god. Thus, as an ideal being, his suffering and sacrificial death can be themselves the ideal of selflessness that the sacrifice of the god is supposed to embody.

Flying in the face of monotheistic beliefs about divine eternity and omnipotence, Hubert and Mauss have in fact argued that sacrifice is *prior* to the god, not, as it were, the other (i.e., generally Christian orthodox) way around. Indeed sacrifice as a social act makes and sustains god.[43] Against claims to Christian exclusiveness, about which Hubert and Mauss are certainly disingenuously silent in the text, they argue that the Roman Catholic Eucharist is built upon ancient pagan "models."[44] It shares the same sacrificial mechanism as found in religions around the world.[45] Similarly, a supposedly exclusive Catholic theological dogma, such as the "real presence" of Jesus in the Eucharist, likewise turns up widely in non-Christian religious traditions of sacrifice. There too, the deceased god once more becomes present in the world after his ritual death.[46]

Hubert and Mauss between Altruism and Self-Interest

In large measure, Durkheim, as well as Hubert and Mauss in *Sacrifice,* repeat much of Renouvier's formulae for reconciling individuals and society. Although usually seen solely as extreme collectivists, the Durkheimians really did eagerly seek to "save" the integrity of the individual, as we have seen in their polemic against the right-wing Catholics. In their treatment of sacrifice, Hubert and Mauss spoke of the necessity of citizens "giving *of*" themselves in behalf of the welfare of the community—but never of "giving *up*" the individual person. Hubert and Mauss's *Sacrifice* moves to the same rhythm of balancing self-interested tendencies against their own conception of an altruistic position, as did other individualists.

Put more abstractly, Durkheim accepted that in practical terms, altruism or perfect civic self-sacrifice—like the sacrifice of the god—is an "ideal," and thus something "that we may approach indefinitely without ever realizing."[47] When we try to live it in reality, says Durkheim, self-sacrificing altruism thus throws up an "antinomy" between the "joy" of release from egoism together with the "pain" of the real loss of pleasure— an "antinomy . . . so deep and so radical that it can never be completely resolved."[48] Thus, Durkheim never quite surrendered his altruism—if we restrict our view to the ideal level—even if he does force the *ideal* of altruism to cohabit with the practical reality and desirability of concrete individuality.

Such a tactic of resistance to extreme views on altruism became even clearer later in Durkheim's life. It confirmed anew Durkheim's sympathy with Renouvier's feeling that altruism and individualism are mutually interdependent "two concurrent and intimately intertwining aspects of all conscious life."[49] Although Renouvier felt altruism was an ideal, like Durkheim, he felt it was difficult to realize in reality. Thus self-sacrifice was the stuff of sanctity; obligation better fit the life of the citizen.[50] Renouvier also undercut the egocentrism of the Kantian principle of duty by allowing no "radical difference between the duty toward oneself and towards others."[51] Yet in the end, he remained an ethical individualist, because he granted the individual human person priority over the claims of others: one needs a self, so to speak, in order to give up oneself.[52] Thus, like Renouvier, Durkheim tried to resist dichotomizing altruism and egoism.[53]

These sentiments of an interplay between the ideal and real worked out in the moral sacrifices of Hamelin, Mauss, and their spiritual kin are repeated in Hubert and Mauss's positive evaluations of *ritual* sacrifice in *Sacrifice: Its Nature and Functions.*

> In any sacrifice there is an act of abnegation since the sacrificer deprives himself and gives. . . . But this abnegation and submission are not without their selfish aspect. The sacrificer gives up something of himself but does not give up himself. Prudently, he sets himself aside. This is because if he gives, it is partly to receive. Thus sacrifice shows itself in a dual light; it is a useful act and it is an obligation. Disinterestedness is mingled with self-interest.[54]

In *Sacrifice*, Hubert and Mauss seem to have taken over Renouvier's view completely, while adding things of their own. Thus, Renouvier's thought, and with it the thought of the Durkheimians, represents an effort to strike a balance between a kind of individualism represented by the liberal Protestants and some free thinkers, on the side of an extreme individualism, against powerful trends of pantheist thought emanating from free thought as well as the anti-individualist annihilationist trends of Roman Catholic theology. In this case, Renouvier represents what we might call a "Protestantizing" of philosophical rationalism or critical idealism. Renouvier and the Durkheimians succeeded in articulating a concept of the individual that sought to avoid both individualism and pantheism, both egoism and altruism.

In contrast to the radical annihilationist teachings of the reactionary Catholics, Hubert and Mauss's *Sacrifice* resisted calls for the effacement of the self—even in face of national calls for heroism. In civic matters, they took a moderate path, urging good citizens to "give of" themselves, but without "giving up" themselves. Duty, in effect, not sanctity, was the normal moral course for humanity. In the domain of ritual, Hubert and Mauss likewise evidence an homologous moderation in their treatment of the sacrifice of the god.[55] No such thing really ever existed—another way of denying the reality of altruism, of saying that people never completely "give themselves up." For Hubert and Mauss, such images as gods pouring themselves out for their devotees are just that—images, ideals, but not records of actual behavior or duties laid upon ordinary people.[56] Thus, Hubert and Mauss's *Sacrifice* assumed their commitment to a variant of philosophical personalism or individualism. Hubert and Mauss's position amounted to an attempt to resist the extreme nationalist propaganda of the day, a propaganda aimed at instilling the uncritical ideal of altruism in the French, while at the same time admitting the validity of sacrificial civic morals.

Therefore, unlike Catholic annihilationist theology of sacrifice, both Durkheimian and Protestant thought reflected enduring commitment to individualism. As a result, their attempts to encourage civic sacrifice were always balanced by doubtless liberal or "bourgeois" considerations for the sanctity of the individual.[57] Their approach to the issue of civic sacrifice always had the look of an "eclectic" compromise, because, like most Durkheimian thinking, it very literally was.[58] Rather than the seamless self-abnegation of the Catholics, Protestant and Durkheimian appeals to civic sacrifice reflected sometimes tortured attempts to balance their ideological or theological preferences for self-interest against the new political need for a theology of altruism. We saw signs of this conflicted thinking in Allier's agonizing treatment of the sacrifice of Isaac at the height of the First World War. Allier's meditations on the meaning of civic sacrifice in the war showed that individualism and self-interest did not exclusively rule the thought of French Protestants. No matter how reluctant, Allier entertained the validity of the civic sacrifice of the *individual*—even including his own son. More conspicuously than the Catholics, who at least since the seventeenth century had made a place for a theological doctrine of sacrifice, the Protestants twisted and turned to reconcile ancient anti-sacrificial doctrines with the new dominance of an officially secular nation-state, to which they were fully committed and which in some sense they directed. Hubert and Mauss's *Sacrifice* reflected the same condition of compromise between individualism and statism, not necessarily because they were "influenced" by Renouvier, although they most likely were, but because they and Renouvier reflected the same reaction to an identical existential situation.

Did It Make a Difference?

Often enough when we consider conflicts of ideas and symbols such as those I have discussed in the course of this book, we neglect to follow through and ask whether intellectual opposition to public policy implications eventuated in real differences of public policy. I have argued that Roman Catholic theology had such consequences. Did a challenge at the level of Durkheimian social theory correspond with one at the level of actual civic life? What, therefore, of the fate of Durkheimian (and for that matter, liberal Protestant) reluctance to affirm the extremes of sacrifice called for by Catholic sacrificial rhetoric?

At least for the Dreyfus Case, we have clear evidence of the radical differences in policy toward the condemned. Catholics, by and large called for condemnation[59] (in extreme cases even if Dreyfus were innocent!), while the liberal Protestants like Albert Réville along with the Durkheimians, called for acquittal and clemency on the grounds of the solemn rights of the individual. In the case of the Great War and the interests of nationalism, both Protestant and Durkheimian moderation seemed less sustainable. The extreme conditions of total war instead called forth a violent theology or ideology of sacrifice on the part of all parties. As the war went on, we have seen how even the Jews and Protestants adopted attitudes closer to those of the intransigent Catholics. The relentless pressures of a national crisis made it hard to resist the "'religion de la patrie.'"[60] We should also recall that leading liberal Protestant intellectuals of the day made explicit calls for a uniquely Protestant ideology of sacrifice at the height of the nationalist fervor.[61] Secular free thought was felt "incapable of deriving an ethic of sacrifice" from abstract philosophical sources.[62] Only a religious basis would do.

As for the Durkheimians, we know that Durkheim led great patriotic efforts during the War, wrote fiery pamphlets indicting German war ideology[63] and suffered the crushing loss of his only son in combat.[64] But Lukes claims that Durkheim's patriotism, like that of his ideological kin, Jean Jaurès, was furthermore nonexclusive and internationalist. As Lukes observes, Durkheim, like Jaurès, felt that "national loyalties are real and valuable, but they should not be exclusive and they should be extended in an internationalist direction."[65] Typical of Durkheim's often infuriating penchant for trying to steer a classically "eclectic" middle course between extremes, this internationalism did not prevent him from defending nationalism—especially when a greater evil attacked it. Thus, when revolutionary syndicalists like Hubert Lagardelle called for the destruction of nations as a preparation for founding a new and, in Lagardelle's mind, more perfect social order, Durkheim objected. Among other reasons, he accepted that if wars between nations were horrible, how much more so would be the massive disorder resulting from a total breakdown of the national system.[66]

Yet, in the nationalist vein, key followers of Durkheim in the all-important educational establishment of the Third Republic took what seemed a rather hard line in favor of extreme forms of civic sacrifice in contemporary society—at least in time of war. Writing in an explicitly Durkheimian manual of civic morals for budding school teachers, the authors begin by assigning education a primarily nationalist role: "The school is, *par excellence*, the agent of national feeling, the means by which a lively and healthy patriotism spreads abroad among us." One strand of feeling that the schools are supposed to inculcate in the citizenry is none other than sacrifice. The school should "recall the sublime sacrifices of those who died so that the *patrie* could live."[67] Indeed, sacrifice should pervade the entire life of a citizen so trained in the schools of the republic:

> Indeed, conforming to the needs of life today, the school should have improved the individual and, at the same time, it should have made him understand that his duty in normal times is to fashion the family which he establishes and which in turn cares for him. But in periods of crisis he should understand that he must devote himself to a reality which transcends him and which is the very condition of the existence of each and every individual—the *patrie*.[68]

What good then is a theory of sacrifice as "giving of" when as soon as war ensued, the second generation followers of the Durkheimians, at least, fell in with the intransigent Catholics and extreme nationalists in favoring one of "giving up" all for the fatherland? What difference did Durkheimian theoretical thinking make—especially thinking about public policy and civic morals?

Yet differences there were. Despite Durkheim's vigorous patriotic words and deeds, Lukes has argued that Durkheim was "not affected by war hysteria, nor, at all by the aggressive integral nationalism evident in the Catholic and conservative sectors of French opinion."[69] While hard evidence of explicit opposition to the intransigent Catholic war policies does not seem available from what has survived of Durkheim's papers, such a view is clearly what one would expect of so close an ideological kin to Jean Jaurès, the principal spokesperson for the policy of a defensive war. In this sense, Durkheim's explicit indictment of war ideology should shed light on this issue. There, in Durkheim's attacks upon the doctrines of Heinrich von Treitschke, the Prussian philosopher of war, one can make a case for what Durkheim's critique of intransigent Catholic war policy might have been—had he published one! To Treitschke, then.

It is remarkable that Durkheim isolates for criticism in the Prussian philosopher's view of war and sacrifice those very things that typify the "language" of civic sacrifice of the French intransigent Catholics, especially Joseph de Maistre. Durkheim, for instance, cites with disapproval Treitschke's glorification of war. Perhaps only a coincidence, but the Prussian Treitschke's worship of war and the warrior seem identical to the views of de Maistre. In France, as early as 1880, de Maistre was recognized by French liberals for representing the very same "admiration for war and the warrior—all those paradoxical theses which have not been easily maintained before the nineteenth century in France."[70] Again, although one does not quite know what to make of these likenesses, they continue to accumulate.

By contrast, for Durkheim and Jean Jaurès, war was a sometimes necessary, but always regrettable, act of the state. But, to Treitschke, says Durkheim, war was "moral and healthy."[71] Treitschke believed this for many reasons, Durkheim tells us: first, because he felt that war disciplines egoism. For him, egoism held the greatest danger to the state. In war, said Treitschke, egoism is submitted to the unqualified discipline of sacrifice. Unlike Durkheim, however, Treitschke did not distinguish egoism from "individualism."[72] War is the "supreme sacrifice," the "sacrifice of the self," in which we "surpass ourselves," this "Prussian de Maistre" says. "Peace, on the other hand, is the triumph of personal interest over the spirit of devotion and sacrifice, of the mediocre and vulgar over the noble . . . the reign of materialism."[73] By contrast, Durkheim argued that even in wartime, persons are not required to "sacrifice" their "individuality."[74] Durkheim argued this, because like his neoliberal ideological kin, Charles Renouvier and Octave Hamelin, he believed that the individual, not the nation, is the highest point of social evolution.[75] We will recall that, despite their neo-Hegelian reworkings of Kant, Renouvier and Hamelin held that the end development of their version of an Hegelian "world spirit" was the Person, not the State.[76] Durkheim and most of his "team," especially Hubert and Mauss, despite their collectivist reputations, remained resolutely bourgeois and liberal as to the ultimate value of the human individual. Although the Durkheimians always believed the individual to be socially embodied and indebted, they always kept at arm's length the more extreme collectivism of the intransigent and integrist Roman Catholic right and radical Marxist left.

What Then Can Be Learned?

What can be learned about the struggle to control the meaning of symbols, such as sacrifice, from the efforts of the Durkheimians battling away in the hallowed halls of academe? Can so rarified and academic a discourse really counter the deeply entrenched, pervasive, and taken-for-granted ideal of sacrifice championed and exploited by almost all sectors of French political life?

For one thing, the Durkheimians well understood that so deeply-rooted and culturally formed a symbol as sacrifice, with its roots in the great seventeenth century of France and its glory, could not be simply thought away. Their ideas needed institutional embodiment. Thus, the Durkheimian effort to control the teaching of civic morals in the schools formed an essential part of their work on sacrifice. What theories they may have concocted would take on concrete form only by being institutionally embodied. The Durkheimians understood this well, as can be seen in their persistent efforts to gain and maintain influence in public education. The *instituteur* of the Third Republic was after all regarded as a kind of lay priest and the *institutrice* as a lay nun. Thus, the future teachers trained by the Durkheimians constituted a kind of new clergy issuing forth from those virtual "seminaries"—the *écoles normales*—which the Durkheimians sought with some degree of success, for at least some while, to influence the domain of civic morals. At best, the transformation of French social morals along Durkheimian lines would take time, if not generations. Durkheim, at least, seemed prepared for a long struggle as he eschewed revolution and moved slowly but deliberately into areas like public instruction.

But, what about the theory? How could it gain plausibility against a deeply entrenched and taken-for-granted viewpoint that most people imbibed with their mother's milk? Here, I think two lessons are to be learned, although these lessons did little in terms to change how we think about sacrifice, even today. The first is to maintain the label "sacrifice" while radically converting its meaning. Thus, while Hubert and Mauss described "sacrifice" as a prudent "giving of" the self, I accept on anecdotal evidence that most people these days (and surely the intransigent Catholics of Durkheim's time), still prefer to think about sacrifice as the sterner act of a total "giving up."

But just changing the meaning of a word without changing its reference will have little effect for changing how people will think about sacrifice. Hubert and Mauss had to show and argue that their definition of sacrifice as "giving of" had empirical grounds sturdier than those of their opponents. Hubert and Mauss had justified their more moderate standard of sacrifice by their arguments concerning the sacrifice of the god. To them, this sacrifice in which everything was given up was so rare a case in the history of religions that it could not serve as a paradigm for sacrifice in general. Far more numerous were the limited sacrifices in which a victim was placed between the persons offering or sponsoring the sacrifice specifically in order that the sponsors or sacrificers would *not* have to offer themselves! Good as such an argument might be, it does not seem to have carried the conceptual day.

It is not clear to me why the Durkheimians failed to change the way we think about sacrifice, especially since their development of the notion of "gift" has provoked radical rethinking in the academic and policy communities.[77] The most prominent recent installment in the theory of sacrifice, the work of René Girard constitutes a moral rejection of the work of Hubert and Mauss—ironically, all the while citing it with approval![78] Girard seeks to save the victim and indict those who would substitute another to protect themselves; Hubert and Mauss want instead to show the good sense of the person offering the victim, how sensible it is to save oneself by offering another in sacrifice.

The reorientation of thinking about sacrifice achieved by Hubert and Mauss arguably remains a brilliant redirection of the extreme collectivism of Roman Catholic thinking, even as someone like Girard must touch the conscience of anyone following in their footsteps. Nevertheless, the mysteries of the more extreme conceptions of sacrifice as a dark self-annihilating "giving up" of everything still draw enthusiastic devotees. Perhaps, the radical intransigent Catholics really hit upon something after all? Perhaps, despite Hubert and Mauss's tidy bourgeois attempt to manage forms of religious exchange like sacrifice, the undomesticated side of human nature remains unaddressed, much as de Maistre argued. Doubtless, this is at least one reason some of the new generation of thinkers, whom Hubert and Mauss themselves trained, veered so sharply away from what I have called their bourgeois theory of sacrifice as a prudent "giving of."

Here, I have in mind extreme thinkers like Georges Bataille. Far from shunning the perversity of sacrifice as unbridled self-destruction and violence, Bataille revels in it. Taking cues from Sade, "cruelty," essential at least to the ritual act of animal sacrifice, is for Bataille a virtue.[79] All this trafficking in the extremism of total giving serves the goal of transcending our bourgeois humanist natures and ascending to the sacred.[80] Bataille, for example, offered to institute human sacrifice in the midst of one of Paris's busiest intersections, the Place de la Concorde. The violence of sacrifice was a kind of "good" evil, which for Bataille and the others made up the essence of sacrifice and the heart of religion: it shattered the safe and self-assured plane of the profane. Bataille thus seeks to bring out the cognitive value of sacrifice: it is for him primarily a way of transcending bourgeois individualist consciousness. In witnessing bloody sacrifice, we should throw ourselves open to the transgressive power of violence; we should feel anguish, so that we can really know death.[81] Sacrifice in this sense is a "limited experience of death"—the very annihilation delicious to the seventeenth-century Oratorians—and one that in the same way is transcendentally pleasurable because it allows us to escape the human order of mundane experience.[82]

Yet, if the Durkheimians failed to capture the vagrant imagination of religious consciousness so seductively recaptured by Bataille, it was not for lack of trying. In their efforts in moral education, they at least had some limited success in forming the bourgeois institutions and ethic of their own time. But having noted this success, it is also just as clear that they were not appreciated for their efforts. Who, for example, would reinstate the Durkheimian program of civic ethics and moral education? In France and elsewhere, if we can judge by the outpouring of writing on sacrifice and ritual violence, the embrace of the dark gods is not easily resisted.

Religion and Nation

That liberals like the Durkheimians essentially embraced sacrifice, even as they tried to make it compatible with their belief in the sacredness of the individual, should make one pause. What are the implications of taking such positions on sacrifice for a normative view of social arrangements? Briefly, seeing how sacrifice was urged and then contested perhaps shows us how easily we can get caught on the horns of what I take to be an impossible dilemma, characteristic of modern times. Those who begin as liberals and seek to preserve the individual from the predations of the collectivity, say, in the form of civic sacrifice in the armed forces, must at some point face the need for collective action and a common life. This, I believe, is what the extreme liberal Protestants of France found out not long after they had assumed positions of power and responsibility in the Third Republic. Much about their theological nurture taught the French Protestants that the height of human being was achieved in an assertion of individuality such as expressed, for example, in the freedom and inviolability of the human conscience or in the ideal of the fullest development of the human individual, which they eagerly embraced along with the Enlightenment.

Yet how long can such values remain pure and uncompromised? Particularly in times of general civic crisis, even the most enthusiastic proponent of self-interest will admit that individuals do not and cannot live in isolation. Simply to insure the survival of their cherished liberal values and all the fruits of civil society, liberal Protestants, in this case, had to insure that these values would become general and would become part of the legally enforceable norms of a republican French collectivity. In the extreme case of war, soldiers ironically had to sacrifice their individual lives to protect the collective values that were enshrined in the belief in the sacredness of the human individual. And even in the routine course of political and public life, individual self-interest would need to be constrained for the purposes of national policy, such as in the need for taxation of incomes or wealth. How then do we justify "sacrificing" the fruits of self-interest in a society that exalts precisely that value?

Those, on the other hand, who begin as standard-bearers for collective life face the opposite set of dilemmas. At some point, they must likewise realize that the strength of collectivities depends in significant part on the integrity of individuals. Even in the extreme case of war—the one event in which collective needs always seem to trump individual self-interest—is an army staffed by human automata, in which individual initiative has no role to play, really likely to perform better than a somewhat decentralized, improvisational, individually motivated fighting team in which all soldiers know that their efforts and welfare are valued? Would the national collectivity really be stronger, as the intransigent Catholic anti-Dreyfusards would have us believe, if the collective "face" of the army and nation were saved by sacrificing a Jewish artillery officer and denying an embarrassing *"erreur judiciare"*? Or does persistence in pursuing a policy of sacrificing Dreyfus for *raison d'état* actually breed a corrosive cynicism about public life and undermine general loyalty to the state itself? Like all those who have tried to promote both liberty and equality in equal measure and at the same time, the French participants in the contest over sacrifice do not seem particularly good at maximizing the values of individualism and collectivism simultaneously. The French of the turn of the century were not much better at resolving such dichotomies than are we.

So now perhaps we can understand more deeply why the Durkheimian theory of sacrifice was such a seemingly shaky, eclectic synthesis. The Durkheimians were unlikely to be any better at resolving seemingly irresolvable dilemmas than anyone else. But having admitted this, we can also appreciate how brilliant—even brave—the Durkheimian theory of sacrifice was as a piece of policy thinking. I say "brave" because Durkheimian aversion for their most deadly enemies—the intransigent Catholics—did not prevent them from admitting what seems certainly true about rightist Catholic insights into the nature of social life. To wit, there can be no durable social life—much less a "nation"—without sacrifice and the transcendent sanctions embodied in it. The Durkheimians, of course, never felt it necessary to invoke theistic sanctions to support sacrifice, but their devotion to "humanity" or "society" (at least as embodied in the French nation) surely counts as a fundamental value as operationally transcendent as traditional beliefs in God. No doubt, the Durkheimians valued society. Yet oddly enough, although Durkheim has been criticized for promoting a religion of society, he also asserted that the human individual is unabashedly "sacred."[83] We can also admire the Durkheimian solution to the problem of sacrifice because of the way in which the Durkheimians wove the data of ethnography and history together with the data of contemporary social and political life in France. Instead of producing two theories—one for ritual sacrifice and another for civic sacrifice—they produced a single theory that was as fully pertinent to explaining ritual sacrifice as it was for making sense of civic sacrifice and social policy. The Durkheimian theory of sacrifice was no small achievement. That it does not answer all the problems it confronts, that it does not win all the contests into which it enters is less important, in my view, than that it offered a theory of sacrifice substantial enough to have made a decent showing.

Notes

CHAPTER ONE

1. Carter Lindberg, *The European Reformations* (Oxford: Blackwell, 1996), 289. See also the links between sacrifice and Eucharist on the one side and ritual murder on the other in R. Po-chia Hsia, *The Myth of Ritual Murder: Jews and Magic in Reformation Germany* (New Haven: Yale University Press, 1988), 226ff.

2. My emphasis on France in no way is to diminish the place of sacrificial discourse in Germany. The French, at any rate the First World War nationalists like Maurice Barrès, have argued that the ideologies of sacrifice differ between the two nations. The French sacrifice to defend their soil, the Germans to impose their wills on others. France is the suffering divinity, Germany, the bearer of a giant sword. Characteristically, when French nationalists represented their cause, they rallied round the symbolic victimized suffering figure of Joan of Arc, rather than that of Napoleon or Louis XIV. See Micheline Tison-Braun, *La Crise de l'humanisme* (Paris: Nizet, 1967), 2:29ff. (Unless otherwise noted, all translations are my own.) In more recent German discourse on sacrifice in the Nazi period, the theme of sacrifice has gained an even stronger voice. See Jay W. Baird's full-length study of the Nazi ideology of sacrifice in his *To Die for Germany: Heroes in the Nazi Pantheon* (Bloomington: Indiana University Press, 1990). Except, however, for the appeal to Norse mythological sources of sacrifice, the German discourse seems for the most part either derivative on or closely related to the French. Nazi ideals of sacrifice for the nation rely on the source of all modern nationalist sacrificial discourse—the French Revolution. Then, when Nazi talk of sacrifice uses Christian language, it again relies on the same sources as the French—typically on Roman Catholic Counter Reformation theologies of Eucharistic sacrifice. These, as we will see, were perfected in France by the Oratorians, the Company of the Most Blessed Sacrament, Jesuits, and various ecstatic mystics. For examples of Nazi uses of Christian notions of sacrifice, often married to Norse mythology, see Baird, *To Die for Germany*, 12, 26, 41, 54–58, 74, 88, 128, 136, 147f, 244, and etc. Many prominent figures in the articulation of Nazi sacrificial rhetoric were Roman Catholic and in some cases educated by the Jesuits. Topping all lists is, of course, the Jesuit-educated Goebbels. But Goebbels is not unique among Catholic recruits to the movement important in the articulation of a discourse of total sacrifice. The Catholic Albert Schlageter was an early model of Nazi sacrificial death (Baird, *To Die for Germany*, 14); Jesuit-educated Hans Baumann was the Hitler Youth's "troubadour" and composer of many of the Nazis' famous marching songs extolling sacrifice (Baird, *To Die for Germany*, xiv, 158f). Gerhard Schumann, a former student of theology, took his place as the leading Nazi poet (Baird, *To Die for Germany*, xv, 41, 54, 88).

3. Carter Lindberg, *The European Reformations* (Oxford: Blackwell, 1996), 278.

4. R. Po-chia Hsia, *The World of Catholic Renewal, 1540–1770* (Cambridge: Cambridge University Press, 1998), 20.

5. In the domain of social thought, it has, in fact, been argued that Hubert and Mauss's *Sacrifice: Its Nature and Functions* remains today, even a hundred years after its publication, still the most frequently cited and formative theoretical work ever written on the subject of sacrifice. No museum piece, Hubert and Mauss's effort still remains "fresh," says Louis Dumont, while, by contrast, Frazer's masterpiece, *The Golden Bough,* the second edition of which appeared a scant two years before *Sacrifice,* is today thoroughly "antiquated." Louis Dumont, "Marcel Mauss: A Science in Becoming," *Essays on Individualism: Modern Ideology in Anthropological Perspective* (Chicago: University of Chicago Press, 1986), 192. Even its critics concede that *Sacrifice* was a "major contribution and without doubt decisive on most points." See Jean Paul Colleyn, "Le Sacrifice selon Hubert et Mauss," in *Le Sacrifice I,* Systèmes de pensée en Afrique noire, bk. 2, ed. Luc de Heusch (Paris: École Pratique des Hautes Études, 1976), 23.

6. See, for instance, John M. Beattie, "On Understanding Sacrifice," in *Sacrifice,* ed. M. F. C. Bourdillon and Meyer Fortes (London: Academic Press, 1980), 34; Colleyn, "Le Sacrifice selon Hubert et Mauss"; Luc de Heusch, *Sacrifice in Africa,* trans. Linda O'Brien and Alice Morton (Bloomington: Indiana University Press, 1985), 16f; Nancy Jay, *Throughout Your Generations Forever* (Chicago: University of Chicago Press, 1992), 134–43; William Beers, *Women and Sacrifice* (Detroit: Wayne State University Press, 1992), chap. 1; Frits Staal, *Rules without Meaning: Ritual, Mantras and the Human Sciences* (New York: Peter Lang, 1989); René Girard, *Violence and the Sacred* (Baltimore: Johns Hopkins University Press, 1977), passim; Victor Turner, "Sacrifice as Quintessential Process, Prophylaxis or Abandonment?" *History of Religions* 16 (1977): 189–215. Regarding Hubert and Mauss's *Sacrifice* as the "first theory" of sacrifice, see my forthcoming *Theology and the First Theory of Sacrifice.*

7. Tison-Braun, *La crise de l'humanisme* (Paris: Nizet, 1967), 2:49.

8. Georges Goyau, *The Church of France during the War* (Paris: Bloud and Gay, 1918), 10.

9. Ibid., 10.

10. An important recent study of the place of certain symbols in the formation of French political culture comes from Laura Mason, *Singing the French Revolution* (Ithaca: Cornell University Press, 1996), 5ff.

11. Suzanne Desan, *Reclaiming the Sacred: Lay Religion and Popular Politics in Revolutionary France* (Ithaca: Cornell University Press, 1990), 18.

12. This was in effect recently argued by John Milbank, *Theology and Social Theory* (Oxford: Blackwell, 1990), 54, 59, 61.

13. Ivan Strenski, "Between Theory and Speciality: Sacrifice in the 90's," *Religious Studies Review* 22 (1996): 10–20.

14. For further discussion, see note 5.

15. Ivan Strenski, "At Home with René Girard: Eucharistic Sacrifice, the 'French School' and Joseph De Maistre," in *Religion in Relation: Method, Application and Moral Location* (London: Macmillan, 1993), 202–16.

16. This is not to repeat the discredited idealism of a Carl Becker, so well dealt with by Peter Gay in his *The Enlightenment, An Interpretation* (New York: W. W. Norton, 1966), 354ff, but it is to reclaim and invigorate the "cultural" approach of French historians like François Furet (*Interpreting the French Revolution* [1978], trans. Elborg Foster [Cambridge: Cambridge University Press, 1981]) and his American admirers like Dale K.

Van Kley (*The Religious Origins of the French Revolution* [New Haven: Yale University Press, 1996]).

17. Roger L. Williams, *The World of Napoleon III* (New York: Collier, 1962), 76.

18. Jay Winter, *Sites of Memory, Sites of Mourning* (Cambridge: Cambridge University Press, 1995).

19. Ibid., 221.

20. Ibid., 206.

21. Ibid., 128.

22. On the persistence of religiously tinged nationalist feelings, see Paul Sabatier, *France To-day*, trans. H. B. Binns (London: J. M. Dent, 1913), 43, chap. 4; Eugen Weber, *The Nationalist Revival in France, 1905–1914* (Berkeley: University of California Publications in History, No. 60, 1959).

23. Daniel Pick, *War Machine: The Rationalization of Slaughter* (New Haven: Yale University Press, 1993), 158.

24. Benedict Anderson, *Imagined Communities*, rev. and ext. ed. (London: Verso, 1991), 7.

25. Ibid., 53.

CHAPTER TWO

1. Selections featuring the persistence, albeit blasphemous, of Catholic language in "Le Ça Ira" (1790), arguably the most popular street song of the French Revolution, quoted in Laura Mason, *Singing the French Revolution* (Ithaca: Cornell University Press, 1996), 42–46.

2. Eugen Weber, "Gauls versus Franks: Conflict and Nationalism," in *Nationhood and Nationalism in France: From Boulangism to the Great War, 1889–1918*, ed. Robert Tombs (London: HarperCollins Academic, 1991), 19.

3. René Rémond, *The Right Wing in France from 1815 to De Gaulle*, trans. James M. Laux (Philadelphia: University of Pennsylvania Press, 1966), 350.

4. Jean Rivière, "La redemption devant la pensée moderne," *La revue du clergé français* 70 (1912): 284; see also 285, 298, 299.

5. Nancy Jay, *Throughout Your Generations Forever: Sacrifice, Religion, and Paternity* (Chicago: University of Chicago Press, 1992), 119–21.

6. Frederick J. McGuinness, "*Roma Sancta* and the Saint: Eucharist, Chastity and the Logic of Catholic Reform," *Historical Reflections/Refléxions Historiques* 15 (1988): 112ff.

7. Ibid., 99.

8. Ibid., 105.

9. John Bossy, "Editor's Postscript," in *The Spirit of the Counter-Reformation*, by H. Outram Evennett (Notre Dame: University of Notre Dame Press, 1968), 140; Dale K. Van Kley, *The Religious Origins of the French Revolution* (New Haven: Yale University Press, 1996), 53.

10. Ralph Gibson, *A Social History of French Catholicism, 1789–1914* (London: Routledge, 1989), 78–80.

11. Van Kley, *The Religious Origins of the French Revolution*, 23.

12. Ibid., 24 (my emphasis).

13. In material terms, minor monuments to this sensibility are witness to the durability of this sacrificial spirituality across the centuries. In Paris, off the great nineteenth-century Boulevard Haussmann, in the Square Louis XVI, the Chapelle Expiatoire was erected between 1815 and 1826 by order of Louis XVIII in memory of his eighteenth-century forebears, Louis XVI and Marie Antoinette. There, in the style of classical "fu-

neral temenos," Louis XVI stands, accompanied by his confessor, while Marie Antoinette is supported (significantly enough) by Corot's image of "Religion." Stuart Rossiter, ed., *The Blue Guides: Paris* (London: Ernest Benn, 1968), 103.

14. Manuel de Diéguez, *L'idole monothéiste* (Paris: Presses universitaires de France, 1981).

15. Natalie Zemon Davis, "The Rites of Violence," in *Society and Culture in Early Modern France* (Stanford: Stanford University Press, 1975), 174.

16. Jacqueline Boucher, "Catholiques royaux et ligeurs: une meme mentalité religieuse des frères ennemis," in *Religion et politique: Les deux guerres mondiales, histoire de Lyon et du Sud-est*, ed. M. Pacaut, J. Gadille, J.-M. Mayeur, and H. Beuve-Méry (Lyon: Université de Lyon, 1972), 67.

17. John Bossy, "The Mass as a Social Institution," *Past and Present* 100 (1983): 29–61. But readers should beware of Bossy's glib and uninformed reading of both Hubert and Mauss's *Sacrifice* and the Durkheimian tradition (49–50).

18. Henri Bremond, *Histoire litteraire du sentiment religieux en France depuis la fin des guerres de religion jusqu'à nos jours*, vol. 9, *La Vie chrétienne sous l'ancien régime* (Paris: Librairie Bloud et Gay, 1932), 132. Attributed to a Dom G. Godu.

19. "Sacrifice in Christian Theology," *The New Catholic Encyclopedia* (New York: McGraw Hill, 1967), 839.

20. Ibid., 837–40.

21. Abbé Kerné, *Le Sacrifice en général et le sacrifice de la messe en particulier* (Landerneau: J. Desmoulins, 1902), 51.

22. Ibid., 20.

23. Ibid., 13–16.

24. Ibid., 15.

25. Ibid., 11–16.

26. Ibid., 18

27. Ibid., 17.

28. Henri Bremond, *A Literary History of Religious Thought in France*, vol. 3, *The Triumph of Mysticism* (1921), trans. K. L. Montgomery (London: Society for the Promotion of Christian Knowledge, 1936). The better-known successors of Bérullean spirituality during the time of "royal religion" were the Jansenists. Especially because Jansenist spirituality called for rigorous cultivation of the interior life and Augustinian awareness of human sinfulness, the Jansenists followed the lead of Bérulle closely. Yet the Jansenists were not wholly faithful followers of Bérulle. To be sure, they, like Bérulle, were constantly conscious of human sinfulness. Yet in place of Bérulle's passionate mysticism of self-annihilation, the Jansenists spoke of God meeting the human soul in a recognition of the divine presence. But, as we will see, not only did the theological features of Bérulle's spirituality put him into a tense relationship with the Jansenists, so too did his politics. Unlike the Jansenists, Bérulle championed the crown and its "royal religion" of absolutism under which the Jansenists were to suffer such deadly blows. Louis Dupré, "Jansenism and Quietism," in *Christian Spirituality: Post-Reformation and Modern*, ed. Louis Dupré and Don E. Saliers (New York: Crossroads, 1991), 129.

29. Geoffrey R. R. Treasure, *Cardinal Richelieu and the Development of Absolutism* (London: Adam and Charles Black, 1972), 111. The spirituality developed by the "École Française de Spiritualité" was also common to opposing Catholic groups such as the Royalists and Leaguers. Jacqueline Boucher, "Catholiques royaux et ligeurs: une meme mentalité religieuse des frères ennemis," in *Religion et politique*, ed. M. Pacaut et al., 71–72.

30. Bremond, *A Literary History of Religious Thought in France*, vol. 3, pp. 17–133.

31. Michael J. Buckley, "Seventeenth-Century French Spirituality," in *Christian Spirituality: Post-Reformation and Modern*, ed. Louis Dupré and Don E. Saliers (New York: Crossroads, 1991), 42.

32. Ibid., 48–49.

33. This perhaps survives from Bérulle's education under the Jesuits and his early devotion to the Spiritual Exercises. See Buckley, "Seventeenth-Century French Spirituality," 42–43, 51–52.

34. This intimate, yet subtle, relation of religion and politics in Bérulle's age was on occasion well appreciated by the theologians of the time themselves. One of the leaders of the Oratorian movement and its one-time general, Charles de Condren (1588–1641), observed that the Council of Trent—from whose edicts much of Bérulle's spirituality took its rise—"had been above all a political assembly." Saint-Beuve quoting de Condren in *Port-Royal* 1. I, 315, as cited in Raoul Allier, *La Compagnie du très saint-sacrement de l'autel: la cabale des dévots* (Paris: Colin, 1902), 164. See also a recent reinterpretation of Trent in David N. Power, *The Sacrifice We Offer* (New York: Crossroad, 1987).

35. Treasure, *Cardinal Richelieu and the Development of Absolutism*, 13–18, 223–24; Bremond, *A Literary History of Religious Thought in France*, vol. 3, p. 254.

36. Alfred Rébelliau, *Bossuet: historien du protestantisme* (Paris: Hachette, 1909), 18.

37. Treasure, *Cardinal Richelieu and the Development of Absolutism*, 13.

38. Bremond, *A Literary History of Religious Thought in France*, vol. 3, p. 16. While Richelieu employed Machiavelli-like principles of Realpolitik and *raisons d'état* in pursuit of the policies of an increasingly absolute monarchy, he did so with great ambiguity because of his enduring commitment to the ideals of a Christian monarchy. Emmanuel LeRoy Ladurie, *The Ancien Regime: A History of France, 1610–1774*, trans. Mark Greengrass (Oxford: Blackwell, 1998), 29–40.

39. Some authors, however, claim that Richelieu promoted Bérulle's spirituality. See Treasure, *Cardinal Richelieu and the Development of Absolutism*, 111; Allier, *La Compagnie du très saint-sacrement*.

40. Eugene A. Walsh, *The Priesthood in the Writings of the French School: Bérulle, De Condren, Olier* (Washington, D.C.: Catholic University Press, 1949).

41. Jean Galy, *Le Sacrifice dans l'école française* (Paris: Nouvelles Editions Latines, 1951).

42. Bremond, *A Literary History of Religious Thought in France*, vol. 3, p. 294.

43. Galy, *Le Sacrifice dans l'école francaise*, 131.

44. Olier, "Preface," *Grand' Messe*, cols. 287–88, quoted in Walsh, *The Priesthood in the Writings of the French School*, 21.

45. Walsh, *The Priesthood in the Writings of the French School*, 56.

46. Galy, *Le Sacrifice dans l'école francaise*, 145.

47. Bremond, *A Literary History of Religious Thought in France*, vol. 3, p. 256.

48. Ibid.

49. Ibid.

50. Ibid.

51. Ibid., 257.

52. Ibid., 270.

53. Renan said he was "repelled" by the seminary and its violence against "personal individuality." R. M. Chadbourne, *Ernest Renan* (New York: Twayne, 1968), 26.

54. Walsh, *The Priesthood in the Writings of the French School*, xi.

55. Even though those touched by Saint Sulpician ideas, like Ernest Renan and Al-

fred Loisy, departed in many ways from the theological straight and narrow, the intransigent lessons taught about the meaning of sacrifice by the Oratorians even survived within their deviant Catholic thought. Renan argued that the only way France could recover from its defeat to the Prussians was to adopt the spirit of sacrifice for the nation, even if this meant submitting to the discipline of a monarchic regime. Ernest Renan, "La Réforme intellectuelle et moral de la France," in *La Réforme intellectuelle et moral de la France*, ed. P. E. Charvet (New York: Greenwood Press, 1968), 45.

56. For example, not only did the Saint-Sulpicians found the first seminary in the United States, but "for a long time, the formation and training of the secular clergy in the whole United States" was in their hands. Even more influential upon the Catholicism of North America was Olier's missionary projects. He personally founded the Seminaire de Saint-Sulpice in Montreal in 1657, only sixteen years after the foundation of the mother house in Paris. Walsh, *The Priesthood in the Writings of the French School*, xi.

57. Louis Chatellier, *The Europe of the Devout*, trans. Jean Birrell (Cambridge: Cambridge University Press, 1989).

58. Suspicions of the Jesuits have of course been legion from early on in their history. And in the end, despite their alignment with the crown, fear of a Jesuit "cabal" or revenge against their secret dealings seem to have been factors leading to their expulsion in France by Louis XV. See Dale van Kley, *The Jansenists and the Expulsion of the Jesuits from France, 1757–1765* (New Haven: Yale University Press, 1975).

59. See the several works of Protestant historian of religion, Raoul Allier on the spirituality of the blessed (i.e., reserved) sacrament and the *dévots:* Allier, *La Compagnie du trés saint-sacrement;* Raoul Allier, *La Compagnie du saint-sacrement. Marseille* (Paris: Honoré Champion, 1909); Raoul Allier, *La Compagnie du trés saint-sacrement de l'autel à Toulouse: une esquisse de son histoire* (Paris: Honoré Champion, 1914).

60. Georges Goyau, "Compagnie du Saint-Sacrement," *The Catholic Encyclopedia* (New York: Robert Appleton, 1908), 4:184–85; Raoul Allier, *Tartuffe et la religion* (Paris: Fischbacher, 1901).

61. Alain Tallon, *La Compagnie du Saint-Sacrement* (Paris: Cerf, 1990).

62. Raoul Allier, *La Compagnie du trés saint-sacrement*, 119.

63. Ibid., 117.

64. Tallon, *La Compagnie du Saint-Sacrement*, 129.

65. Allier, *La Compagnie du trés saint-sacrement*, 119.

66. Tallon, *La Compagnie du Saint-Sacrement*, 129.

67. Ibid., 133.

68. Ibid., 129.

69. Benedict Anderson, *Imagined Communities*, rev. and ext. ed. (London: Verso, 1991), 7.

70. Tallon, *La Compagnie du Saint-Sacrement*, 136.

71. This was also the position Bérulle took against Richelieu's employment of *raison d'état*. See Ladurie, *The Ancien Regime*, 40.

72. Tallon, *La Compagnie du Saint-Sacrement*, 130.

73. At first, the rise of the cult split the world of French Catholic spirituality between the Jesuits and the "parti dévot." Jean-Jacques Olier as well as the members of the "parti dévot" in the French School and their Jansenist successors objected fiercely to the emotionalism of the Jesuit devotion to the Sacred Heart. See Keith P. Luria, "The Counter-Reformation and Popular Spirituality," in *Christian Spirituality*, ed. Dupré and Saliers, 118; and Louis Dupré, "Jansenism and Quietism," in *Christian Spirituality*, ed. Dupré and Saliers, 125.

74. Van Kley, *The Religious Origins of the French Revolution,* 116.

75. Luria, "The Counter-Reformation and Popular Spirituality," 117.

76. Ibid.

77. Van Kley, *The Religious Origins of the French Revolution,* 115.

78. Luria, "The Counter-Reformation and Popular Spirituality," 117.

79. Van Kley, *The Religious Origins of the French Revolution,* 118.

80. Treasure, *Cardinal Richelieu and the Development of Absolutism,* 111; Van Kley, *The Religious Origins of the French Revolution,* 115.

81. Jean-Marie Mayeur, "Le Catholicisme français et le Première Guerre mondiale," *Francia* 2 (1974): 388.

82. Ibid.

83. Van Kley, *The Religious Origins of the French Revolution,* 118.

84. Mayeur, "Le Catholicisme français," 388.

85. Ibid., 389.

86. While Susan Dunn argues persuasively that the rhetoric of Jacobin regicide and Michelet's celebration of Jeanne d'Arc's death should be seen as sacrificial, she stops short of reaching back for the theological precedents of the kind of thinking, which is marked only from the end of the eighteenth century and then only among republicans. Susan Dunn, *The Deaths of Louis XVI: Regicide and the French Political Imagination* (Princeton: Princeton University Press, 1994), 23ff.

87. Ibid.

88. Van Kley, *The Religious Origins of the French Revolution,* 23, 68.

89. Ibid., 116–18.

90. Dunn, *The Deaths of Louis XVI,* 39ff.

91. Georges Goyau, *The Church of France during the War* (Paris: Bloud and Gay, 1918), 10.

92. Daniele Menozzi, *Les Interprétations politiques de Jésus de l'ancien régime à la Révolution,* trans. Jacqueline Touvier (Paris: Cerf, 1983), 155ff.

93. Ibid., 160.

94. Menozzi, *Les Interprétations politiques.*

95. Jacques-Bénigne Bossuet, *Politique tirée des propres paroles de l'Écriture sainte,* ed. J. le Brun (Geneva: Droz, 1967), 446–47, cited in Menozzi, *Les Interprétations politiques,* 125.

96. Menozzi, *Les Interprétations politiques,* 126.

97. Ibid., 156.

98. Ibid., 152, 153, 155, 158.

99. Ibid., 152.

100. Quoted from page 14 of Mille's *A la piété patriotique: Discours apologétique sur la Constitution du clergé* (1791), in Menozzi, *Les Interprétations politiques,* 152.

101. Mona Ozouf, *Festivals and the French Revolution,* trans. Alan Sheridan (Cambridge: Harvard University Press, 1988). For a Marxist perspective on these questions, see Michel Vovelle, *Ideologies and Mentalities,* trans. Eamon O'Flaherty (Chicago: University of Chicago Press, 1990).

102. Simon Schama, *Citizens: A Chronicle of the French Revolution* (Knopf: New York, 1989), 350.

103. Patrice Higonnet, *Goodness beyond Virtue: Jacobins during the French Revolution* (Cambridge: Harvard University Press, 1998), 205.

104. Saint-Just, "Esprit de la révolution et de la constitution de France," *Oeuvres complètes,* ed. Michèle Duval (Paris: Editions Gérard Lebovici, 1984), 338.

105. Higonnet, *Goodness beyond Virtue*, 187.

106. Ibid., 317–18.

107. It is worth noting that Mona Ozouf argues that these attempts by the revolutionaries to efface their immediate Catholic past were largely failures; the revolutionaries were just not very adept at manipulating the religious imagination. Even prominent figures of French history, sympathetic to the republic and Revolution, such as Auguste Comte and Edgar Quinet, were singularly appalled at the "sterility" of the religious imagination of the Revolution. Thus, given the Revolution's failure at religious invention, it is perhaps no wonder that the Revolutionaries engaged in the "quite unprincipled imitation" of Catholic traditions. See Ozouf, *Festivals and the French Revolution*, 271.

108. Schama, *Citizens*, 259, 343, 360, 380f, 440, 494f, 504, 564, 577.

109. Ibid., 504.

110. Howard C. Barnard, *Education and the French Revolution* (Cambridge: Cambridge University Press, 1969), chap. 1.

111. Harold T. Parker, *The Cult of Antiquity and the French Revolutionaries: A Study in the Development of the Revolutionary Spirit* (New York: Octagon Books, 1965), 31.

112. Camille Desmoulins, *La France libre*, in *Les oeuvres de Camille Desmoulins recueillies et publiées d'après les textes originaux augmentées de fragments inédits, de notes et d'un index et précédées d'une étude biographique et littéraire par Jules Claretie* (Paris: Bibliothèque-Charpentier, 1906), 1:120–21, quoted in Parker, *The Cult of Antiquity*, 75.

113. Claude Mossé, *L'Antiquité dans la Révolution française* (Paris: Albin Michel, 1989), 82–86.

114. Schama, *Citizens*, 259; Edith Flamarion, "Brutus ou l'adoption d'un mythe romain par la Révolution française," in *La Révolution française et l'antiquité*, ed. R. Chevallier (Tours: Centre de Recherches A. Piganiol, 1991), 91–112.

115. Higonnet, *Goodness beyond Virtue*, 138.

116. Here the reference is to Marcus Brutus. Ibid., 196. Higonnet, however, does not always distinguish which Brutus is at issue. See ibid., 138, 205, where the identity of Brutus is not made clear. It was, for example, Lucius Junius Brutus who was immortalized by the paintings of Jacques-Louis David and the play *Brutus* (1730) by Voltaire, while Marcus Junius Brutus was featured in his *Mort de César*. Edith Flamarion argues that in fact a third Brutus is to be found among those revered by the French Revolution—another Lucius Junius Brutus, celebrated by Robespierre and discussed in her "Brutus ou l'adoption d'un Mythe romain par la Révolution française," 98ff.

117. It is interesting how Plutarch becomes a target for those who wish to disenchant the national patriotic rhetoric of devotion—even as remote from the French Revolution as the First World War. In Henri Barbusse's *Feu: Journal d'une escouade*, an embittered French soldier flings his republican lessons of patriotic devotion back into the face of the republic herself:

> "The future!" he cried all at once as a prophet might. "How will they regard this slaughter, they who'll live after us, to whom progress—which comes as sure as fate—will at last restore the poise of their conscience? How will they regard these exploits which even we who perform them don't know whether one should compare them with those of Plutarch's and Corneille's heroes or with those of hooligans and apaches?"

From the English translation, Henri Barbusse, *Under Fire: The Story of a Squad*, trans. Fitzwater Wray (London: J. M. Dent & Sons Ltd., 1929), 256.

118. Plutarch, "Brutus (85−42 B.C.)," in *Makers of Rome: Nine Lives by Plutarch,* trans. Scott Kilvert (New York: Dorset Press, 1965), 231.

119. Flamarion, "Brutus ou l'adoption d'un Mythe romain par la Révolution française," 91, 98ff.

120. Peter France, "Voltaire," *The New Oxford Companion to Literature in French* (Oxford: Oxford University Press, 1995), 844.

121. Emmet Kennedy, *A Cultural History of the French Revolution* (New Haven: Yale University Press, 1989), 363. It is no small wonder that the French Revolution should have honored Marcus Brutus, given his depiction in Voltaire's play as uttering the following lines typical of his character there.

> Would Caesar be a Roman citizen,
> I should adore him, and would sacrifice
> My life and fortune to defend his cause;
> But Caesar, as a king, I must abhor.
> (Act 3, scene 4)

Voltaire, *The Death of Caesar,* in *The Dramatic Works of Voltaire,* trans. William F. Fleming (Akron, Ohio: Werner Company, 1905), 5:131.

122. William Doyle, *The Oxford History of the French Revolution* (Oxford: Oxford University Press, 1989), 259.

123. Flamarion, "Brutus ou l'adoption d'un Mythe romain par la Révolution française," 95.

124. Ibid., 105.

125. Ibid., 97.

126. Schama, *Citizens,* 564. On the cult of Brutus, see Kennedy, *A Cultural History of the French Revolution,* 86f; Robert I. Herbert, *David, Voltaire, Brutus and the French Revolution: An Essay in Art and Politics* (London: Penguin, 1972).

127. Higonnet, *Goodness beyond Virtue,* 205.

128. Schama, *Citizens,* 738.

129. Higonnet, *Goodness beyond Virtue,* 205.

130. Ibid.

131. Voltaire, *La Mort de César,* ed. André-M. Rousseau (Paris: Société d'Enseignement Supérieure, 1964), 78ff.

132. Barnard, *Education and the French Revolution,* 9−11; Flamarion, "Brutus ou l'adoption d'un Mythe romain par la Révolution française," 102.

133. Barnard, *Education and the French Revolution,* 11.

134. Parker, *The Cult of Antiquity and the French Revolutionaries,* 8ff.

135. David P. Jordan, *The Revolutionary Career of Maximilien Robespierre* (Chicago: University of Chicago Press, 1985), 24.

136. Parker, *The Cult of Antiquity and the French Revolutionaries,* chap. 2; Flamarion, "Brutus ou l'adoption d'un mythe romain par la Révolution française," 102.

137. Parker, *The Cult of Antiquity and the French Revolutionaries,* 26.

138. Ibid.

139. Ibid., 32.

140. Schama, *Citizens,* 602; Van Kley, *The Religious Origins of the French Revolution,* 12, chap. 2.

141. Schama, *Citizens,* 449.

142. François Furet, *Interpreting the French Revolution,* trans. Elborg Foster (Cambridge: Cambridge University Press, 1981), 77.

143. Schama, *Citizens,* 671 (expiation), 595 (total immolation).

144. Ibid., 633.

145. Dunn, *The Deaths of Louis XVI*, 66; Zev Sternhell, "The Political Culture of Nationalism," in *Nationhood and Nationalism in France*, ed. Tombs, 30–31.

146. Susan Dunn argues persuasively that the rhetoric of Jacobin regicide and Michelet's celebration of Jeanne d'Arc's death should be seen as sacrificial. Dunn, *The Deaths of Louis XVI*, chaps. 1, 2.

147. Ibid., 39.

148. Conor Cruise O'Brien, foreword to Dunn's *The Deaths of Louis XVI*, xi.

149. Dunn, *The Deaths of Louis XVI*, 66.

150. Ibid., 53

151. Ibid., 46.

152. Ibid., 47.

153. Ibid., 66.

154. Ibid., 50.

155. Ibid., 27.

156. Richard A. Lebrun, *Throne and Altar: The Political and Religious Thought of Joseph de Maistre* (Ottawa: University of Ottawa, 1965), chap. 4.

157. Joseph de Maistre, *Considerations on France* (1797), ed. and trans. Richard A. Lebrun (Cambridge: Cambridge University Press, 1994), xxxv–xxxvii.

158. Joseph de Maistre, *Les Soirées de Saint-Petersbourg, ou entretiens sur le gouvernement temporel de la providence suivis d'un traite sur les sacrifices*, vol. 2 (Paris: La Librairie Ecclesiastique de Rusand, 1822).

159. While I have been unable to trace a direct lineage between them and de Maistre nor find explicit reference to them in Maistre's major writings on sacrifice, this may not be of much consequence. The sacrificial Eucharistic theology of the French School and the devotion to the Sacred Heart were then so widespread and popular in the France of the eighteenth century, we must presume that a pious Catholic like de Maistre was informed by them. We can say this with certainty of the theology of the French School because it had attained a classic status in the seventeenth century and was fundamental in the formation of the clergy. Likewise, devotion to the Sacred Heart was a spiritual commonplace in the eighteenth century, indeed in some ways defining the essence of rococo spirituality. As a sophisticated, pious, and educated lay theologian, Joseph de Maistre could not have avoided their influence and knowledge of them. They formed part of the spiritual taken-for-granted core of the Catholicism which would have shaped Maistre. See Joseph de Maistre, "Dixième Entretien" and "Eclaircissement sur les sacrifices," in *Les Soirées de Saint-Petersbourg*, vol. 2. See also the discussion of expiation in de Maistre's work in Joyce O. Lowrie, *The Violent Mystique: Thematics of Retribution and Expiation in Balzac, Barbery d'Aurevilly, Bloy and Huysmans* (Geneva: Droz, 1974), 17–24.

160. Joseph de Maistre, *St. Petersburg Dialogues, or Conversations on the Temporal Government of Providence*, ed. and trans. Richard A. Lebrun (Montreal/Kingston: McGill/Queen's University Presses, 1993), 384, 385. De Maistre differs from other Catholics, however, in his view that the suffering of the victim is the just amends for sin. De Maistre is interesting and perhaps perverse because it is precisely the suffering of the innocent in sacrifice that attracts his inquiries. See Owen Bradley, *A Modern Maistre* (Lincoln: University of Nebraska Press, 1999), 39.

161. De Maistre, *St. Petersburg Dialogues*, 385.

162. René Girard, *Violence and the Sacred*, trans. Patrick Gregory (Baltimore: Johns Hopkins University Press, 1977).

163. Bradley, *A Modern Maistre*, 194–95.

164. De Maistre, *St. Petersburg Dialogues*, 385; see especially "The Christian Theory of Sacrifice," ibid., 379–91; de Maistre, *Considerations on France*, 30–31; Bradley, *A Modern Maistre*, 189–95.

165. De Maistre, *Les Soirées de Saint-Petersbourg*, 2:456.

166. Ibid., 457. Note that this is one of the points where Girard picks up on Joseph de Maistre. Girard, *Violence and the Sacred*, 4.

167. Lebrun, *Throne and Altar*, 76.

168. Maistre's *Etude sur la souveraineté*, quoted in Lebrun, *Throne and Altar*, 76.

169. Ibid.

170. Van Kley, *The Religious Origins of the French Revolution*, 29.

171. Regarding the revival of de Maistre's reputation at the *fin-de-siècle*, see Georges Goyau, "La Modernité d'un 'réactionnaire' catholique: Joseph de Maistre," in *Catholicisme et politique* (Paris: Editions de la Revue des Jeunes, 1923), 69–93.

172. Isaiah Berlin has recently argued that it is just this forward-looking aspect of de Maistre's thought that anticipates twentieth-century developments—the Catholic revival, the new nationalism, and later the backlash against a triumphant Dreyfusard movement. Isaiah Berlin, "Joseph de Maistre and the Origins of Fascism," parts 1 and 2, *New York Review of Books*, 27 September 1990, 57–64; 11 October 1990, 54–65. See also Goyau, "La Modernité d'un 'réactionnaire' catholique Joseph de Maistre"; and Abbé Bouquerel, *Le Sacrifice dans l'économie des religions* (Paris: n.p., 1912), 18. The charge that de Maistre was a protofascist is contested by Owen Bradley, as at least anachronistic, in his *Modern Maistre*, xv ff.

173. Berlin, "Joseph de Maistre and the Origins of Fascism," part 1, 64.

174. Berlin, "Joseph de Maistre and the Origins of Fascism," part 2, 57.

175. Ernst Nolte, *Three Faces of Fascism*, trans. L. Vennewitz (New York: New American Library, 1965), 57–61. On Veuillot, see Lebrun, *Throne and Altar*, 143; Louis Veuillot, *La Guerre et l'homme de guerre*, 3d ed. (Paris: Société Générale de Librairie Catholique, 1878).

176. De Maistre, *Les Soirées de Saint-Petersbourg*, 2:184. Bouquerel also cites Joseph de Maistre throughout. Bouquerel, *Le Sacrifice dans l'économie des religions*, 3. Owen Bradley argues that de Maistre differs from Catholicism in rejecting the view that the suffering of the victim is the just amends for sin. Bradley, *A Modern Maistre*, 39.

177. Jacques Soustelle, *Daily Life of the Aztecs* (Stanford: Stanford University Press, 1961), 97–102.

178. De Maistre quoting from Johann Jung-Stilling, *Die Siegesgeschichte der christlichen Religion in einer gemeinnützigen Erklärung der Offenbarung* (Nuremburg: n.p., 1799), 429, in de Maistre, *St. Petersburg Dialogues*, 336 n. 1.

179. De Maistre, *St. Petersburg Dialogues*, 381.

180. Girard, *Violence and the Sacred*, 96ff.

181. Rémond, *The Right Wing in France*, 1966 ed., 261.

182. Dunn, *The Deaths of Louis XVI*, chap. 1.

183. Ibid., chap. 2.

184. Rémond, *The Right Wing in France*, 1966 ed., 184, 187.

185. Richard Griffiths, *The Reactionary Revolution: The Catholic Revival in French Literature, 1870–1914* (London: Constable, 1966), 157. See also Rémond, *The Right Wing in France*, 1966 ed., 184–89.

186. Griffiths, *The Reactionary Revolution*, passim.

187. Ibid., 157, 217.

188. René Rémond, *The Right Wing in France from 1815 to De Gaulle*, trans. James M. Laux, 2d American ed. (Philadelphia: University of Pennsylvania Press, 1969), 184–86.

189. Griffiths, *The Reactionary Revolution*, 156, and see also 190–93.

190. Lowrie, *The Violent Mystique*; Griffiths, *The Reactionary Revolution*, 156.

191. Griffiths, *The Reactionary Revolution*, 167ff.

192. Ibid., 171.

193. Ibid., 200.

194. Ibid., 198.

195. Ibid., 193.

196. Ernest Psichari, "Les Voix qui crient dans le désert," in *Oeuvres complètes de Ernest Psichari* (Paris: Louis Conard, 1920), 354.

197. Griffiths, *The Reactionary Revolution*, 217.

198. Richard D. Sonn, *Anarchism and Cultural Politics in Fin de Siécle France* (Lincoln: University of Nebraska Press, 1989), 287–88.

199. Ibid., 264ff.

200. Ibid., 289.

201. John L. Stanley, *The Sociology of Virtue* (Berkeley: University of California Press, 1981), 6. See also discussions of the revival of Maistre's reputation at the *fin-de-siècle* such as Goyau, "La Modernité d'un 'réactionnaire' catholique," 69–93.

202. Georges Sorel, "Modernisme dans la religion et dans le socialisme," *Revue critique des idées et des livres* 2 (1908): 182.

203. Rémond, *The Right Wing in France*, 1966 ed., 225.

204. Alfred Loisy, *La Religion* (Paris: Nourry, 1917), 64.

205. Albert Houtin and Felix Sartiaux, *Alfred Loisy: sa vie, son oeuvre* (Paris: Editions du CNRS, 1960), 235.

206. Maude D. Petre, *Alfred Loisy: His Religious Significance* (Cambridge: Cambridge University Press, 1944), 94.

207. Loisy, *La Religion*, 101.

208. Alfred Loisy, *La Discipline intellectuelle* (Paris: Nourry, 1919), 42, quoted in Petre, *Alfred Loisy*, 96.

209. Alfred Loisy, *La Morale humaine* (Paris: Nourry, 1923), 290.

210. Jay Winter, *Sites of Memory, Sites of Mourning* (Cambridge: Cambridge University Press, 1995), 221.

211. Loisy, *La Morale humaine*, 290.

212. Ibid., 291.

213. Ibid., 289–91.

214. Gibson, *A Social History of French Catholicism*.

215. Georges Goyau, "Disciplines catholiques et disciplines socialistes," in *Catholicisme et politique*, 65–66.

216. Goyau, *The Church of France during the War*, 10.

217. Rémond, *The Right Wing in France*, 1966 ed., 189. There are even much earlier (sixteenth-century) traces of a common spirituality even among groups who staunchly opposed each other such as the Catholic League and the Royalists. See Boucher, "Catholiques royaux et ligeurs," 67–82.

218. Sternhell, "The Political Culture of Nationalism," 23, 28; Michel Despland, "A Case of Christians Shifting Their Moral Allegiance: France 1790–1914," *Journal of the American Academy of Religion* 52 (1984): 672–90; Peter Steinfels, "The Failed Encounter: The Catholic Church and Liberalism in the Nineteenth Century," in *Catholi-*

cism and Liberalism, ed. R. Bruce Douglas and David Hollenbach (Cambridge: Cambridge University Press, 1994), 19–44.

219. Rémond, *The Right Wing in France,* 1969 ed., 56.

220. Ibid., 57.

221. Roger L. Williams, *The World of Napoleon III* (New York: Collier, 1962), 76.

222. Rémond, *The Right Wing in France,* 1966 ed., 188.

223. Paul M. Cohen, *Piety and Politics: Catholic Revival and the Generation of 1905– 1914 in France* (New York City: Garland, 1987), 32–38. See Cohen's nuancing of the term "liberal." Nonetheless, I shall use it in a more encompassing sense than is often the practice of historians such as Cohen with other aims than mine. I am not troubled, for example, by whether or not given figures or movements, such as some of the right-wing movements, embraced *economic* liberalism.

224. Mayeur, "Le Catholicisme français," 393.

225. Despland, "A Case of Christians Shifting Their Moral Allegiance," 681.

226. Cohen, *Piety and Politics,* 37.

227. Diéguez, *L'idole monothéiste.*

CHAPTER THREE

1. Charles de Gaulle, *The Edge of the Sword,* trans. Gerard Hopkins (New York: Criterion, 1960), 10.

2. Paul Fussell's *The Great War in Modern Memory,* for example, records the voices of both remembrance and literature as disillusionment with the First World War gradually grew in the ranks of Americans and Englishmen. Paul Fussell, *The Great War and Modern Memory* (London: Oxford University Press, 1975).

3. Among the more significant French writers of the twentieth century, Melvin Gallant notes Roger Martin du Gard's repugnance for patriotic propaganda, especially about the so-called glories of war and combat. See his *Le Thème de la mort chez Roger Martin du Gard* (Paris: Klincksieck, 1971), chap. 2.

4. From Henri Barbusse *Under Fire: The Story of a Squad,* trans. Fitzwater Wray (London: J. M. Dent & Sons Ltd., 1929), 316.

5. Henri Barbusse, *Feu: Journal d'une escouade* (Paris: Flammarion, 1916); Barbusse, *Under Fire;* Henri Bordeaux, *Les Derniers jours du Fort de Vaux* (Paris: Plon, 1916); Georges Duhamel, *Vie des martyrs: 1914–1916* (Paris: Hachette, 1917); Georges Duhamel, *The New Book of Martyrs,* trans. Florence Simmonds (London: William Heinemann, 1918); Georges Duhamel, *Civilisation, 1914–1917* (Paris: Mercure de France, 1951).

6. Barbusse, *Under Fire,* 343.

7. Ibid., 298–99.

8. Eugen Weber, *The Nationalist Revival in France, 1905–1914* (Berkeley: University of California Publications in History, No. 60, 1959), 6.

9. Ibid., 58.

10. Robert Tombs, introduction to *Nationhood and Nationalism in France: From Boulangism to the Great War, 1889–1918,* ed. Robert Tombs (London: HarperCollins, 1991), 5.

11. Weber, *The Nationalist Revival in France,* 57.

12. Ibid., 58.

13. Ibid., 11.

14. Adrien Bertrand, *L'Appel du sol* (Paris: Calmann-Lévy, 1916), 83.

15. Ibid., 114ff.

16. Micheline Tison-Braun, *La Crise de l'humanisme* (Paris: Nizet, 1967), 2:50ff.

17. Annette Becker, "Les Dévotions des soldats catholiques pendant la Grand Guerre," in *Chrétiens dans la Première Guerre mondiale,* ed. Nadine-Josette Chaline (Paris: Cerf, 1993), 18. Becker here cites P. D. Dupouey's comment on Claudel in his *Lettres et essais* (Paris: Cerf, 1935), 319.

18. Paul Claudel, *The Tidings Brought to Mary,* in *Two Dramas: Paul Claudel,* trans. Wallace Fowlie (Chicago: Henry Regnery, 1960), 286.

19. Becker, "Les Dévotions des soldats catholiques," 18, citing J. D'Arnoux, *Les Sept colonnes de l'héroisme* (Paris: Plon, 1938), 418.

20. Becker, "Les Dévotions des soldats catholiques," 18.

21. Tison-Braun, *La Crise de l'humanisme,* 2:50ff.

22. Maurice Barrès, *Chronique de la Grande Guerre: 1914–1920* (Paris: Plon, 1968), 154.

23. Bertrand, *L'Appel du sol,* 142.

24. Liah Greenfeld, *Nationalism: Five Roads to Modernity* (Cambridge: Harvard University Press, 1992), 175ff.

25. Regarding Robespierre, see Norman Hampson, "La Patrie," in Colin Lucas, *The French Revolution and the Creation of Modern Political Culture,* vol. 2, *The Political Culture of the French Revolution* (Oxford: Pergamon Press, 1988), 130. The relevant passages from Rousseau can be found in *The Social Contract,* bk. 2, chap. 5, and bk. 3, chap. 5. See, in this connection, Greenfeld, *Nationalism,* 172–77.

26. Adrien Dansette, *Religious History of Modern France,* vol. 1, *From the Revolution to the Third Republic* (Edinburgh/London: Nelson, 1961), 95

27. James L. Osen, *Royalist Protestant Political Thought during the French Revolution* (Westport, Conn.: Greenwood Press, 1995), 29.

28. Ibid., 68.

29. Ibid., 35.

30. Chaline, ed., *Chrétiens dans la Première Guerre mondiale.*

31. The great neo-Kantian public philosopher of the Third Republic, Charles Renouvier, argued in vain that the French should convert en masse to Protestantism, making it the de facto national religion! See Theodore Zeldin, *France 1848–1945: Intellect and Pride* (Oxford: Oxford University Press, 1980), 156. Although this appeal was made primarily to Catholics, Renouvier also urged Free Thinkers or "laïcs" to "declare themselves Protestants" so as to make common cause against the revanchist Catholic forces threatening the republic. See Daniel Robert, "Les intellectuels d'origine non-protestante dans le protestantisme des debuts de la Troisième République," in *Actes du colloque: Les protestants dans les débuts de la Troisième République (1871–1885)* (Paris, 3–6 Octobre 1978), ed. André Encrevé and Michel Richard (Paris: Société de l'histoire du protestantisme français, 1979), 95.

32. Paul Sabatier, *France To-day,* trans. H. B. Binns (London: J. M. Dent, 1913), 194.

33. Paul was no relation to his contemporary the great liberal Protestant theologian, Auguste Sabatier, although Auguste was Paul's theological mentor. Paul Sabatier is best known for his "modernist" biography of St. Francis of Assisi (1893). By 1918, this book had been produced in 43 French editions. See Albert Houtin and Felix Sartiaux, *Alfred Loisy: sa vie, son oeuvre* (Paris: Editions du CNRS, 1960), 399–400.

34. Sabatier, *France To-day,* 191.

35. For him, since his (liberal) brand of Judaism was an ethical and critical religion, it embraced the irreverent spirit of modern thought. See James Darmesteter, *Les Prophètes d'Israel* (Paris: Calmann Lévy, 1892), vi. And, even Protestant commentators

of the time agreed with Darmesteter that modern Judaism suited modern France perfectly. See Jean Réville's review of Darmesteter's *Les Prophètes d'Israel* in *Revue d'histoire des religions* 25 (1892): 253–56.

36. Weber, *The Nationalist Revival in France*, 36.

37. Sabatier, *France To-day*, 55.

38. Dom Besse, *Les religions laiques: un romanticisme religieux* (Paris: Nouvelle Librairie Nationale, 1913), 22

39. Paul Gerbod, "L'Ethique héroique en France (1870–1914)," *Revue historique* 268 (1982): 413.

40. Pierre Nora, "Ernest Lavisse: son role dans la formation du sentiment national," *Revue historique* 228 (1962): 103.

41. Brian Jenkins, *Nationalism in France: Class and Nation since 1789* (Savage, Md.: Barnes and Noble, 1990), 83.

42. Gerbod, "L'Ethique héroique en France," 414.

43. Richard D. Sonn, *Anarchism and Cultural Politics in Fin de Siècle France* (Lincoln: University of Nebraska Press, 1989), 274.

44. Part of the motive behind Loisy's move toward the religion of patriotism was moral expedience. The war reduced loyalties to a common denominator. In 1917, Loisy wrote Maude Petre, "I have one reason for insisting on the religion of the fatherland; it is the one thing on which men of good will can meet in France." Maude D. Petre, *Alfred Loisy: His Religious Significance* (Cambridge: Cambridge University Press, 1944), 117. The war only accentuated what had become a perennial feature of the new religious life of humanity living with the daily reality of nationalism. Loisy sees that for the French, the new religion of patriotism had replaced traditional religion as a locus of real religious feeling for the foreseeable future. In his 1917 correspondence with Maude Petre, Loisy notes that "'it seems to me better to give a concrete form to our French ideal of humanity by starting from France.'" Ibid.

45. Alfred Loisy, *La Religion* (Paris: Nourry, 1917), 31

46. In retrospect, Loisy therefore judged the Catholic revival of the first decade of the twentieth century rather superficial. Loisy, *La Religion*, 24ff.

47. Ibid., 290.

48. Ibid., 33.

49. Alfred Loisy, *La Morale humaine* (Paris: Nourry, 1923), 289–91.

50. Zev Sternhell, "The Political Culture of Nationalism," in *Nationhood and Nationalism in France*, ed. Tombs, 30–33.

51. D. G. Charlton, *The Secular Religions of France (1815–1870)* (Oxford: Oxford University Press, 1963), 90.

52. Ibid., 72, 73.

53. In this connection, Henri Guillemin distinguished between what we might call religious and secular nationalisms. The "nationalistes" proper were those who deified the nation; the "nationaux" simply loved it. Henri Guillemin, *Nationalistes et "nationaux"* (Paris: Gallimard, 1974).

54. Stéphane Audoin-Rouzeau, "The National Sentiment of Soldiers during the Great War," in *Nationhood and Nationalism in France*, ed. Tombs, 89–100; Susan Dunn, *The Deaths of Louis XVI: Regicide and the French Political Imagination* (Princeton: Princeton University Press, 1994), 66. She discusses Dunn's arguments regarding Michelet's investment in Catholic symbolism, such as Joan of Arc, the Passion, and so on.

55. Georges Goyau, *The Church of France during the War* (Paris: Bloud and Gay, 1918), 11.

56. Maurice Barrès, "Young Soldiers of France," in *War and the Spirit of Youth* (Boston: Houghton and Mifflin, 1917), 21ff.

57. Commentators of the times, such as Salomon Reinach, also thought that he recognized a peculiar preoccupation with "blood" in French Catholic discourse. Salomon Reinach, "L'Accusation du meurtre rituel en 1892," *Cultes, mythes et religions* (Paris: Ernst Leroux, 1923), 5:471–73.

58. Tison-Braun, *La Crise de l'humanisme*, 2:44.

59. Ibid., 51.

60. Gerbod, "L'Ethique héroïque en France," 414.

61. Ibid., 414, 419.

62. Jean-Marie Mayeur, "Le Catholicisme français et le Première Guerre mondiale," *Francia* 2 (1974): 388.

63. Ibid., 396.

64. Weber, *The Nationalist Revival in France*, 102; J. A. Gunn, *Modern French Philosophy* (New York: Dodd, Mead, 1922), 278.

65. Gunn, *Modern French Philosophy*, 278.

66. Mayeur, "Le Catholicisme français," 387.

67. Jacques Fontana, *Attitudes et sentiments du clergé et des catholiques françaises devant et durant la guerre de 1914–1918* (Lille: Service de Reproduction des thèses, 1973), 96.

68. Victor Bucaille, ed., *Lettres de prêtres aux armées* (Paris: Payot, 1916), 21–22.

69. The Germans—even German Catholics—were deemed equally culpable by the intransigents because it was from Germany that that bugbear of intransigent Catholic sensibility, religious modernism, came. See Mayeur, "Le Catholicisme français," 383.

70. Ibid.

71. Ibid., 396.

72. Bertrand, *L'Appel du sol*, 193.

73. Ibid., 141–42.

74. Mayeur, "Le Catholicisme français," 383.

75. Ibid., 381.

76. Ibid., 386.

77. Ibid., 387.

78. Goyau, *The Church of France during the War*, 11.

79. Mayeur, "Le Catholicisme français," 384.

80. Ibid., 396.

81. Norman Ravitch, *The Catholic Church and the French Nation, 1589–1989* (London: Routledge, 1990). This theme recurs in Ravitch's work from his treatment of Louis XIV (21–27, 40) through to the French Revolution (52ff), Napoleon (56–58) and into the nineteenth century (62–63).

82. Monsignor Guérard, bishop of the diocese of Coutance, pastoral letter, 2 February 1915, cited in Jacques Fontana, *Les Catholiques français pendant la Grande Guerre* (Paris: Cerf, 1990), 225.

83. Fontana, *Les Catholiques français pendant la Grande Guerre*, 225.

84. Ibid., 58.

85. Richard Griffiths, *The Reactionary Revolution: The Catholic Revival in French Literature, 1870–1914* (New York: Frederick Ungar, 1965), 330.

86. Sternhell, citing "La Reforme intellectuelle," in "The Political Culture of Nationalism," 35.

87. Fontana, *Attitudes et sentiments du clergé*, 81–82. See also Fontana, *Les Catholiques français pendant la Grande Guerre*, 59.

88. Bishop Gauthey of Besançon, pastoral letter, 11 February 1915, cited in Fontana, *Les Catholiques français pendant la Grande Guerre*, 226.

89. Fontana, *Les Catholiques français pendant la Grande Guerre*, 59.

90. Richard Griffiths, *The Reactionary Revolution: The Catholic Revival in French Literature, 1870–1914* (London: Constable, 1966), passim; René Rémond, *The Right Wing in France from 1815 to De Gaulle*, 2d American ed., trans. James M. Laux (Philadelphia: University of Pennsylvania Press, 1969), 185–88.

91. Ronald N. Stromberg, *Redemption by War: The Intellectuals and 1914* (Lawrence: Regents Press of Kansas, 1982), 190.

92. Fontana, *Les Catholiques français pendant la Grande Guerre*, 58.

93. Bishop Chapon of the diocese of Nice, pastoral letter, 2 February 1915, cited in ibid., 226.

94. Cardinal archbishop Luçon of Reims, pastoral letter, 27 January 1917, cited in ibid., 228.

95. The "vicaire titulaire" of Rouen, pastoral letter, 24 February 1916, cited in ibid., 227.

96. Incidentally, the same pairing of redemption and expiation for sin dominates the Irish Catholic ideology of revolution. See John Newsinger, "'I Bring Not Peace but a Sword': The Religious Motif in the Irish War of Independence," *Journal of Contemporary History* 13 (1978): 615, 618.

97. Gerbod, "L'Ethique héroique en France," 425–26.

98. Paraphrase of Bishop of Nantes, pastoral letter, 12 February 1917, cited in Fontana, *Les Catholiques français pendant la Grande Guerre*, 229.

99. Gabriel Langlois, *Le Clergé, les catholiques et la guerre* (Paris: Bibliothèque des Ouvrages Documentaires, 1915).

100. Frère Ambroise Soudé, "L'âme du prêtre," in *Lettres de prêtres aux armées*, ed. Bucaille, 9.

101. Bucaille, ed., *Lettres de prêtres aux armées*, 11.

102. Ibid., 12.

103. Ibid., 65.

104. Désiré Cardinal Mercier, pastoral letter, "Patriotisme et endurance," Christmas 1914, in *Le Cardinal Mercier contre les barbares*, ed. Cardinal Amette and Antoine Monsignor Baudrillart (Paris: Bloud and Gay, 1917), 16ff.

105. Isaiah Berlin, "Joseph de Maistre and the Origins of Fascism," part 2, *New York Review of Books*, 11 October 1990, 56.

106. Joseph de Maistre, *Les Soirées de Saint-Petersbourg, ou entretiens sur le gouvernement temporel de la providence suivis d'un traite sur les sacrifices* (Paris: La Librairie Ecclesiastique de Rusand, 1822), 2:456.

107. Joseph de Maistre, *St. Petersbourg Dialogues*, ed. and trans. Richard A. Lebrun (Montréal/Kingston: McGill/Queen's University Presses, 1993), 381.

108. Louis Veuillot, *La Guerre et l'homme de guerre*, 3d ed. (Paris: Société Générale de Librairie Catholique, 1870), 369.

109. Ibid., 36.

110. Ibid., 84.

111. Ibid., 95.

112. Ibid., 95ff.

113. Ibid., 97.

114. Ibid., 366–67.

115. Ibid., 369.

116. Barrès, "Young Soldiers of France," 10.

117. Bordeaux, *Les Derniers jours de Fort de Vaux,* 112, 117. I quote the official English translation in my text rather than attempting to best professional translators. Henry Bordeaux, *The Last Days of Fort de Vaux,* trans. Paul Cohen (Edinburgh/New York: Thomas Nelson and Sons, 1917), 78, 82.

118. Loïs Dabbadie, *Une Croisade au vingtième siècle: civilisation chrétienne contre pan-germanisme* (Port-Louis, Ile Maurice: General Printing, 1917), 72.

119. Ibid., 71.

120. Ibid., iii.

121. Ibid., i.

122. Geoffroy de Grandmaison, *Un Caractère de Soldat: le Capitaine Pierre de Saint-Jouan (1888–1915)* (Paris: Plon, 1920).

123. Ibid., 267

124. Ibid., 266.

125. Newsinger, "'I Bring Not Peace but a Sword,'" 615.

126. Bishop Grellier of the diocese of Laval, pastoral letter, 2 February 1915, cited in Fontana, *Les Catholiques français pendant la Grande Guerre,* 225.

127. Bishop Gouraud of Nice, in his "Devoirs de la famille pendant la guerre," 2 February 1916, cited in ibid., 232.

128. Mayeur, "Le Catholicisme français," 383. See the numerous citations from wartime pastoral letters by many prominent Catholic bishops in Fontana, *Les Catholiques français pendant la Grande Guerre,* 58, 225, 228, 229, 232, 242.

129. Louis de Grandmaison, *Dressage de l'infanterie en vue du combat offensif,* 3d ed. (Paris: Berger-Levrault, 1908), 4.

130. Ibid., 2.

131. Ibid.

132. Ibid., 3.

133. Ibid., 9.

134. Ibid., 5.

135. Ferdinand Foch, *The Memoirs of Marshal Foch,* trans. T. Bentley Mott (New York: Doubleday, 1931), lxi.

136. Jack Snyder, *The Ideology of the Offensive: Military Decision Making and the Disasters of 1914* (Ithaca: Cornell University Press, 1984), 16.

137. Basil H. Liddell Hart, *Foch: Man of Orléans* (Harmondsworth: Penguin Books, 1937), 1:76. See also Leonard V. Smith, *Between Mutiny and Obedience* (Princeton: Princeton University Press, 1994), 29.

138. Bordeaux, *Les Derniers jours de Fort de Vaux,* 251, 255; Bordeaux, *The Last Days of Fort de Vaux,* 183, 186.

139. Joseph Joffre, *The Personal Memoirs of Joffre,* trans. T. Bentley Mott (New York: Harper, 1932), 26.

140. Grandmaison, *Dressage de l'infanterie en vue du combat offensif.*

141. Joffre, *The Personal Memoirs of Joffre,* 29.

142. Ibid.

143. Ibid., 30.

144. Natalie Zemon Davis, "The Rites of Violence," in *Society and Culture in Early Modern France* (Stanford: Stanford University Press, 1975), 174.

145. Simon Schama, *Citizens: A Chronicle of the French Revolution* (Knopf: New York, 1989), 259, 445ff.

146. Ibid., 406.

147. Patrice Higonnet, *Goodness beyond Virtue: Jacobins during the French Revolution* (Cambridge: Harvard University Press, 1998), 187.

148. Ibid., 317–18.

149. Daniel Pick, *War Machine: The Rationalization of Slaughter* (New Haven: Yale University Press, 1993), 162.

150. Ibid., chap. 15. See also Audoin-Rouzeau, "The National Sentiment of Soldiers during the Great War," 89–100.

151. Pick, *War Machine*, 104 n. 41, 267.

152. On the broad popular influence of Bergson's ideal of *"élan vital,"* see Tison-Braun, *La Crise de l'humanisme*, 1:385–90.

153. Liddell Hart, *Foch*, 1:76.

154. Roger Martin du Gard, *Jean Barois*, trans. Stuart Gilbert (1914; reprint, New York: Bobbs Merrill, 1969), 317. "Duty" translates *devoir*.

155. Ibid., 319.

156. Ibid., 312ff.

157. Bertrand, *L'Appel du sol*, 193.

158. Ibid., 194.

159. Ibid., 192.

160. Foch, *The Memoirs of Marshal Foch*, xxii.

161. Ferdinand Foch, cited in André Tardieu, *Avec Foch* (Paris: n.p., 1929), 32, cited in Stefan T. Possony and Etienne Mantoux, "Du Picq and Foch: The French School," in *Makers of Modern Strategy*, ed. Edward Mead Earle (Princeton: Princeton University Press, 1971), 230.

162. Maistre's influence on the military is also confirmed by intransigent Catholic Ernest Psichari's views in his *L'Appel des armes*. For Psichari, de Maistre is a perfect "model of the 'pensée catholique' for soldiers.'" See Robert Triomphe, *Joseph de Maistre: Étude sur la doctrine d'un matérialiste mystique* (Droz: Genéve, 1968), 14.

163. Possony and Mantoux, "Du Picq and Foch," 228.

164. Richard Griffiths, *The Use of Abuse: The Polemics of the Dreyfus Affair and Its Aftermath* (New York: Berg, 1991), chap. 6.

165. Bertrand, *L'Appel du sol*, 140, 259.

166. Ibid., 194.

167. On Vaissette's affection for Lucretius, see ibid., 259. We are "animals" who submit themselves to nature. They "accept what the universe wants."

168. Ibid., 281.

169. Ibid., 282.

170. Ibid., 196.

171. Jack Snyder, in his study *The Ideology of the Offensive*, also comes close to engaging religious factors in writing of how the First World War was fought according to an "ideology" informing the excessive character of the French offensive.

172. Pick, *War Machine*, 158.

173. Audoin-Rouzeau, "The National Sentiment of Soldiers during the Great War," 99.

174. Barrès, "Young Soldiers of France," 21ff.

175. Pick, *War Machine*, 158, 257.

176. Barrès, "Young Soldiers of France," 17.

177. That sacrifice was essential to the existence of the nation was Renan's position in his highly influential "What Is a Nation?" (1882) in *Poetry of the Celtic Races and Other Essays*, ed. William G. Hutchinson (London: Walter Scott Publishing, 1896), 61–83, cited in Sternhell, "The Political Culture of Nationalism," 33.

178. Barrès, "Young Soldiers of France," 55.

179. Audoin-Rouzeau, "The National Sentiment of Soldiers during the Great War," 94ff.

180. Ibid., 99.

181. Ibid.

182. Ibid.

183. Suzanne Desan, *Reclaiming the Sacred: Lay Religion and Popular Politics in Revolutionary France* (Ithaca: Cornell University Press, 1990), 18. For continuities between Catholic and revolutionary values, see Dale K. Van Kley, *The Religious Origins of the French Revolution* (New Haven: Yale University Press, 1996); Daniele Menozzi, *Les Interprétations politiques de Jésus de l'ancien régime à la Révolution*, trans. Jacqueline Touvier (Paris: Cerf, 1983); Hugh R. Trevor Roper, "The Religious Origins of the Enlightenment," in *The European Witchcraze of the Sixteenth and Seventeenth Centuries and Other Essays* (New York: Harper, 1967), chap. 4. Old, but still useful for its documentary sources, is Augustin Louis Gazier, *Études sur l'histoire religieuse de la révolution française d'après des documents originaux et inédits* (Paris: A. Colin, 1887). See also the vast literature on the Constitutional Church and Abbé Grégoire, its leading thinker: Frank Paul Bowman, *L'Abbé Grégoire: évêque des Lumières* (Paris: France-Empire, 1988); Bernard Plongeron, *L'Abbé Grégoire: (1750–1831) ou l'arche de la fraternité* (Paris: Letouzey et Ané, 1988). For the perspective of African American liberationist concerns and Roman Catholic revolutionary ideals, see Ruth F. Necheles, *The Abbé Grégoire, 1787–1831* (Westport, Conn.: Greenwood Press, 1971). Higonnet (*Goodness beyond Virtue*) and Schama (*Citizens*, 350, 602) offer more general viewpoints on the relation of Catholicism and the ideals of the French Revolution.

184. As I discussed in chapter 2, I am not denying or playing down the importance during the French Revolution of models drawn from the ancient world, especially from Rome.

185. Jay Winter, *Sites of Memory, Sites of Mourning* (Cambridge: Cambridge University Press, 1995), 204.

186. Ibid., 128ff, 204.

187. Barrès, "Young Soldiers of France," 57.

188. Audoin-Rouzeau, "The National Sentiment of Soldiers during the Great War," 92.

189. Bertrand, *L'Appel du sol*, 132.

190. Ibid., 133.

191. Ibid., 132

192. Ibid., 133.

193. Ibid., 134.

194. Snyder, *The Ideology of the Offensive*, 57.

195. Ibid., 58.

196. Ibid., 215.

197. Ibid., 214.

198. Ibid., 216ff.

199. Ibid., 51ff; Veuillot, *La Guerre et l'homme de guerre*, 366.

200. Carole Fink, *Marc Bloch: A Life in History* (Cambridge: Cambridge University Press, 1989), 54, citing Snyder, *The Ideology of the Offensive*, 15–16.

201. What is truly remarkable was the "ubiquity" of this belief in the years 1870–1914, and how thoroughly this belief dominated especially Catholic, but also Jewish and to a much lesser extent Protestant, religious sensibility in late nineteenth-

and early twentieth-century France. Griffiths, *The Reactionary Revolution*, 1966 ed., 149.

202. Bertrand, *L'Appel du sol*, 193.

203. Liddell Hart, *Foch*, 1:76.

204. On the Jew as outsider and pollutant, see Shmuel Trigano, "From Individual to Collectivity: The Rebirth of the 'Jewish Nation' in France," in *The Jews in Modern France*, ed. Frances Malino and Bernard Wasserstrom (Hanover, N.H.: University Press of New England, 1985), 245–81.

205. Philippe Landau, "'La Patrie en danger': D'une guerre à l'autre," in *Histoire politique des juifs de France*, ed. Pierre Birnbaum (Paris: Presses de la Fondation Nationale des sciences politiques, 1990), 74–91.

206. See Michael R. Marrus, *The Politics of Assimilation: A Study of the French Jewish Community at the Time of the Dreyfus Affair* (Oxford: Oxford University Press, 1971), 122ff.

207. Armand Bloch, "Le patriotisme juif," allocution prononcée à l'inauguration de la statue de Jeanne D'Arc, Nancy, 28 June 1890 (Nancy: Imprimerie Nouvelle, 1890).

208. Ibid., 6.

209. Jacques Henry Dreyfuss, "L'esprit de sacrifice," sermon, 15 September 1890, Israelite Temple, Brussels, 4. See also Marrus, *The Politics of Assimilation*, 111f.

210. Dreyfuss, "L'esprit de sacrifice," 5.

211. Hyppolite Prague, "Kippour et l'esprit du sacrifice," *Archives israélites*, 5 October 1916, 157.

212. Ibid.

213. "Le Soldat Juif," *Archives israélites*, 8 April 1915, 53.

214. *Archives israélites*, 15 July 1915, 114.

215. *Archives israélites*, 28 October 1915, 173.

216. Hyppolite Prague, "Purim," *Archives israélites*, 16 March 1916, 41.

217. Prague, "Kippour et l'esprit du sacrifice," 159.

218. Dreyfuss, "L'esprit de sacrifice," 5.

219. Ibid., 6.

220. *Archives israélites*, 13 May 1915, 77.

221. Annie Kriegel, *Les juifs et le monde moderne* (Paris: Éditions du Seuil, 1977), 137–66. See also Salomon Reinach's favorable account of the Russian revolution, published under the initials S. R., *Histoire de la révolution Russe (1905–1917)* (Paris: Librairie Militaire Berger-Levrault, 1917).

222. Salomon Reinach, "Le Réveil religieux en France avant la guerre" (1914), in *Cultes, mythes et religions*, 5:378.

223. Salomon Reinach, "Pendant et après la guerre" (1922), in *Cultes, mythes et religions*, 5:382.

224. André Spire, *Les juifs et la guerre* (Paris: Payot, 1917), 18ff.

225. Charles Péguy, *Notre jeunesse* (Paris: Gallimard, 1933), 68.

226. Hubert Bourgin, *De Jaurès à Leon Blum* (Paris: Artheme Fayard, 1938), 484.

227. Spire, *Les juifs et la guerre*, 158. On Spire, see Michel Abitbol, *Les Deux terres promises: Les juifs de France et le sionisme* (Paris: Olivier Orban, 1989), 82. On Spire, see Paula Hyman, *From Dreyfus to Vichy* (New York: Columbia University Press, 1979), passim.

228. Spire, *Les juifs et la guerre*, 32.

229. Gerbod, "L'Ethique héroique en France," 417.

230. Ibid., 418.

231. Daniel Robert, "Les Protestants français et la guerre de 1914–1918," *Francia* 2 (1974): 415–30.

232. Ibid., 420.

233. Ibid., 421.

234. Ibid.

235. Ibid., 416.

236. Ibid., 417.

237. Ibid., 418.

238. Ibid.

239. Ibid., 420.

240. Ibid., 422.

241. Ibid., 423.

242. Barrès, "Young Soldiers of France," 11ff.

243. See the biography of a devoted student, Gaston Richard, *La Vie et l'oeuvre de Raoul Allier* (Paris: Berger-Levrault, 1948). Allier also served as head of the Protestant faculty of theology in Paris.

244. Raoul Allier, *La Compagnie du trés saint-sacrement de l'autel: la cabale des dévots* (Paris: Colin, 1902); Raoul Allier, *La Compagnie du saint-sacrement. Marseille* (Paris: Honoré Champion, 1909); Raoul Allier, *La Compagnie du trés saint-sacrement de l'autel à Toulouse: une esquisse de son histoire* (Paris: Honoré Champion, 1914).

245. Jean Réville, review of *La Cabale des dévots*, by Raoul Allier, *Revue de l'histoire des religions* 48 (1903): 256.

246. Raoul Allier, *Le Sacrifice vivant* (Paris: Librarie de Foi et Vie, 1915). See also Raoul Allier, *Sacrifice et récompense* (Paris: Librairie de Foi et Vie, 1915).

247. Richard, *La Vie et l'oeuvre de Raoul Allier*, 192.

248. Ibid., 201.

249. Ibid., 205.

250. This is a view Allier shared with his philosophical mentor, Charles Renouvier. See Richard, *La Vie et l'oeuvre de Raoul Allier*, 224.

251. Ibid., 197.

252. Allier, *Le Sacrifice vivant*, 3ff.

253. Genesis 22 nowhere speaks of Abraham's hesitation. On the contrary, the patriarch is dutiful to the letter.

254. Allier, *Le Sacrifice vivant*, 5.

255. Ibid., 6.

256. Ibid., 7.

257. Richard, *La Vie et l'oeuvre de Raoul Allier*, 204.

CHAPTER FOUR

1. Charles Péguy, *Notre Jeunesse* (1910; reprint, Paris: Gallimard, 1933), quoted in *Charles Péguy: Basic Verities*, ed. Ann and Julian Green (New York City: Pantheon, 1943), 131.

2. Micheline Tison-Braun, *La Crise de l'humanisme* (Paris: Nizet, 1967), 1:246.

3. Ibid., 251.

4. Péguy, *Notre Jeunesse*, 115–16.

5. Richard Griffiths, *The Use of Abuse: The Polemics of the Dreyfus Affair and Its Aftermath* (New York: Berg, 1991), chap. 3.

6. Péguy, *Notre Jeunesse*, 117.

7. A. Daspre, "L'héroisation de Dreyfus," in *Les Écrivains et l'affaire Dreyfus*, ed. Géraldi Leroy (Paris: Presses Universitaires de France, 1983), 219, 221ff.

8. Griffiths, *The Use of Abuse*, chap. 6.

9. While these distinctions among the "case," "affair," and "mystique" are separable analytically, they are not always separable chronologically. Richard Griffiths also develops a similar distinction in ibid., chap. 2.

10. Ibid., 18.

11. Bernard Lazare, *Une Erreur judiciare: l'affaire Dreyfus*, 2d ed. (Paris: P.-V. Stock, 1897).

12. Jean-Denis Bredin, *The Affair: The Case of Alfred Dreyfus*, trans. Jeffrey Melman (New York: George Braziller, 1986), chap. 6.

13. Roger Dadoun, "Une affaire de mystique," in *Les Écrivains et l'affaire Dreyfus*, ed. Leroy, 13.

14. One of the earlier articles actually was so potent that it occasioned Bernard Lazare's entry into the fray. See Bredin, *The Affair*, 137.

15. For a full account of Zola's *parcours*, consult Béatrice Laville, "Zola et ses représentations de L'Affaire," *Littérature et Nation*, hors série, Les Représentations de l'affaire Dreyfus dans la presse en France et à l'étranger: Actes du colloque de Saint-Cyr-sur-Loire, November 1994 (1998): 145–50.

16. Ibid., 149.

17. Géraldi Leroy, "L'affaire Dreyfus dans la *Revue Blanche*," *Littérature et Nation*, hors série, Les Représentations de l'affaire Dreyfus dans la presse en France et à l'étranger: Actes du colloque de Saint-Cyr-sur-Loire, November 1994 (1998): 30.

18. This, at any rate, is the opinion of Roger Dadoun ("Une affaire de mystique," 14–15). As such, it represents the intention to differ from the implications of Charles Péguy's claim that the two realms are continuous, as Péguy implies in his saying "La politique se moque de la mystique, mais c'est encore la mystique qui nourrit la politique même."

19. Charles Maurras, *Au Signe de flore* (Paris: Editions Bernard Grasset, 1933), 52.

20. P. E. Charvet, introduction to Ernest Renan, *La Réforme intellectuelle et morale de la France*, ed. P. E. Charvet (New York: Greenwood, 1968), xxvi–ii. Here it is worth noting how the new antipositivist epistemology of the turn of the century, embraced by Bernard Lazare, aided him in piercing the shell of official opinion against Dreyfus. As a critic of positivism, Bernard Lazare was already prepared to look beyond what struck the naked eye, to retain a skepticism of received authoritative opinion. To him, the dogged resistance to an acquittal of Dreyfus pointed to deeper causes than those that appeared to everyday opinion. Dreyfus's condemnation had a distinct "theological" character. See Nelly Wilson, *Bernard Lazare* (Cambridge: Cambridge University Press, 1978), 172.

21. In the same way that Dreyfus was caught up in mythological constructions, there are the perhaps better-known Jewish victims of the accusation of "'ritual murder.'" See R. Po-chia Hsia, *The Myth of Ritual Murder: Jews and Magic in Reformation Germany* (New Haven: Yale University Press, 1988); Norman Ravitch, *The Catholic Church and the French Nation, 1589–1989* (London: Routledge, 1990), 97.

22. Daspre, "L'héroisation de Dreyfus," 220.

23. Pierre Bénard, "Maurice Barrès regarde Alfred Dreyfus," *Littérature et Nation*, hors série, Les Représentations de l'affaire Dreyfus dans la presse en France et à l'étranger: Actes du colloque de Saint-Cyr-sur-Loire, November 1994 (1998): 170.

24. Maurice Barrès seems to have been first to direct the rhetoric of "Judas" against

Dreyfus. On 8 December 1894, only weeks after Dreyfus's condemnation and a full month *before* his degradation, Barrès published an analysis of Dreyfus as Judas. Bénard, "Maurice Barrès regarde Alfred Dreyfus," 170.

25. See, in particular, the fine collection assembled by Norman L. Kleeblatt in his edited volume *The Dreyfus Affair: Art, Truth, and Justice* (Berkeley: University of California Press, 1987).

26. Un Français, "Le Traitre," *Le Pélerin,* 30 December 1894, 718.

27. Nelly Wilson, "Bernard Lazare et le syndicat," in *Les Écrivains et l'affaire Dreyfus,* ed. Leroy, 27ff.

28. Bredin, *The Affair,* 138.

29. Wilson, *Bernard Lazare,* 207.

30. Robert S. Wistrich, "Three Dreyfusard Heroes: Lazare, Zola, Clemenceau," in *Les Intellectuels face à l'affaire Dreyfus alors et aujourd'hui,* ed. Roselyne Koren and Dan Michman (Paris: Harmattan, 1998), 17.

31. This epithet actually appeared in the Lyon newspaper, *La France Libre,* 11 January 1898, as "Judas Dreyfus." See Pierre Pierrard, *Les Chrétiens et l'affaire Dreyfus* (Paris: Les Editions de L'Atelier, 1998), 77. See also Maurice Barrès's early declaration of Dreyfus as Judas in Bénard, "Maurice Barrès regarde Alfred Dreyfus," 170.

32. Wistrich, "Three Dreyfusard Heroes," 28. See also Griffiths, *The Use of Abuse,* 97–99.

33. Griffiths, *The Use of Abuse,* 97.

34. Quoting Zola's "Lettre à Madame Alfred Dreyfus," *L'Aurore,* 29 September 1899, in Griffiths, *The Use of Abuse,* 98.

35. Wistrich, "Three Dreyfusard Heroes," 30.

36. René Girard, *The Scapegoat,* trans. Yvonne Freccero (Baltimore: Johns Hopkins University Press, 1986).

37. Daspre, "L'héroisation de Dreyfus," 219.

38. Pierre Pierrard claims that Judas was "a *leitmotif* countless times repeated in the Catholic press." Pierrard, *Les Chrétiens et l'affaire Dreyfus,* 59.

39. See in particular the comments of John Grand-Carteret listing Judas as one of the chief images representing Dreyfus in the popular press in his *L'Affaire Dreyfus et l'image* (Paris: Flammarion, 1898), 2.

40. Bénard, "Maurice Barrès regarde Alfred Dreyfus," 170.

41. Ibid. This identification of Dreyfus with Job was reasserted by Barrès as late as 1902. Ibid., 171.

42. Pierrard, *Les Chrétiens et l'affaire Dreyfus,* 48. In his writings for *La Croix,* Bailly used the *nom de plume* "Le Moine" (ibid., 18). Pierre Bénard argues that Maurice Barrès considers the figure of Dreyfus as a "sacrifice" in his "Maurice Barrès regarde Alfred Dreyfus," 171.

43. Daspre, "L'héroisation de Dreyfus," 221.

44. Matthew 27:5: After learning of Jesus' arrest, Judas throws down the forty silver pieces in the temple and commits suicide; Acts 1:18−19: Judas falls to his death on the field which he had bought with the forty pieces of silver. He bursts open and his insides fall out.

45. J. M. Robertson, *Jesus and Judas, a Textual and Historical Investigation* (London: Watts & Co., 1927). Although the work of Robertson may in general be considered outdated, it is interesting to note that he records that the price of thirty *shekels* or pieces of silver paid to Judas was the standard price paid for a slave and that victims for sacrifice were always bought with a price.

46. Pierrard, *Les Chrétiens et l'affaire Dreyfus*, 203–7; Eric Cahm, *The Dreyfus Affair in French Society and Politics* (London and New York: Longman, 1996), 123.

47. Daspre, "L'héroisation de Dreyfus," 221ff.

48. Bénard, "Maurice Barrès regarde Alfred Dreyfus," 170.

49. Ibid., 172.

50. Ibid., 170. This identification of Dreyfus with Job was reasserted by Barrès as late as 1902. Ibid., 171.

51. Edith Flamarion, "Brutus ou l'adoption d'un mythe romain par la Révolution française," in *La Révolution française et l'antiquité*, ed. R. Chevallier (Tours: Centre de Recherches A. Piganiol, 1991), 91, 98ff.

52. Maurice Barrès also held the same opinion. See Bertrand Joly, "Les Antidreyfusards, croyaient-ils Dreyfus coupable?" *Revue historique* 291/590 (April–June 1994): 404.

53. Ravitch, *The Catholic Church and the French Nation*, 97.

54. Maurras, *Au Signe de flore*, 61.

55. Joly, "Les Antidreyfusards," 405.

56. Girard, *The Scapegoat*, 113.

57. René Girard, *Violence and the Sacred*, trans. Patrick Gregory (Baltimore: Johns Hopkins University Press, 1977), 2.

58. Bredin, *The Affair*, 139.

59. Émile Durkheim, *Textes*, vol. 2, *Religion, morale, anomie*, ed. Victor Karady (Paris: Minuit, 1975), 252.

60. Albert S. Lindemann, *The Jew Accused* (Cambridge: Cambridge University Press, 1991), 108ff.

61. Ibid., 107.

62. Léon Blum, quoted from *Souvenirs sur l'Affaire* (n.p., 1935); Wladimir Rabi, "Écrivains juifs face à l'affaire Dreyfus," in *Les Écrivains et l'affaire Dreyfus*, ed. Leroy, 18. See also Tony Judt on Blum's criticism of his French Jewish peers in *The Burden of Responsibility* (Chicago: University of Chicago Press, 1999), 43.

63. Léon Blum, apparently quoted from *Souvenirs sur l'affaire*, 1935 ed.; Rabi, "Écrivains juifs face à l'affaire Dreyfus," 19.

64. Léon Blum, *Souvenirs sur l'affaire* (Paris: Gallimard, 1937), 97, quoted in *The Dreyfus Affair: Art, Truth, and Justice*, ed. Norman L. Kleeblatt (Berkeley: University of California Press, 1987), 31. Also cited in Judt, *The Burden of Responsibility*, 43.

65. Michael R. Marrus, *The Politics of Assimilation: A Study of the French Jewish Community at the Time of the Dreyfus Affair* (Oxford: Oxford University Press, 1971), 141ff.

66. Girard, *Violence and the Sacred*, 4.

67. Wistrich, "Three Dreyfusard Heroes," 19.

68. I, at least, have not found such reference.

69. Girard, *The Scapegoat*, 117.

70. Cahm, *The Dreyfus Affair in French Society and Politics*, 185.

71. Nor, as Lindemann argues, did the original army tribunal seize on Dreyfus as some sort of scapegoat for their problems. Lindemann, *The Jew Accused*, 97ff.

72. Cahm, *The Dreyfus Affair in French Society and Politics*, 185; Nicholas Halasz, *Captain Dreyfus: The Story of Mass Hysteria* (New York: Simon and Schuster, 1955), 266.

73. Daspre, "L'héroisation de Dreyfus," 220.

74. Pierrard, *Les Chrétiens et l'affaire Dreyfus*.

75. Lindemann, *The Jew Accused*, 106ff.

76. Ibid., 110.

77. Blum, *Souvenirs sur l'affaire,* 1937 ed., 97, quoted in *The Dreyfus Affair,* ed. Kleeblatt, 31; also cited in Judt, *The Burden of Responsibility,* 43; Wistrich, "Three Dreyfusard Heroes," 19.

78. Léon Blum, quoted from *Souvenirs sur l'Affaire,* 1935 ed., in Rabi, "Écrivains juifs face a l'affaire Dreyfus," 18.

79. Rabi, "Écrivains juifs face a l'affaire Dreyfus," 18.

80. Lindemann, *The Jew Accused,* 117.

81. Péguy, *Notre Jeunesse,* 68.

82. One might recall the remarkably ambivalent reactions of some Jewish commentators to the nomination of an Orthodox Jew, Senator Joseph Lieberman, to be the vice-presidential candidate of the Democratic party in 2000. One such fear voiced over this nomination was that raising Jews to public prominence only raises the likelihood that Jews will be blamed if events should go wrong. See David Margolick, "For American Jews, Hope and Uncertainty," *New York Times,* 12 August 2000.

83. Quoted from Barrès's *Scènes et doctrines du nationalism,* in Robert Soucy, *Fascism in France* (Berkeley: University of California, 1972), 100.

84. For a list of anti-Dreyfusards who persisted in saying that even though Dreyfus was innocent he should still be punished, see Joly, "Les antidreyfusards," 401–38.

85. Eugen Weber, *Action Française* (Stanford: Stanford University Press, 1962), 4.

86. Joly, "Les antidreyfusards," 432.

87. Charles Maurras, *Revue de l'Action Française* 3 (1901): 753, cited in Weber, *Action Française,* 6.

88. Maurras, *Au Signe de flore,* 55. See as well the discussion by Micheline Tison-Braun in *La Crise de l'humanisme,* 1:250.

89. Pierrard, *Les Chrétiens et l'affaire Dreyfus,* 101. Notable was the support for Henry from *La Croix* and *Les Annales Catholiques* (ibid., 102).

90. Pierre Félix, *Deux Cas de conscience: les catholiques français, l'affaire Dreyfus et l'Action Française* (Camp de Sathonay: private, 1911), 69ff.

91. Liah Greenfeld, *Nationalism: Five Roads to Modernity* (Cambridge: Harvard University Press, 1992), 175ff. Recall as well that Robespierre, among others, followed Rousseau's absolutizing of the General Will and held aloft the transcendent ideal of the nation as superior to any individual will. See Norman Hampson, "La Patrie," in Colin Lucas, *The French Revolution and the Creation of Modern Political Culture,* vol. 2, *The Political Culture of the French Revolution* (Oxford: Pergamon Press, 1988), 130. The relevant passages from Rousseau can be found in *The Social Contract,* bk. 2, chap. 5, and bk. 3, chap. 5. See, in this connection, Greenfeld, *Nationalism,* 172–77.

92. Adrien Dansette, *Religious History Modern France,* vol. 1, *From the Revolution to the Third Republic* (Edinburgh/London: Nelson, 1961), 95.

93. James L. Osen, *Royalist Protestant Political Thought during the French Revolution* (Westport, Conn.: Greenwood Press, 1995), 35.

94. Ibid., 68.

95. Theodore Herzl, *Die Judenstaat* (Vienna: Breitenstein, 1896).

96. For examples of the sacrificial language surrounding Israeli patriotism, see Yael Tamir, "Pro Patria Mori! Death and the State," *The Morality of Nationalism,* ed. Robert McKim and Jeff McMahan (New York: Oxford University Press, 1997), 227–44.

97. Natan Altermann, "The Silver Platter," quoted in Tamir, "Pro Patria Mori!" 235, 240–41.

98. An exception here is Léon Blum, who felt that his very Frenchness dictated his being Zionist. See Judt, *The Burden of Responsibility,* 43.

99. Ernst Nolte, *Three Faces of Fascism*, trans. L. Vennewitz (New York: New American Library, 1965), 57–61.

100. Georges Goyau, "La Modernité d'un 'réactionnaire' catholique: Joseph de Maistre," in *Catholicisme et politique* (Paris: Editions de la Revue des Jeunes, 1923).

101. Citing Charles Maurras, *Revue de l'Action Française* 1 (1899): 316, in Weber, *Action Française*, 8.

102. Weber, *Action Française*, 11.

103. Ibid., 16.

104. Isaiah Berlin, introduction to *Joseph de Maistre: "Considerations on France,"* ed. Richard A. Lebrun (Cambridge: Cambridge University Press, 1994), xxx.

105. See Julien Benda, *The Treason of the Intellectuals* (1928), trans. Richard Aldington (Boston: W. W. Norton, 1969), 104, cited in Soucy, *Fascism in France*, 101.

106. Regarding the revival of Maistre's reputation at the *fin-de-siècle*, see Georges Goyau, "La Modernité d'un 'réactionnaire' catholique," 69–93.

107. Girard, *Violence and the Sacred*.

108. Isaiah Berlin, "Joseph de Maistre and the Origins of Fascism," part 1, *New York Review of Books*, 27 September 1990, 64.

109. Isaiah Berlin, "Joseph de Maistre and the Origins of Fascism," part 2, *New York Review of Books*, 11 October 1990, 57.

110. L. Vérax [pseud.], *Essai sur la mentalité militaire* (Paris: V.-P. Stock, 1898).

111. Ibid., 2.

112. Ibid., 3.

113. See Bertrand Joly on the military's habits of sacrifice for the greater good in his "Les antidreyfusards," 431.

114. Vérax, *Essai sur la mentalité militaire*, 13.

115. Ibid.

116. Ibid.

117. Ibid., 75.

118. Ibid., 87.

119. Ralph Gibson, *A Social History of French Catholicism: 1789–1914* (London: Routledge, 1989), 78–80.

120. Quentin Skinner, *Foundations of Modern Political Thought* (Cambridge: Cambridge University Press, 1978), 1:131ff.

121. Dale K. Van Kley, *The Religious Origins of the French Revolution* (New Haven: Yale University Press, 1996), 33.

122. Ernst H. Kantorowicz, *The King's Two Bodies: A Study in Mediaeval Political Theology* (Princeton: Princeton University Press, 1981).

123. Van Kley, *The Religious Origins of the French Revolution*, 22.

124. Ibid., 36.

125. Ibid.

126. Ibid., 72.

127. One may well argue with Norman Ravitch that the state had effectively co-opted and politicized the church as early as the sixteenth century, attaining total domination in the reign of Louis XIV and perfecting this domination bureaucratically with Napoleon. Ravitch, *The Catholic Church and the French Nation*, 17, 21, 40. Assertions of *raison d'état* in cases like these express the claim to superiority of the state over the church. Indeed, if we reflect on the fact that Machiavelli asserted the principle of *raison d'état* in face of the stiff opposition by the church, Ravitch's view gains further strength. See Skinner, *Foundations of Modern Political Thought*, 1:129. Royal religion, the

religion of "immanence," the "Confessional state," and such are examples of religion that had lost its prophetic character. It cannot oppose the state because it is merely one of its agents. Confirming this, we know further that Machiavelli anticipated Gibbon, Nietzsche, and Sorel in arguing that Christianity was unfit for a place in the proper ordering of the state—certainly for any prophetic role. Christianity only encouraged lamblike weakness. See Skinner, *Foundations of Modern Political Thought*, 1:167. But as in every process of identification, when religion and politics are identified, the energies and characteristics of both flow toward the other, often producing unanticipated results. When the French crown identified its interests with those of the Church, it not only co-opted the Church, depriving it of its prophetic role, it also assumed for itself a religious character, later inherited by the nation-state. A politicized Church calls forth a sacred nation.

128. Greenfeld, *Nationalism*, 172–77.

129. Ibid., 176.

130. Van Kley, *The Religious Origins of the French Revolution*, 367.

131. Ibid.

132. Ibid., 51.

133. John McManners, *Church and State in France, 1870–1914* (New York: Harper, 1972), 74.

134. Eugen Weber, "Gauls versus Franks: Conflict and Nationalism," in *Nationhood and Nationalism in France: From Boulangism to the Great War, 1889–1918,* ed. Robert Tombs (London: HarperCollins Academic, 1991), 19.

135. Van Kley, *The Religious Origins of the French Revolution,* 369–754, citing especially Quinet's *La Révolution* (1865; Paris: Claude Lefort, 1987).

136. Jules Arboux, "Maistre (Maire-Joseph, Comte de)," in *Encyclopédie des sciences religieuses,* ed. Frédéric Lichtenberger (Paris: Sandoz et Fischbacher, 1889), 8:575.

137. Ibid., 577.

138. Ibid., 576.

139. For details of Réville's biography, see Philippe Alphandéry, "Albert Réville," *Revue d'histoire des religions* 54 (1906): 401–23; Albert Houtin and Felix Sartiaux, *Alfred Loisy: sa vie, son oeuvre* (Paris: Editions du CNRS, 1960), 396–97.

140. Weber, "Gauls versus Franks," 19.

141. These include *Le Temps, Revue de Deux Mondes, L'Impartial, La Flandre libérale,* and *Revue Bleu.*

142. Jacques Marty, *Albert Réville: sa vie, son oeuvre* (Cahors: Conesdant, 1912), 54.

143. Albert Réville, "Conditions and Outlook for a Universal Religion," in *The World Parliament of Religions,* ed. John Henry Barrows (London: Review of Reviews, 1893), 2:1363–67.

144. Albert Réville, *Les étapes d'un intellectuel* (Paris: Stock, 1898).

145. Stephen Wilson, *Ideology and Experience: Antisemitism in France at the Time of the Dreyfus Affair* (Rutherford, N.J.: Fairleigh Dickinson University Press, 1982), 80–82.

146. Ibid., 476, 561.

147. Samples of this writing may be found in Albert Réville's *Fernand Cortez et les causes réeles de la conquête du Mexique* (Paris: Ve Ethiou-Perou, 1882), or "Contemporaneous Materialism in Religion: the Sacred Heart," *Theological Review* 11, no. 44 (1874): 138–56.

148. As might be expected, Réville favored the "radical" (that is to say, bourgeois) economics of someone like Gambetta who, in turn, reciprocated Réville's feelings by appointing him to take charge of the study of religions in the capital.

149. So much did Réville love the country that he even wrote several books on Holland during his stay there. See Alphandéry, "Albert Réville," 419. See also the *Revue des deux mondes* 1870–72.

150. Ernst Troeltsch, *The Social Teaching of the Christian Churches*, trans. Olive Wyon (London: George Allen and Unwin, 1931), 2:635, 683ff.

151. See especially Hugh Trevor-Roper, "Hugo Grotius and England," in *From Counter-Reformation to Glorious Revolution* (Chicago: University of Chicago Press, 1992), 47–82.

152. Ibid., 164.

153. Albert Réville, "Dutch Theology: Its Past and Present State," *Theological Review* 1, no. 3 (1864): 283.

154. Albert Réville, *Théodore Parker* (Paris: Reinwald, 1865). For a sample of Parker's views, see Theodore Parker, *Sermons of Theism, Atheism and Popular Theology* (Boston: Rufus Leighton, Jr., 1859).

155. Stuart R. Schram, *Protestantism and Politics in France* (Alençon: Corbière et Jugan, 1954), 54. About the same time, but in different circumstances, the great theorist of a humanist *"religion laïque,"* Ferdinand Buisson, was expelled by the Consistory from his orthodox Protestant congregation for advocating freedom of conscience against attempts to require doctrinal discipline. See George Chase, "Ferdinand Buisson: *Moraliste Laïque,*" Western Society for French History, Proceedings of the 10th Annual Meeting, 1982, 323.

156. Steven Lukes, *Individualism* (Oxford: Blackwell, 1973) 125–27; Louis Dumont, *Essays on Individualism: Modern Ideology in Anthropological Perspective* (Chicago: University of Chicago Press, 1986).

157. Albert Réville, *Lectures on the Origin and Growth of Religion*, 2d ed., trans. P. H. Wicksteed (London: Williams and Norgate, 1905), 40.

158. Ibid., 40–41.

159. Réville, *Les étapes d'un intellectuel.* Réville also wrote openly about his conversion during the Affair, even to Anglophone audiences, in "The Dreyfus Affair," *New World* 8 (1899): 601–25.

160. Réville, *Les étapes d'un intellectuel*, 4.

161. Ibid., 22, 24–28, 38–44.

162. Ibid., 33.

163. Ibid., 38.

164. Ibid., 24, 29.

165. Ibid., 40.

166. Lukes, *Individualism*, chap. 7.

167. Van Kley, *The Religious Origins of the French Revolution*, 24ff. The Jansenists shared much of the Calvinist position too. Ibid., 63, 66ff, 72.

168. Ibid., 23ff.

169. Ibid., 33.

170. Ibid., 13.

171. It should be noted that Norman Ravitch argues that instead of a sacralization of politics, such principles as *raison d'état* constitute a secularization or domestication of religion. Ravitch, *The Catholic Church and the French Nation*, 17, 22ff.

172. Émile Durkheim, "Individualism and the Intellectuals" (1898), in *Durkheim on Religion*, comp. W. S. F. Pickering (London: Routledge, 1975).

173. Ibid., 62.

CHAPTER FIVE

1. Ferdinand Buisson, ed., *French Educational Ideals of Today*, trans. Frederic E. Farrington (Yonkers: World Book Company, 1919), 205.

2. This was published two years later in *Revue d'histoire des religions* 44 (1901): 16–39.

3. Ibid., 35.

4. Ibid., 39.

5. Here I follow the analysis of transformations from monarchy to republican politico-religious forms worked out by Dale K. Van Kley, *The Religious Origins of the French Revolution* (New Haven: Yale University Press, 1996), 13–14.

6. Jay Winter, *Sites of Memory, Sites of Mourning: The Great War in European Cultural History* (Cambridge: Cambridge University Press, 1995), 128f.

7. Ibid., 204.

8. J. A. Gunn, *Modern French Philosophy* (New York: Dodd, Mead, 1922), 270.

9. See a similar conclusion drawn by Nancy Jay in *Throughout Your Generations Forever* (Chicago: University of Chicago Press, 1992), chap. 8.

10. Ravitch notes that the Jansenists wholeheartedly accepted all of the decrees of Trent, which would of course include the sacrificial reading of the Eucharist as well as transubstantiation. Norman Ravitch, *The Catholic Church and the French Nation, 1589–1989* (London: Routledge, 1990), 15.

11. Mack P. Holt notes that the Huguenots had drafted a republican constitution as early as 1572. Mack P. Holt, *The French Wars of Religion, 1562–1629* (Cambridge: Cambridge University Press, 1995), 98.

12. Van Kley, *The Religious Origins of the French Revolution*, 23, 24.

13. Ibid., 24f.

14. Ibid., 23.

15. Jean Laporte, ed., *La Doctrine de Port-Royal: La Morale (d'après Arnaud)* (Paris: Vrin, 1952), 202, 210.

16. Ibid., 234, 260.

17. Ibid., 225.

18. Ibid., 234.

19. Van Kley, *The Religious Origins of the French Revolution*, 22, 65. Kley asserts, however that during the 1600s, the challenge to absolutism by Jansenist thought was "latent." Ibid., 63.

20. Ibid., 78, 94. Van Kley argues as well that this collective ideal of the church may have been the precursor of the "General Will." Ibid., 78.

21. Ibid., 66f.

22. Jean Réville, *Les origines de l'Eucharistie (Messe—Sainte Cène)* (Paris: Ernest Leroux, 1908).

23. Jean Galy, *Le Sacrifice dans l'école française* (Paris: Nouvelles Editions Latines, 1951), 131.

24. Réville, *Les origines de l'Eucharistie*, 116.

25. Ibid., 117, see also 149.

26. Ibid., 19.

27. Ibid., 117.

28. Alain Tallon, *La Compagnie du Saint-Sacrement* (Paris: Cerf, 1990).

29. Ibid., 155.

30. Ibid., 157.

31. Georges Goyau, "Compagnie du Saint-Sacrement," in *The Catholic Encyclopedia* (New York: Robert Appleton, 1908), 4:184.

32. Ibid., 185.

33. Tallon, *La Compagnie du Saint-Sacrement,* 58–61. While Tallon admits the antagonism of the Compagnie to Protestantism, he argues that the evidence does not support Allier's view that this meant that the Compagnie either had or exercised as much power as Allier suggests. In fact, Tallon argues that the Compagnie's exercise of power reflects its relative impotence, its failure to persuade the Crown to march to its orders.

34. Raoul Allier, *La Compagnie du trés saint-sacrement de l'autel: la cabale des dévots* (Paris: Colin, 1902), 108–9.

35. Tallon, *La Compagnie du Saint-Sacrement,* 59.

36. Allier, *La Compagnie du trés saint-sacrement de l'autel* (1902), 214.

37. Raoul Allier, *La Compagnie du très saint-sacrement de l'autel à Toulouse: une esquisse de son histoire* (Paris: Honoré Champion, 1914), 80.

38. Allier, *La Compagnie du très saint-sacrement de l'autel* (1902), 137.

39. Pierre Goubert, *Louis XIV and Twenty Million Frenchmen* (New York: Vintage, 1970), 157.

40. I do not claim that to embrace a sacrificial theology of the Eucharist *necessarily* entails political absolutism. There is the example of the Jansenists, who embraced a sacrificial theology of the Eucharist while opposing royal absolutism. By contrast, Luther affirmed absolute obedience to the state, while *rejecting* a sacrificial theology of the Eucharist. What I am arguing is that the case can be made for a natural affinity between the two and that, under the right circumstances, one may trade on this affinity. If we deny that such a link may be made we have to say it was simply a coincidence that the *révocation* and its political consequences conform to the spirit of the new annihilationist theologies of Eucharist and sacrifice of the same period, and thus also reformation notions of the value of the individual coincided with the new anti-sacrificial theologies being created by reformers.

41. Tallon, *La Compagnie du Saint-Sacrement,* 15.

42. Ibid., 97.

43. Ibid., 119.

44. Ibid., 129.

45. Ibid.

46. Ibid., 119.

47. Ibid., 131.

48. Ibid., 136.

49. See Jean Réville's review of *La Compagnie du trés saint-sacrement de l'autel: la cabale des dévots,* by Raoul Allier, *Revue d'histoire des religions* 48 (1903): 255–60.

50. Ralph Gibson, *A Social History of French Catholicism: 1789–1914* (London: Routledge, 1989), 148. See the recent study of the cult of the Sacred Heart. Raymond Jonas, *France and the Cult of the Sacred Heart: A Tale for Modern Times* (Berkeley: University of California Press, 2000).

51. Tallon, *La Compagnie du Saint-Sacrement,* 46, 76, 129.

52. Albert Réville, "Contemporaneous Materialism in Religion: the Sacred Heart," *Theological Review* 11, no. 44 (1874): 152. Interestingly enough, Réville is equally hard on the Anglican liturgical reformers of the mid-nineteenth century, saying that "it enjoins participation in its mysterious ceremonies as necessary for the salvation of souls." Albert Réville, "Evolution in Religion, and Its Results," *Theological Review* 11, no. 42 (1873): 243.

53. Albert Réville, "The Religious Situation in France after the War," *Theological Review* 10, no. 40 (1873): 115–35.

54. Contrary then to what Renan thought, sacrificial polities were not strong-willed in being ready for any sacrifice. Ernest Renan, "La Réforme intellectuelle et morale de la France" (1871) in *La Réforme intellectuelle et morale de la France,* ed. P. E. Charvet (New York: Greenwood, 1968), 27–36.

55. Albert Réville, *Fernand Cortez et les causes réeles de la conquête du Mexique* (Paris: Ve Ethiou-Perou, 1882), 3.

56. Ibid., 17.

57. Ibid., 29. Renan voiced similar militarist sympathies in "La Réforme intellectuelle et morale de la France," 78.

58. D. G. Charlton, *The Secular Religions of France (1815–1870)* (Oxford: Oxford University Press, 1963), 90.

59. Ibid., 72, 73.

60. Ibid., chap. 4; Ivan Strenski, "Durkheim, Hamelin and the 'French Hegel,'" *Historical Reflections/Réflexions Historiques* 16 (1989): 146–49.

61. Georges Goyau, *The Church of France during the War* (Paris: Bloud and Gay, 1918), 10.

62. Renouvier's conversion came slowly and fitfully. Although he affiliated with the Lutherans in 1873, he only converted officially in about 1884–86, and then never took communion. See Daniel Robert, "Les intellectuels d'origine non-protestante dans le protestantisme des debuts de la Troisième République," in *Actes du colloque: Les protestants dans les débuts de la Troisième République (1871–1885)* (Paris, 3–6 October 1978), ed. André Encrevé and Michel Richard (Paris: Société de l'histoire du protestantisme français, 1979), 95–96.

63. That Durkheim should write an *hommage* at all was remarkable. During his entire life, Durkheim wrote only four obituaries. The first was for Victor Hommay (1877), the second for Hamelin (1907), the third for Robert Hertz (1916), the last for his son, André (1917). See Émile Durkheim, *Textes,* vol. 3, *Fonctions sociales et institutions,* ed. Victor Karady (Paris: Editions de Minuit, 1975), 490, 525, 536, 537. The task of writing such *nécrologies* was typically left to his nephew, Marcel Mauss—as was the great work of editing the posthumous works of valued colleagues. Yet Durkheim took a large part in preparing Hamelin's *Le Système de Descartes.* For an account of Durkheim's part in editing Hamelin's papers, see Jean Nabert, "Les Manuscrits d'Hamelin à la Bibliothèque Victor-Cousin," *Études philosophiques* 2 (1957): 171. The actual redaction of Hamelin's manuscript for *Le Système de Descartes* (Paris: Alcan, 1921) was realized by Léon Robin. But for the details of Durkheim's involvement, see the letters (31) sent Robin by Durkheim between 1914 and 1917 kept in the Bibliothèque Victor Cousin, côte 356/ 2f.

64. Émile Durkheim, "Nécrologie d'Octave Hamelin," *Le Temps,* 18 September 1907, reprinted in Émile Durkheim, *Textes,* vol. 1, *Éléments d'une theorie sociale,* ed. Victor Karady (Paris: Minuit, 1975), 429.

65. Durkheim's French is rhetorically interesting in trading on sacrificial imagery. "Dévouement" is both "devotion" and "self-sacrifice." A stiffly literal English rendition of "mourait victime de son dévouement" as "died a victim of his devotion" eliminates heroism and substitutes "victimization." Émile Durkheim, preface to *Le Système de Descartes,* by Octave Hamelin (Paris: Alcan, 1921), v. On Hamelin as Protestant, see Protestant Gaston Richard's celebration of Hamelin's theism in W. S. F. Pickering, ed., *Durkheim on Religion* (London: Routledge and Kegan Paul, 1975), 265, 272, 275 n. 92.

66. Theodore Zeldin, *France, 1848–1945: Politics and Anger* (Oxford: Oxford University Press, 1979), 263–64.

67. Protestant interest in education can be traced back to Huguenot affection for literacy, arising from the practice of reading the Bible.

68. Stuart R. Schram, *Protestantism and Politics in France* (Alençon: Corbière et Jugan, 1954), 37.

69. Pécaut was no rank-and-file liberal Protestant, but one of the founders of the liberal Protestant movement itself. Along with Pécaut, we can also list other founders of the liberal movement, Eduoard Schérer and Albert Réville—both of whom will figure in the discussion to follow.

70. Zeldin, *France, 1848−1945: Politics and Anger,* 263.

71. Renan, "La Réforme intellectuelle et morale de la France," 45.

72. Buisson, ed., *French Educational Ideals of Today,* 43.

73. George Chase, "Ferdinand Buisson: *Moraliste Laïque,*" Western Society for French History, Proceedings of the 10th Annual Meeting, 1982, 321−31.

74. Steven Lukes, *Emile Durkheim* (New York: Harper and Row, 1972), 360; Zeldin, *France, 1848−1945: Politics and Anger,* 263−64.

75. Chase, "Ferdinand Buisson," 321−31.

76. Lukes, *Emile Durkheim,* 360.

77. Jean-Marie Mayeur, "La Foi laïque de Ferdinand Buisson," *Libre pensée et religion laïque en France* (Strasbourg: Cerdic, 1980), 254.

78. Chase, "Ferdinand Buisson," 328.

79. Ibid., 324.

80. Paul Gerbod, "L'Ethique héroique en France (1870−1914)," *Revue historique* 268 (1982): 413.

81. Pierre Nora, "Ernest Lavisse: son role dans la formation du sentiment national," *Revue historique* 228 (1962): 74.

82. Ibid., 103.

83. Robert J. Smith, *The Ecole Normale Supèrieure and the Third Republic* (Albany: State University of New York Press, 1982), 118.

84. Buisson, ed., *French Educational Ideals of Today,* 196.

85. Ibid., 199.

86. Ibid., 197.

87. Ibid., 204−5.

88. Ibid., 205.

89. Added confirmation of this may be had by referring to an article by J. J. Gourd (1850−1909), a revisionist Renouvierian philosopher, "Le sacrifice," *Revue de métaphysique et de morale* 10 (1902): 131−63. There, in somewhat verbose and contorted prose, Gourd repeats many of the same conclusions reached by Hubert and Mauss's *Sacrifice* only a few years earlier about the exceptional nature of sacrifice in the human moral economy. On Gourd, see Isaac Benrubi, *Contemporary Thought in France,* trans. Ernest B. Dicker (London: Williams and Norgate, 1926), 126f; and Gunn, *Modern French Philosophy,* 72.

90. Renouvier worked primarily in the areas of epistemology, politics, and morals. Of his twenty-one books, the most interesting to us are his manuals of government and citizenship: Charles Renouvier, *Manuel républicain de l'Homme et du citoyen* (1848), *Gouvernement direct et organisation communale et centrale de la République* (1851). He also wrote a difficult and uncompromising anti-utilitarian moral treatise, *Science de la morale,* 2d ed. (Paris: Alcan, 1908); a revision of Kant, *Critique de la doctrine de Kant* (Paris: Alcan, 1906); and a statement of his idea of person as the culmination of the categories, *Le Personnalisme* (Paris: Alcan, 1903).

91. Marcel Méry, *La critique du christianisme chez Renouvier*, 2 vols., 2d ed. (Paris: Ophrys-Gap, 1963); Louis Prat, *Charles Renouvier, philosophe: sa doctrine, sa vie* (Ariége: Labrunie, 1937), chaps. 23, 24; Louis Foucher, *La Jeunesse de Renouvier et sa première philosophie (1815–1854)* (Paris: Vrin, 1927), 216–28.

92. Charles Renouvier was at least listed on the roles of the Avignon Lutheran community in 1873, although Daniel Robert believes he did not fully convert until 1884 or 1886. In any event, Renouvier apparently never took communion. Robert, "Les intellectuels d'origine non-protestante," 95–96.

93. Méry, *La critique du christianisme chez Renouvier*, 1:239, 494.

94. Theodore Zeldin, *France, 1848–1945: Intellect and Pride* (Oxford: Oxford University Press, 1980), 156.

95. Charles Renouvier, *La Critique philosophique* 1873:145–46, cited in Gunn, *Modern French Philosophy*, 290.

96. *La Critique religieuse* was published in seven volumes from 1878 to 1884.

97. Gunn, *Modern French Philosophy*, 291.

98. Méry, *La critique du christianisme chez Renouvier*, 1:278–79.

99. Ibid., 2:303.

100. Ibid., 291.

101. Gunn, *Modern French Philosophy*, 294–95, 298–99.

102. Baron de Montesquieu, *The Spirit of the Laws* (1748), trans. Thomas Nugent (New York: Hafner, 1949), 2:29.

103. Gunn, *Modern French Philosophy*, 300–301.

104. Foucher, *La Jeunesse de Renouvier*, 24.

105. Gunn, *Modern French Philosophy*, 292–93.

106. Ibid., 236.

107. It is noteworthy that Robert Soucy claims that Maurice Barrès drew much of the inspiration for his approval of the sacrifice of Dreyfus from his opposition to the individualism fostered by the neo-Kantian philosophy he had been taught while a lyceén at Nancy. Robert Soucy, *Fascism in France* (Berkeley: University of California, 1972), 102–3.

108. Hamelin, *Le Système de Renouvier*, 382–83.

109. Ibid., 382.

110. Gunn, *Modern French Philosophy*, 239.

111. Although not published until 1950, this work actually dates from course of lectures given in 1904.

112. Émile Durkheim, *Professional Ethics and Civic Morals* (1950 posth.), trans. Cornelia Brookfield (Westport, Conn.: Greenwood Press, 1957), 72.

113. Émile Durkheim, *Moral Education* (1925), trans. Everett K. Wilson and Herman Schnurer (New York: Free Press, 1961), 217.

114. William Bruneau, "Altruism and Opportunism: Two Poles of Moral Instruction in France, 1880–1920," Western Society for French History, Proceedings of the 10th Annual Meeting, 1982, 338–39.

115. But as Albert Réville's slow conversion to the cause of Dreyfus and as Raoul Allier's tortured testament about civic sacrifice during the war also indicate, this movement proceeded cautiously, as we will see in the next chapter.

116. Chase, "Ferdinand Buisson," 322.

117. It is well to remember in this connection that Protestants were equally happy to be royalists while the French crown acted as their protector.

118. Bruneau, "Altruism and Opportunism," 340.

119. Paul Sabatier, *France To-day*, trans. H. B. Binns (London: J. M. Dent, 1913), 194.

120. Bruneau, "Altruism and Opportunism," 332–44.

121. Paul was no relation to his contemporary, the great liberal Protestant theologian Auguste Sabatier, although Auguste was Paul's theological mentor. Paul Sabatier is best known for his "modernist" biography of St. Francis of Assisi (1893). By 1918, this book had been produced in 43 French editions. See Albert Houtin and Felix Sartiaux, *Alfred Loisy: sa vie, son oeuvre* (Paris: Editions du CNRS, 1960), 399–400.

122. Sabatier, *France To-day*, 191.

123. Here Vernes argued against the anticlerical party. Michel Despland, "Maurice Vernes et Ernst Troeltsch: histoire et science sociale des religions," unpublished manuscript.

124. Maurice Vernes, *Le spiritualisme dans l'enseignement* (Saint-Maud, Cher: Imprimerie Bussière, 1911); Maurice Vernes, *Coopération des idées* 15 Juin 1911 (Niort: B. Clouzot), 10, quoted in Michel Despland's "Histoire et science sociale des religions: Maurice Vernes et Ernst Troeltsch," in *Histoire et théologie chez Ernst Troeltsch*, ed. Pierre Gisel (Geneva: Labor et Fides, 1992), 201 n. 9, 202 n. 20.

125. Quoted from Renan's "What Is a Nation?" pages 80–81, cited in Tzvetan Todorov, *On Human Diversity: Nationalism, Racism, and Exoticism in French Thought* (Cambridge: Harvard University Press, 1993), 225.

126. Quoted from the preface to Renan's *Mélanges d'histoire et de voyages*, page 314, in Todorov, *On Human Diversity*, 221.

127. It should be noted that despite the tendency of French Protestants of the *fin-de-siècle* to rally to the republican side of the French political spectrum, some Protestant families maintained monarchist traditions into the present while other individual Protestants supported Charles Maurras's "Action Française," even to the extent of founding their own parallel movement, "Action Protestante." See Grace Davie, "Protestants de droite et *Action Française* au temps de la condamnation," *Études maurrassiennes* 5 (1986): 169–80.

CHAPTER SIX

1. See my *Four Theories of Myth in the Twentieth Century* (London/Iowa City: Macmillan/Iowa University Press, 1987).

2. Émile Durkheim, "Individualism and the Intellectuals," in *Durkheim on Religion*, ed. W. S. F. Pickering (London: Routledge, 1975), chap. 4; Steven Lukes, *Individualism* (Oxford: Blackwell, 1973), 41–42.

3. Ivan Strenski, "Henri Hubert, Racial Science and Political Myth," *Journal of the History of the Behavioral Sciences* 23 (1987): 353–67.

4. Émile Durkheim, remarks made at the 12 March 1905 meeting of the Union pour la Verité, *Libres Entretiens*, 1st ser. (1904/5): 369.

5. Henri Hubert, review of *L'Evangile et l'église*, by Alfred Loisy, *L'Année sociologique* 8 (1905): 291.

6. Henri Hubert, review of *Orpheus*, by Salomon Reinach, *L'Anthropologie* 20 (1909): 594.

7. Henri Hubert, review of *Orpheus*, by Salomon Reinach, *L'Année sociologique* 11 (1910): 73.

8. Marcel Mauss, review of *Esquisse d'une philosophie de la religion*, by Auguste Sabatier, *L'Année sociologique* 1 (1898); Marcel Mauss, *Oeuvres*, vol. 1, *Les Fonctions sociales du sacré*, ed. Victor Karady (Paris: Éditions de Minuit, 1968), 536.

9. Marcel Mauss, "La Prière," in *Oeuvres*, vol. 1, p. 375.

10. Emile Durkheim, *The Evolution of Educational Thought: Lectures on the Formation and Development of Secondary Education in France*, 2d ed. (1938), trans. Peter Collins (London: Routledge and Kegan Paul, 1977).

11. Durkheim, "Individualism and the Intellectuals," 68.

12. For Dumont's view, see Louis Dumont, "A Modified View of Our Origins: The Christian Beginnings of Modern Individualism," *Religion* 12 (1982): 1–27.

13. Henri Hubert and Marcel Mauss, *Sacrifice: Its Nature and Functions* (1899), trans. W. D. Halls (Chicago: University of Chicago Press, 1964), 93.

14. Ivan Strenski, "Henri Hubert," 353–67.

15. Hubert, 1909 review of *Orpheus*, 596.

16. Unlike the French Catholic community, liberal Protestantism utterly overshadowed its conservative brethren. Although speaking from a certain bias as a major liberal representative himself, Albert Réville said that the reason more of the French did not convert to Protestantism was because "Protestant orthodoxy has nothing very attractive about it." Albert Réville, "The Religious Situation in France subsequent to the War of 1870–71," *Theological Review* 10, no. 40 (1873): 124. Whatever the general merits of Réville's assessment, it was certainly true in the venue where Protestants most mattered to the Durkheimians—in the academic world. As a result, we can virtually ignore a *distinct* orthodox or evangelical French Protestant contribution to the milieu in which the Durkheimians operated. For an extensive discussion of the polemic between the Durkheimians and the French liberal Protestants, see my forthcoming book *Theology and the First Theory of Sacrifice*.

17. Compare, for example, Mauss's rather soft criticism of leading liberal Protestant theologian Auguste Sabatier's work, while seeking appointment to the Fifth Section, with his much more outspokenly critical attack on Sabatier after having been safely awarded his post. In 1898, before election to the Fifth Section, Mauss complimented Sabatier's *Esquisse d'une philosophie de la religion* for having put the "social and external character of dogma into bold relief." Mauss, *Oeuvres*, vol. 1, p. 535. Compare the sharp critique leveled at Auguste Sabatier in 1909 in Mauss's (never completed) doctoral thesis, "La Priere." Ibid., 373ff.

18. And, so too were the political groupings bearing the marks of intransigent Catholic culture on the extreme left, whom we have mentioned earlier—notably the anarchists. See Richard D. Sonn, *Anarchism and Cultural Politics in Fin de Siècle France* (Lincoln: University of Nebraska Press, 1989), 287–88.

19. Ivan Strenski, "Durkheim's Bourgeois Theory of Sacrifice," in *Durkheim's "Elementary Forms of the Religious Life,"* ed. N. J. Allen, W. S. F. Pickering, and W. Watts Miller (London: Routledge, 1998), 116.

20. Ibid., passim.

21. Although there are other things to be said, we can boil down the matter to a number of points. First, is the sacrificial victim sacred before the sacrifice—as Robertson Smith assumes—or does sacrifice make the victim sacred—the position of Hubert and Mauss? Thus, while it seems at first that Durkheim sides with Smith in declaring the pre-existence of the sacred, he nonetheless adds a comment that reverses this view. Thus, regarding the sacrificial ritual of *Intichiuma*, Durkheim says that "the only difference we find here is that the animal is naturally sacred while it *ordinarily* acquires this character artificially in the course of sacrifice." Emile Durkheim, *The Elementary Forms of the Religious Life*, trans. J. W. Swain (New York: Free Press, 1915), 378. In saying that the "ordinary" situation is one in which sacrificial ritual makes the victim sacred,

Durkheim thus accepts the position of Hubert and Mauss that sacrifice makes the sacred—not the other way round, as in the exceptional case of the *Intichiuma*, as related by Smith where the sacred totemic principle already resides in the victim. This acceptance, in effect, makes Hubert and Mauss's theory of sacrifice, *the* Durkheimian theory of sacrifice.

22. Louis Dumont, "Marcel Mauss: A Science in Becoming," in *Essays on Individualism: Modern Ideology in Anthropological Perspective* (Chicago: University of Chicago Press, 1986), 192.

23. Jean Paul Colleyn, "Le Sacrifice selon Hubert et Mauss," in *Le Sacrifice I*, Systèmes de pensée en Afrique noire, bk. 2, ed. Luc de Heusch (Paris: École Pratique des Hautes Études, 1976), 23.

24. See, for instance, John M. Beattie, "On Understanding Sacrifice," in *Sacrifice*, ed. M. F. C. Bourdillon and Meyer Fortes (London: Academic Press, 1980), 34; Colleyn, "Le Sacrifice selon Hubert et Mauss"; Luc de Heusch, *Sacrifice in Africa*, trans. Linda O'Brien and Alice Morton (Bloomington: Indiana University Press, 1983), 16ff; Nancy Jay, *Throughout Your Generations Forever* (Chicago: University of Chicago Press, 1992), 134–43; William Beers, *Women and Sacrifice* (Detroit: Wayne State University Press, 1992), chap. 1; Frits Staal, *Rules without Meaning: Ritual, Mantras and the Human Sciences* (New York: Peter Lang, 1989); René Girard, *Violence and the Sacred* (Baltimore: Johns Hopkins University Press, 1977), passim; Victor Turner, "Sacrifice as Quintessential Process, Prophylaxsis or Abandonment?" *History of Religions* 16 (1977), 189–215.

25. Émile Durkheim, preface to *L'Année sociologique*, vol. 2 (1899), trans. J. French, in *Émile Durkheim: Contributions to "L'Année Sociologique,"* ed. Yash Nandan (New York: Free Press, 1980), 54.

26. In a letter to Hubert written shortly after the publication of *Sacrifice*, Durkheim himself declared that he was "ever more convinced that [sacrifice] is a fundamental notion playing a capital role in the evolution of morals and ideals." Émile Durkheim, Letter to Henri Hubert, 5 June 1898, in "Lettres de Émile Durkheim à Henri Hubert," ed. Philippe Besnard, *Revue française de sociologie* 28 (1987): 497.

27. Émile Durkheim, preface to *L'Année sociologique*, vol. 2, p. 54 (my emphasis). In the preface to the inaugural volume of *L'Année sociologique*, Durkheim says that these "Mémoires" attempted "to show by means of a few examples how . . . materials ('essential for science') may be put to work." Ibid., 49.

28. Émile Durkheim, "The Dualism of Human Nature and Its Social Conditions" (1914), in *Essays on Sociology and Philosophy*, ed. Kurt Wolff (New York: Harper and Row, 1960), 328.

29. Letter of Henri Hubert to Marcel Mauss, n.d., 1898. I thank Marcel Fournier for this citation (Marcel Fournier, *Marcel Mauss* [Paris: Fayard, 1994], 151).

30. *Revue d'histoire et de litterature religieuses* 7 (1902): 281 (my emphasis).

31. Marcel Hebert, *Revue d'histoire et de litterature religieuses*, n.s., 1 (1909): 71.

32. Hubert and Mauss, *Sacrifice: Its Nature and Functions*, 100.

33. Ivan Strenski, "Durkheim, Hamelin, and the 'French Hegel,'" *Historical Reflections/Réflexions Historiques* 16 (1989): 153.

34. Hubert and Mauss, *Sacrifice: Its Nature and Functions*, 101.

35. Contrast this to Mark C. Taylor's reading of Bataille's devotion to self-immolation in "The Poli-tics of Theo-ry," *Journal of the American Academy of Religion* 59 (1991): 26–27. Although Taylor is right to bring out Bataille's extremism, he is not right in implicitly laying it at the door of the Durkheimians.

36. Hubert and Mauss, *Sacrifice: Its Nature and Functions*, 14.

37. Ibid., 17. On Bonald, see John Milbank, *Theology and Social Theory* (Oxford: Blackwell, 1990), 56, citing Louis de Bonald, *Essai analytique sur les lois naturelles de l'ordre sociale* (Paris: n.p., 1800), 79ff.

38. Hubert and Mauss, *Sacrifice: Its Nature and Functions*, 13.

39. Ibid., 94.

40. Ibid., 69, 81.

41. Ibid., 69.

42. Ibid., 81.

43. Ibid., 80, 88, 91.

44. Ibid., 94.

45. Ibid., 93–94.

46. Ibid., 91.

47. Durkheim, "The Dualism of Human Nature and Its Social Conditions," 329.

48. Ibid., 328.

49. Émile Durkheim, *Moral Education* (1925), trans. Everett K. Wilson and Herman Schnurer (New York: Free Press, 1961), 217.

50. J. A. Gunn, *Modern French Philosophy* (New York: Dodd, Mead, 1922), 239.

51. Octave Hamelin, *Le Système de Renouvier* (Paris: Alcan, 1927), 383.

52. Gunn, *Modern French Philosophy*, 237.

53. Durkheim, *Moral Education*, 209, 210.

54. Hubert and Mauss, *Sacrifice: Its Nature and Functions*, 100.

55. Ibid., chap. 5.

56. Ibid., 81–82.

57. Strenski, "Durkheim's Bourgeois Theory of Sacrifice."

58. John I. Brooks III, *The Eclectic Legacy: Academic Philosophy and the Human Sciences in Nineteenth-Century France* (Newark: University of Delaware, 1998), chap. 6.

59. Jean-Marie Mayeur, "Les catholiques dreyfusards," *Revue historique* 530 (1979): 337–62.

60. Eugen Weber, *The Nationalist Revival in France, 1905–1914* (Berkeley: University of California Publications in History, No. 60, 1959), 36.

61. Here Vernes argued against the anticlerical party. See Michel Despland, "Maurice Vernes et Ernst Troeltsch: histoire et science sociale des religions," unpublished manuscript.

62. Maurice Vernes, *Le spiritualisme dans l'enseignement* (Saint-Maud, Cher: Imprimerie Bussiére, 1911); Maurice Vernes, *Coopération des idées*, 15 June 1911 (Niort: B. Clouzot), 10, quoted in Michel Despland's "Histoire et science sociale des religions. Maurice Vernes et Ernst Troeltsch," in *Histoire et théologie chez Ernst Troeltsch*, ed. Pierre Gisel (Genève: Labor et Fides, 1992).

63. Emile Durkheim, *"L'Allemagne au-dessus de tout": la mentalité allemande et la guerre* (Paris: Armand Colin, 1915).

64. Émile Durkheim and Ernest Lavisse, *Lettres à tous les français*, ed. Michel Maffesoli (Paris: Armand Colin, 1992).

65. Steven Lukes, *Emile Durkheim: His Life and Work* (New York: Harper and Row, 1972), 350.

66. Ibid., 542.

67. André Hesse and André Gleyz, *Notions de sociologie appliquée à la morale et à l'éducation* (Paris: Alcan, 1922), 139.

68. Ibid., 140.

69. Lukes, *Emile Durkheim*, 552.

70. Jules Arboux, "Maistre (Maire-Joseph, Comte de)," *Encyclopédie des sciences religieuses*, ed. Fréderic Lichtenberger (Paris: Sandoz et Fischbacher, 1889), 8:577.

71. Durkheim, *"L'Allemagne au-dessus de tout,"* 12.

72. Durkheim, "Individualism and the Intellectuals," 59–74.

73. Durkheim, *"L'Allemagne au-dessus de tout,"* 12.

74. Émile Durkheim, *Professional Ethics and Civic Morals* (1904), trans. Cornelia Brookfield (Westport, Conn.: Greenwood Press, 1983) 72.

75. Ibid., 73.

76. Strenski, "Durkheim, Hamelin, and the 'French Hegel,'" 135–70.

77. The literature on gifts that is attributable to Mauss's *The Gift* is vast. See, for example, in literary theory, the recent work of Jacques Derrida, *Given Time: 1. Counterfeit Money*, trans. Peggy Kamuf (Chicago: University of Chicago Press, 1991). The influence of *The Gift* on policy, while perhaps not nearly as great, is significant. Here I have in mind economist Karl Polanyi's *The Great Transformation* (New York: Farrar and Rinehart, 1944), and former director of Britain's National Health Service, Richard M. Titmuss's *The Gift Relationship* (New York:Vintage, 1971).

78. Ivan Strenski, "At Home with René Girard," in *Religion in Relation* (London/Columbia: Macmillan/South Carolina, 1993), chap. 11.

79. Alice Owen Letvin, *Sacrifice in the Surrealist Novel: The Impact of Early Theories of Primitive Religion on the Description of Violence in Modern Fiction* (New York: Garland, 1990), 112.

80. Ibid., 57.

81. Ibid., 74ff.

82. Ibid., 112.

83. Émile Durkheim, "Individualism and the Intellectuals," chap. 4.

Index

annihilationist spirituality 157

Add. et corrigenda

59   for Albert, read Alfred

77   word missing

75   syntax lost in quotation

103   for "produce to" read "produces..."?

145 bottom   wd missing

146 top   missing close-quotes
160   2/5 ls down — word missing
167   top   for "mythologicly" read mythologically